PRESTON STURGES

BY PRESTON STURGES

Adapted and edited by Sandy Sturges

SIMON AND SCHUSTER

New York London Toronto Sydney Tokyo Singapore

Simon and Schuster
Simon & Schuster Building
Rockefeller Center
1230 Avenue of the Americas
New York, New York 10020

Designed by Laurie Jewell
Manufactured in the United States of America

Photos courtesy of the Sturges family.

1 3 5 7 9 10 8 6 4 2

Library of Congress Cataloging in Publication Data

Sturges, Preston.
Preston Sturges / by Preston Sturges ; adapted and edited by Sandy Sturges.
p.   cm.
1. Sturges, Preston.   2. Motion picture producers and directors—
United States—Biography.   3. Screenwriters—United States—Biography.
I. Sturges, Sandy.   II. Title.
PN1998.3.S78A3 1990
791.43′0233′092—dc20   90-34024
[B]   CIP

ISBN 0-671-67929-5

ACKNOWLEDGMENTS

MY WARMEST THANKS to Allan Mayer, my first editor, who received each installment of this book with such enthusiasm that I could hardly wait to get his opinion on the next; to Susanne Jaffe, who took over as editor with such an easy expertise when Allan left Simon & Schuster; to David Streiff, who at the 40th Locarno Film Festival in the summer of 1989 presented the largest retrospective of Preston's films ever assembled, invited me to attend as a guest of honor, and then provided the first public platform for a reading of a portion of this book at a conference of film critics, students, and enthusiasts from all over the world. But most of all, for their interest and love, I thank my Tom and his bride, Antonina Armato Sturges, who spent many an evening of their first year of marriage reading the manuscript, asking questions, making suggestions, and providing unfailing support at all hours.

Sandy Sturges

To my sons,
Preston and Tom,
and
to the memory of my brother,
Bill Nagle

FOREWORD

LIKE MANY OF YOU who will read this book, I never knew Preston Sturges either. He died just after I turned three. He was my father.

I came to appreciate his talent during my adolescence—film by film and laugh by laugh—in a series of gradual steps that one day led me to be invited to speak about him for a film course at the college I was attending. I stood before a room of my fellow students and realized, to my dismay, that beyond a couple of anecdotes one might tell at a cocktail party, I probably knew less about my father than most of the people in this class did. But I told both my stories anyway, not very well, and quickly sat down. The lights dimmed, and a black and white image flickered on the screen.

The film was an irreverently funny, beautifully paced journey through Hollywood and its dream machine that also gave seven chilling, silent minutes to a somber walk through the streets of homeless, post-depression America. During the last reel—when the hero got himself out of a southern prison, got the girl, and still had enough of his wits about him to say "There's a lot to be said for making people laugh . . . do you know that's all some people have?"—there was an outpouring of appreciation from the audience that was nothing if not amazing to me.

I left the auditorium stunned. I had seen *Sullivan's Travels* twice before, but never in a room stuffed with believers like this one was. While speaking to the professor afterwards, and accepting his thanks (for watching a movie?), it did not escape me that a certain fact that I had always taken for granted, namely, that my father was a pretty good filmmaker, was the reason and inspiration not only for this class and this course, but also for many others like it all over the world.

A father who dies when his children are young usually leaves behind the nagging question of what might have been. But my father did leave us, my brother Preston and me, with a way to understand who he was and how he thought about the world he lived in. I couldn't actually go to him and ask: How do you know when it's time to get married? or, When do you leave a job and start your own business? or, What were you like when you were my age? or, When did you realize you were *really* good at what you do? But I could see his films and read his plays and through them trace a faint image of what he must have thought about love, and children, and luck versus opportunity, and fighting your way out of a lousy circumstance, and being true to your friends, and some of the other things boys learn from their fathers by just having them around.

Some years after that film class, fate stepped in, in the person of an off-Broadway producer, Ms. Marlene Swartz, who wanted to do a series of Lost American Plays. I sent her *Cup of Coffee,* a play my father wrote in 1930. She got the play on the boards, and from it came interviews and articles, and one in particular in the *New York Times* caught the eye of Mr. Allan Mayer, then an editor for Simon and Schuster. He contacted me and asked if I would be interested in writing a book about my father. Being in much the same situation as I was that day in college, I told my two anecdotes and suggested that the person he really needed to speak to about such a project was my mother. They spoke, contracts followed, and it was done.

My mother took a year to put together everything my father wrote about himself—from letters, diaries, and an unfinished autobiography— to create what you hold in your hand: a seamless narrative that tells the story of his life. It is a sharper, clearer picture of him than I could ever have hoped to see.

A book will never replace the person I've wanted to meet and get to know for so long, but now, for the first time, I can say that I have met him and I do know him . . . in a way.

Thank you, Mama, for making this book.

Tom Sturges
Los Angeles, California
January 16, 1990

INTRODUCTION

fade in

THIS BOOK IS IN NO SENSE a farewell letter to the world. I happen merely to have noticed that everyone I have been privileged to observe behaved as if life were going to continue forever. Looking around me, I discover sadly that practically everyone I knew fifty-five, fifty, or even a measly forty-five years ago, is gone from this planet, usually without a trace—or spurlos versenkt, as this form of total disappearance was known in submarine circles during the 1914–1918 war to end all wars.

These regretted persons, most of them at least, did not quit this gloomy globe because of untoward accidents or by the contraction of tularemia, psittacosis, or some other exotic disease, but simply because they had reached the end of their lives, like butterflies, or snakes, or orchids which shrivel up one day and vanish despite all one's efforts to make them last with glass and rubber tubes.

A good reason for writing one's *auto*biography is that it may prevent some jerk from writing one's biography. And this is all to the good, if only because what one writes oneself about persons and facts one knew firsthand will contain only such voluntary departures from the truth as one considers necessary to prevent a few husbands from shooting their wives, for instance (or vice versa), as opposed to the mountains of false statements, misspelled names, wrong dates, and incorrect loci the well-meaning biographer usually comes up with after tracking one down through the morgues of defunct newspapers, the old letters of some of one's friends, and the very unreliable memories of people who knew one slightly. This is the tremendous advantage of even the most analphabetic autobiography over even the most scholarly biography. Baron Münchhausen himself will be closer to the truth, describing what he himself has done, than the most conscientious outsider trying to relate the same thing a couple of centuries later. It is often stupefying to read a piece about somebody one knew intimately, in a time which appears still quite recent, and to discover its extraordinary inaccuracy. It makes one doubt all the history studied in school, rarely written down by those who made it.

Along about here, I believe, custom requires the hero of an autobiography to lower his eyes shyly, clear his throat a couple of times, then mutter some self-deprecating remarks for the purpose of disarming his readers with his frankness, whilst at the same time charming them with his modesty. I have much to be modest about, as a matter of fact. Between flops, it is true, I have come up with an occasional hit, but compared to a good boxer's record, for instance, my percentage has been lamentable. It is a little like that of my friend Dr. Leach Cross, the great lightweight who fought when this century was new. "In my first fight," said Dr. Cross, "I got knocked out in the first round. In my second fight, I got knocked out in the second round. In my third fight, I got knocked out in the third round. I thought I was improving."

My own record was equally painful. I fought a draw in my first fight, stupefied everyone by winning the championship in my second, got a couple of wins with picture rights, then was knocked out three times in a row. Dragging my weary carcass to Hollywood, I was immediately knocked out again, won a big fight some six months later, then marked time for six years as an ordinary ham-and-beaner, picking up what I could. Suddenly I saw a chance and offered to fight for the world championship for a dollar. To everyone's astonishment, I won that championship and defended it successfully for a number of years, winning nine times by knockout, fighting three draws, losing twice and getting one no-decision in Europe. I have just come over to America for a fight, but it was called off at the last moment, one of the promoters having gone nuts and having to have been locked up. Why I'm not walking on my heels after all this, I don't know. Maybe I *am* walking on my heels. It would be surprising if I weren't.

Preston Sturges
New York, 1959

COLD ARE THE HANDS of time that creep along relentlessly, destroying slowly, but without pity, that which yesterday was young. Alone our memories resist this disintegration and grow more lovely with the passing years.

Preston Sturges

LIKE NEARLY EVERYONE ELSE, with the exception of a few crowned heads, hereditary multimillionaires, and other neurotic characters, I know little of whence I came. No scribes have burned the midnight oil on my account, nor have crusty genealogists chiseled the branches of my family tree into the enduring stone. My forebears *may* all have been aristocratic loafers who spent their days *couchant* on fields of *argent*, *regardant* concupiscently the *passant* maidens or wetting their whistles at *bars sinister*, but if so, somebody forgot to tell me about it.

I am, of course, directly descended from Brian Boru, the last king of Ireland, a fact certified by my mother and therefore beyond dispute. But as everybody else with a drop of Irish blood in his carcass is also a guaranteed descendant of the old billy goat, I am not overly arrogant because of this royal strain.

I would like to think that I had as many ancestors as the next fellow, of course, and I have always treasured the reply of Irvin S. Cobb, one of the great humorists of our time, whom I knew slightly and who, when questioned about his antecedents, said, "I come of a very old Southern family. As a matter of fact, my family goes straight back to the garden of Eden . . . without a break on either side."

Personally, I have always thought my original ancestor came up out of a swamp. Occasionally, in the shadowland between wakefulness and sleep, I have seen this character arise, steaming, from the greenish depths of a primeval peat bog, squeeze the water from his eyes, blow the mud out of his nose and then, with evident displeasure, sample his very first lungful of the searing, sulphurous air. Now, his eye meeting that of an unusually large and disagreeable-looking brontosaurus, he stiffens with alarm, then by means of a full gainer one-and-a-half twist from a standing position, regains the warm protection of his previous habitat with a loud splash.

What my original grandmother (there must have been one) could have seen in this athlete, I have no idea. But since I have been equally perplexed upon viewing the daguerreotypes of some of my later, whiskered grandsires, I presume that beauty lies in the eyes of the beholder.

My mother's father prospered under the name of Dominic Dempsey and, according to my mother, was six feet four, a sailing master out of Dublin, and an absolute smasher with the fair sex. Escaping by the length of his coattails from Flint, Michigan, where he had been one of the original instigators of a movement to conquer Canada by water and annex it to the United States, he settled in the Irish section of Quebec, where, in a pair of black bearskin gloves, startling against the white sheets, he died of consumption at the age of thirty-six, leaving a widow and six children. The youngest of these was my mother, then about four or five years old.

My Grandmother Dempsey managed somehow to get her hungry brood as far south and west as Chicago. She chose the Windy City because one of her sisters had married a saloon keeper down there whose place of business—or workingman's club, as those ale houses were known at the time—was situate in a choice but gently perfumed district near the stockyards. A saloon in those days meant a free lunch, and that custom implied enough leftovers to keep body and soul together for one's widowed sister and her small children. This proved correct. I do not know the name of the boniface who married my grandaunt, but I thank him for his largesse and salute his beery memory.

These are the few slender facts I know about my mother's progenitors.

Until one terrible night in Glencoe, Illinois, when I was about eight years old, I did not know that my father, Solomon Sturges, was not my father. How I managed not to know this as a child, I will never understand. I don't think I was a particularly stupid little boy; in fact, everybody thought I was quite bright. At eight, I could speak and sing in several languages, and recite pieces, and roller skate, and box, and I could draw, and do simple tricks with cards. But the fact that there were three names in my family had never struck me as peculiar nor caused me to draw any conclusions about it. What I mean is this: I knew that my father's name was Sturges. I knew that my mother's maiden name was Dempsey. And I knew that my Grandmother Biden's name was Biden. But why I had a grandmother called Isabelle Missouri Biden when my father's name was Sturges and my mother's name was Dempsey never aroused the slightest curiosity. Other people had two names in their families, I had three. This was merely some sort of superiority.

Nobody ever tried to conceal anything from me. My Grandmother Biden came freely to our house and brought me lovely presents. I visited her son, my uncle Sidney Biden, in Berlin, where he was a successful lieder singer. I knew my Grandfather Biden, a drinking man, who had fought for the North during the Civil War, my grandmother hissing him from the sidewalk during his entire military career. Grandmother Biden was from the South and according to her, my grandfather's military career was accomplished in one march around the block. Nonetheless, he was thereafter known as the Commodore. But never, until that terrible night, did I realize that I was the son of a certain Edmund C. Biden, that I had been born Edmund Preston Biden, and that I wasn't my father's son at all, but had only been adopted by him in January 1902, after he had married my mother.

My Grandmother Biden, born Isabelle Missouri Parry, was the daughter of a Miss Preston of Virginia and a building contractor in St. Louis named Parry. On August 16, 1864, she married one Edmund S. Biden in St. Louis. For a southern belle, my grandmother was remarkably modern. She threw my grandfather out for one thing—some kind of argument about bourbon whiskey—shortly after the birth of their third child, and then went back to school to get herself a teaching certificate. She became a tutor to the children of George Pullman and subsequently the first teacher in the first school in the town of Pullman, Illinois, which Mr. Pullman had founded. One of the regular visitors to the Pullman house was Mary Delafield Sturges, presently to become my Aunt Mary Sunshine. Maybe it was she who introduced her brother, Solomon Sturges, to Mrs. Biden's son's wife, my mother. But maybe not, because I remember hearing that Mother had known Mr. Sturges even before she knew Mr. Biden.

At the beginning of this chapter I said I knew little of whence I came. I was mistaken. I know almost nothing, and I realize now that I waited much too long before trying to gather a few facts about my foregoers. All the people who would have been willing to help me document the past are deader than doornails. My uncle Sidney Biden said to me once, "I must tell you someday where you came from, Preston, who the Bidens were and how they happened to settle around Rochester in upper New York State." But I didn't ask him any more about it. I didn't care at all then why the Bidens had settled around Rochester. Now I will never know. I'll never know about the name Biden either. Somebody told me once it wasn't German, as it sounded, but English, possibly Bidden.

I do know that one day in 1897, Dominic Dempsey's youngest daughter, my mother, and Isabelle Parry Biden's second son, Edmund C. Biden, both then residents of Chicago, ran off and got married in Milwaukee, Wisconsin. I don't know how Mr. Biden earned his living during the greater part of his life, but I think around the time I was born, he was connected with a collection agency. It's an awful thing to say, but I think it is the truth. He was five feet seven, parted his hair in the middle and drank some during the evenings. He was also an expert on the trapeze—the single one, not the romantic flying one. Among his possessions was a revolver, with which he often threatened to shoot himself, and my mother, who didn't like him, would urge him to go ahead. One night, improvising on this familiar theme, he locked himself in the bathroom with the revolver and hollered through the keyhole, "This is it, Mamie . . . farewell!" then fired straight into the ceiling over his head to frighten her. The character who really got frightened, however, was the man in the bathroom immediately above, who was brushing his teeth when the bullet went between his toes, though it fortunately removed nothing but the toilet tank from his wall. They had to get the janitor out of bed to shut off the water.

Mr. Biden never sounded like much of a husband to me, but it must be remembered that he was one of Mother's very first ones, and, like the celebrated Mrs. Simpson, she did better later.

I saw Mr. Biden only once in my life, and by then I was almost sixteen. That was in the summer of 1914, when my mother sent me from France to America so that I wouldn't enlist too young in a war that wasn't mine anyway. Mr. Biden heard that I was in New York and invited me to dinner. I went, but during the evening he said something rude about my mother, so I left and never saw him again during his lifetime.

They must have liked each other better in the winter of 1897, though, or I wouldn't be here now.

According to my mother, positively no one, least of all herself, had even the faintest suspicion that she was heavy with child at the time of my birth. On the contrary, for the very first time in her life, those signs whose cessation normally indicates a case of galloping gravidity had been appearing with startling regularity. I was thought to be a tumor, and Mr. Biden, who was fond of operations and given to snap judgments, was on the verge of taking us down to the hospital to have me removed when the Commodore, standing sympathetically at the foot of Mother's bed, is supposed to have noticed a thumping under the covers and to have roared, "Why goddamit! What the hell is the matter with you bunch of nitwits? This here girl is a'goin' to have a goddam baby!"

That was during the evening of August 28, 1898. On the following morning around five o'clock, the Commodore was proved to be one hundred percent goddam right!

THE WORDS "ACCORDING TO MY MOTHER" will continue to appear from time to time, and I had better explain what they mean.

My mother was in no sense a liar, nor even intentionally unacquainted with the truth . . . as she knew it. She was, however, endowed with such a rich and powerful imagination that anything she had said three times, she believed fervently. Often, twice was enough. This gave rise to some tall stories around our house and eventually, although reluctantly, to some mild disbelief on the part of her son regarding some of the stories he heard.

The tender tale she told me about finding her mother's valuable sealskin coat in the attic when she was three years old and cutting it up into tippets for all the other little girls in Quebec until her mother began wondering where all the sealskin was coming from, I was willing enough to believe.

I believed, too, the one about her having had me at fifteen, although I found it faintly unpleasant. I was relieved to learn after her death that she was about twenty-seven when she had me. As a matter of fact, I never had the faintest idea *what* my mother's age was during all the time I knew her. I was brought up on such a tissue of lies on this subject that I never even tried to figure it out.

Then there was the tale of Doctor Dimples. Doctor Dimples, it turned out, was none other than my mother, this time a brilliant medical student of sixteen in the Herring Homeopathic Hospital in Chicago, where her pretty smile and extreme youth caused her to be known by that charming sobriquet. This time I definitely smelled a herring. What had she done with me, for instance, during classes, since I had been around for a couple of years already? This she did not bother to explain, but I nearly choked on the formaldehyde as she regaled me with charming details, interesting sidelights, and gay anecdotes about the autopsy rooms and the jolly pranks the students used to play in them. The delicious "I offer you my hand and my heart," with these items presented in an accompanying shoebox, always convulsed me and was my favorite.

The witty "I only have eyes for you," similarly presented, ran a close second.

How long Doctor Dimples pursued her studies, I will never know. She must have come within shouting distance of some kind of degree, at least in her mind, because in 1905 she was certainly one of the founders and principal whoopers-up of the Chicago Home for Convalescent Women and Children, a free institution for young and needy mothers in that period before Social Security. On the other hand, by 1905 she had been married to Father for a few years, and charitable endeavors, then as now, were customary pastimes for the ladies.

Among the many fantasies with which my mother surrounded herself, the one that gave her the most satisfaction, and lasted the longest, was undoubtedly the figment concerning her maiden name and her illustrious Italian origin. No such plebian name as 'Dempsey' could possibly have been hers, my mother felt. With this thought as a starter, it was but one leap to the conclusion that the name was a misnomer, bestowed upon the family in error by the vulgar Irish varlets attending her ancestor, a distinguished Italian prince, unfortunately on the lam in Ireland because of a romantic duel. What these uneducated flunkies were trying to say was "d'Este," the distinguished prince being a member of that celebrated Italian family, only they couldn't pronounce it.

Thus my mother, in her mind an Italian princess, simply resumed her true name and became Mary d'Este Dempsey, a moniker that adorns most of her works and many of her marriage certificates. When she founded her excellent perfumery house at 4, rue de la Paix in Paris in 1911, she quite naturally called it the Maison d'Este. Her furious indignation was terrible to behold when the French descendants of the great Italian family dared to demand—under pain of huge damages—the instant disappearance of the large electric sign bearing their name. Forgetting that she herself was an Italian princess, she raged against these upstart spigotis and only most reluctantly, on the advice of a whole team of celebrated lawyers, considered changing the name of the establishment to the Maison Desti. Thus my mother became and remained Madame Desti. As such she lived, conducted her business, wrote, and died.

This then is what I mean by "according to my mother." I would not care to dig too deeply in some spot where she indicated the presence of buried treasure, nor to erect a building on a plot she had surveyed. Also, since we have only her description of him, it is entirely possible that my Grandfather Dempsey was four feet six, rather than six feet four, that he died of drink rather than of consumption, and that, finally, rather than the master of a sailing ship, he was actually an oiler on a banana boat.

3

CHAPTER

A LETTER IN MY FILES from Mr. Biden, who wrote to me in 1930 seeking reimbursement for medical expenses incurred by him on my behalf some thirty years earlier, when I was not quite a year old, reports that I was attacked by tuberculosis of the throat, operated on and taken with my mother and grandmother to Thomasville, Georgia, to recuperate for the winter months. I remember none of this, of course, but I carry a long, jagged scar on my neck connected with the removal of tubercular or scrofulous glands, which turned out to be a little swollen because I was teething, rather than heir to the king's evil.

As my memory at this time was not as good as it became soon afterwards, any facts about this period of my life will have to be based on the say-so of someone else.

Happily, my mother wrote a book called *The Untold Story* about her meeting, friendship with, and tragic parting from Isadora Duncan, and in Chapter II she writes:

> In January 1901, after a disastrous runaway marriage and later divorce, I tucked my little year-and-a-half-old babe under my arm and started for Paris to study for the stage. This I did under the advice of Dr. Ziegfeld, Flo Ziegfeld's father, who had the Conservatoire of Music in Chicago. At this moment, I had rather an extraordinary voice and, as I was scarcely more than a child myself, great things were hoped for from my Paris trip.

The year-and-a-half-old babe was of course myself, except that the most elementary calculation establishes that in January 1901, I was approximately *two* and a half years old, rather than *one* and a half. But this is probably just dull male logic. If it pleased my mother to be "scarcely more than a child myself" in Paris in 1901, well, I have already commented sufficiently upon the reliability of facts and figures issued by my mother—to continue would be boorish.

On her very first day in Paris, Mother met a Mrs. Duncan, also an American, at the office of a real-estate agent, another American and expatriate, who sat up nights figuring out ways to rent vile apartments without any windows in them to pathetic young American mothers like mine. Mrs. Duncan invited the young mother and her baby to her own apartment to meet one of her sons, Raymond Duncan, and her daughter, a young dancer. That was the beginning of my mother's lifelong and devoted friendship with Isadora Duncan.

On the second or third day in Paris, in a dark apartment which indeed turned out to have no windows, I came down with a desperate case of pneumonia. Everybody started to pray, and Mother, who was trying it for the first time, went so far as to make a deal in which she promised that if the life of her child were saved, she would never complain about anything for the rest of her existence. And I think she kept this promise pretty well. She was not a complainer. While Mother was negotiating with the Lord, Isadora's mother was busy saving my life with a remedy of her own: a spoonful of champagne every so many hours. This seems an unusual treatment for an infant, but it is clearly stated on page 27 in Mother's book, so it must be true. I woke the next morning without a trace of pneumonia.

Mother did find a more pleasant apartment. Isadora went to live with her, and together they enjoyed the bohemian life in Paris, surrounded by many celebrities of the artistic, social, and political worlds: Carrère, Besnard, Mounet-Sully, the Prince de Polignac, and the not-yet-old tiger, Clemenceau, among them. Raymond Duncan tucked the little year-and-a-half-old babe who was really two and a half under his arm, and I was taken down to Giverny with old Mrs. Duncan. Mother and Isadora spent weekends with us sometimes.

A couple of weeks after my third birthday, Mother and I sailed back to America, and on October 2, 1901, in Memphis, Tennessee, Mother became Mrs. Solomon Sturges. I must have been there, because many years later I was told by a member of the family that Father disappeared for a week one time and then reappeared with a wife and child.

Three months later, Father adopted me and I became Preston Sturges. Father and Mother must have explained things to me then, but if they did, I retained no memory of it.

Of the Sturges family, much more is known than is available about poor Irish immigrants and obscure Scottish-English settlers around

Rochester. That the name was originally Turgesius and stemmed from a Danish freebooter who landed on the coast of Cornwall in the twelfth century and founded the dynasty by exterminating all the men and raping all the women, may or may not be true. But of the family's subsequent honors, distinctions, and great wealth, there is no doubt whatsoever. From a John Sturges who came from England and settled in Fairfield, Connecticut, in 1660, the family produced members who in time financed railroads and grain elevators and tugboat lines, established banks and founded timber companies. By 1860, Father's antecedents were already long and well established in Chicago and its environs.

When Father married Mother, he was almost thirty-six years old, a member of the stock-brokerage house of Alfred L. Baker & Co. of Chicago, and he had never been married before.

4
CHAPTER

ACCORDING TO MY MOTHER, Father agreed to let her spend six months of the year in Europe and the other six months in Chicago. Whether this extraordinary promise originated in Father's generous heart or was wheedled out of him, I don't know. Of course, Mother always tucked her however-many-years-old babe under her arm when she decamped, so that my memory of these early days embraces without distinction a couple of continents and several languages.

I can turn on this memory newsreel for more or less any period of my life, but what I get in summoning up my very early youth are scenes like the component parts of what we used to call a Vorkapitch, one of those artistic cinematographic montages extensively used, if not invented, by the character of the same name, in which at one point, one is looking between the hind legs of a horse, two feet later up the nose of a grimacing wrestler, and two feet after that at a racing automobile bearing straight for the viewer.

These very early times unreel, sharp and immediate, but without dates and rarely chronologically. A scene might run for only seconds and be followed instantly by another so unrelated as to call into question the process of memory. Yet somehow the scenes are spliced together, maybe because they were imprinted around the same time, or maybe because they fell into an already established memory file.

I push the projection button . . .

. . . I see five Chinamen in Canton blue with long queues down their backs being delivered in a horse-drawn express wagon to our house on Elm Street. Snow is falling, and after a while the youngest one, called Wong, hurries onto the sidewalk to sweep this stuff off. He has never seen snow before. His efforts are not successful.

. . . It must be later, and there is Mother leaning over laying a fire. Suddenly I give her a big humorous push from behind. Her hair tangles in an andiron. She frees it furiously and rushes toward me to give me my first good licking. Screaming, I run into the stairway. Here I am snatched up by Wong, who runs with me to the top of the house and locks me in his room with him so that I will not get the beating I so richly deserve. My mother pounds on the door and threatens Wong with instant dismissal and corporal punishment when my father comes home, but Wong is adamant.

. . . Now we're on Thirty-first Street in New York, at the Hotel Wolcott, designed by Stanford White. Father is taking me to see Buffalo Bill and his Wonderful Wild West Show in old Madison Square Garden, also designed by Stanford White. On the way across town in a hansom cab, our cabbie hooks wheels with another cab. The other cabbie calls ours a son of a bitch. I ask Father what that means. Father seems rather embarrassed and says it is just like saying our cabbie was the son of a cow. That doesn't seem so terrible to me. The show is wonderful, with many scenes of the taming of the West. Thousands of Indians get killed, but then get up again, which is pleasant for everybody. There is an exhibition of shooting, and the announcer says that Mr. Cody will now shoot the glass balls off a horse. I heard many years later that this announcer only said this when he was drunk, which was only part of the time. I think Father introduced me to Mr. Cody during some kind of intermission relieved by pink lemonade. I'm pretty sure I remember somebody with long hair down his back and a lot of fringes on his clothes, but it might have been one of Mr. Cody's stand-ins. How I loved Father and going places with him.

. . . Then, there I am, riding bareback inside a dark old riding academy, taking little jumps over logs about a foot above the tanbark.

. . . Morning sunlight at the Onwentsia Club, where Father has just given me a beautiful pony of my own, a retired polo pony. I go riding with a groom from the club's stables. My retired polo pony is, of course, neck-broken, he works with one hand, but I don't know this and I must do something wrong with the reins, because abruptly the pony has started back where we came from and I am swinging in the air on the other end of the reins doing the big loop.

. . . Then, aboard ship: it seems to be some kind of French or German liner with four funnels, it could be the *Deutschland*. I am on Caruso's shoulders, my short legs around his neck, and he is hollering with laughter because he's got my mother's squirrel-lined cape on inside out. He has a little black waxed mustache, which, if I didn't see it right here in front of me, I might have forgotten he had.

. . . Caruso draws caricatures—of himself, of Scotti, the great baritone, of Madame Sembrich, and one of my mother, which I don't think she liked, asleep in her deck chair, little z-z-z's rising above her.

5

I DON'T REMEMBER GETTING THERE, but one day in the very early spring of 1904, Mother and I arrived at Isadora's apartment in Berlin. Mrs. Duncan was there and so was lovely little Temple Duncan, Isadora's niece, a few months older than I and my first and desperate sweetheart.

It was on our first evening here that Isadora talked Mother out of her fashionable clothes and high heels and into bare feet, gold sandals, and loose flowing Grecian gowns. After a couple of years in Chicago playing society matron, Mother must have longed for the simplicity of the unconventional, because for the rest of the time, that's the only kind of costume in which she ever appeared, the formality of any particular occasion notwithstanding.

The next day, Mother and Isadora left for Bayreuth, where Frau Cosima had at last persuaded Isadora to participate in the Wagner Festival. According to my mother, she and Isadora were brought to Frau Wagner, who, rather surprised at their Grecian attire, wondered if all Americans dressed like that. "Oh, no," Isadora assured her, "some wear feathers!"

Left behind with Mrs. Duncan and Temple, I remember vaguely being put in something called a Gymnasium there in Berlin, and sitting dumbly, unable to understand a word, amongst a bunch of little, short-cropped German boys until the kindly professor took pity on me. He came and sat beside me and showed me how to draw a fish by attaching an unending quantity of U's to each other, and how to make a tree by working the same principle with Y's. I perfected these two drawings during the rest of my stay in the Gymnasium. Since I learned somehow to sing "O Tannenbaum" ("Oh, Christmas Tree") and "Fuchs Du Hast die Gans Gestohlen" ("Fox You Have the Goose Geswiped") in passable German, I was later considered quite a German scholar in Chicago circles.

After a few months, Mrs. Duncan, Temple, and I joined Mother and Isadora in Bayreuth. Mother and Isadora shared a sort of villa there that was really a peasant's cottage, or bauernhaus. The non-music-loving locals would move out during the festival period and shack up in their cow sheds while extorting fancy rents for their vacated cottages from the simpleminded Wagner enthusiasts. The villa was small, not large enough to accommodate Mrs. Duncan, Temple and me, and the governess we shared. We were put up at an inn not too far away. There, besides the governess, Temple and I shared, I think, a bed. Bayreuth was aswarm with musicians, artists, vagabonds, painters, tramps, and scholars. We were probably lucky not to have been housed in a tree.

The sounds of rehearsals were nearly continuous. *Tannhäuser, Parsifal,* and *The Ring* commenced, stopped, recommenced, stopped. Boys who seemed to be only a little older than I whistled leitmotive in the streets. Happily, only those taking part in the performances were ever allowed in the theatre during rehearsals, probably the only reason my life wasn't poisoned by having to accompany my mother and Isadora there, ever.

Very soon after our arrival, it might even have been the very same day, Temple and I were stripped of our wardrobes and we found ourselves decked out, like Mother and Isadora, exclusively in bare feet, sandals, and little Grecian dresses.

I remember a day when three of us, Temple and I and a Siegfried Wagner son who had yellow hair down to his shoulders, were playing in the ruins of the Roman theatre. While I stood at stage level looking out into the ruins, he sneaked up behind me and gave me a murderous push from the back. I was lucky and only skinned my legs when I landed on the broken marble below. Temple yelled, "I've got him!" And she had. When I got back around, she was sitting on him, holding him down by his long yellow hair. I gave him the going-over he had earned in spades for his sneakiness and delivered it with all the fury a five-year-old can muster. When his grandmother, Frau Cosima, saw him with his eyes blacked and his hair glued together with blood, she became quite indignant and wished to know if all small American children treated their dear little playmates so roughly. She didn't realize her grandson was an embryonic murderer who may have been set back on the straight and narrow path by Temple's and my good offices.

I remember the grotto where the old guard gave a demonstration of waterworks every afternoon, sending brightly painted metal crowns spinning high up on the fountain's stream.

One time, calling on Mother at the villa, I wandered into Isadora's room and stopped suddenly in horrified indignation. "A lady," I remarked waspishly, "wouldn't stand around in front of a gentleman without any clothes on at all!" Isadora looked slowly around from the mirror, down at me, then let me have it. "A *gentleman*," she said, "wouldn't come crashing into a lady's room without knocking!"

That summer we spent a little time at a place called Schevening, too, where the bath cabins for changing clothes were on wheels and were pulled out over the sand at low tide by horses. All I remember is a guy with a beard and a red woolen shirt standing in the ocean up to his wishbone and holding me by the slack of my bathing suit to teach me to swim. My head was always going under the water and I screamed bloody murder . . .

Another time that summer, Mother and Isadora, accompanied by Beregay Oskar, Isadora's by then discharged firstest of the firstests, left Bayreuth for a few days, taking Temple and me with them to Helgoland, the island rock fortress in the North Sea. According to my mother, Isadora wanted to swim, an inconceivable exercise in the angry waves assaulting Helgoland, so the four of us—I don't think Beregay Oskar came—were rowed to a flat sandy spit of an island nearby so Isadora could swim that afternoon. On the sandy spit was a small house, the only structure standing on the little island, which rejoiced in calling itself a hotel. Enchanted with the place, Isadora announced that we would stay here instead of on Helgoland. Temple and I were left with the housewife who helped run the place, while Mother and Isadora were rowed back to Helgoland for their baggage. That would have taken about an hour. But they didn't come back. Daylight drained away while Temple and I stood waiting at the window, watching the world disappear in the deep, deep dark.

Later that night, one of the most terrible storms ever known in the North Sea burst in a fury all around us. The wind raged, the sea pounded the sandy spit, washed over it, washed over the house. Temple and I huddled at the window.

According to my mother, she and Isadora had intended to come right back, but after dinner Isadora decided to wait till the next day, so that she and Mother could spend the evening with Beregay Oskar, who was leaving in the morning. When the storm broke, Mother and Isadora asked about the safety of the little island and were told that every now and then a good storm swept it bare. But the children were there! It was possible that the hotel would weather the storm, they were told, it had withstood a few already. But Mother and Isadora both recalled that flimsy little structure and far from being reassured, they became frantic. No means of communicating with the hotel existed. They ran out into the storm, down to the little port, and begged some fishermen there to take them over in one of their boats. They had to get their children! The fishermen refused. That sea was a grave. They ran to the lifeguards and pleaded until one of guards gave in. Then, refusing to be left behind, these two brave women jumped into the boat and headed into the violent seas. They found Temple and me, "faces peering out the window, terrified, waiting for us to come to get them."

Then we were in the tossing lifesaving boat—I crouched at my mother's feet, Temple at Isadora's, the snarling icy sea crashing over us as the lifeguards fought to bring us into Helgoland. At the port, a crowd of fishermen stood cheering and lending a hand. Temple and I were rubbed down, wrapped up, given hot tea and whiskey and put to bed. Mother and Isadora sat up till daylight, and then we all went back to Bayreuth.

The great German tenor, von Bary, met us with crossness and perplexed anxiety. He was a serious admirer of Mother's and thought he should have been, if not invited along, at least forewarned of the Helgoland excursion.

Gathered in, once in a while, by my mother and Isadora for a mandatory dose of exposure to great minds, Temple and I sat on the lap of Ernst Haeckel, who discovered the invisible organisms in seawater and looked like Father Time. We also graced the lap of Frau Cosima, and the tenor Burgstahler's lap, and Humperdinck's lap, and Frau Thode's lap, and the laps of the King and Queen of Württemberg, and that of the Ab-Princess of Meiningen, the Kaiser's sister, and many others. Temple and I came pretty close to being professional lap-sitters that summer of 1904.

Oh, yes, I remember that little Bavarian village. But most of all I remember Temple.

6

AT THE END OF THAT AUGUST, the festival was over, and I became six years old. According to my mother's book, our little troupe then went to Florence, where, allegedly, I danced over Dante's bridge in the middle of the night with Isadora and my mother.

Incidentally, when I look back over what I was exposed to as a child, I realize how extraordinarily lucky I was never to have become a (God forbid) male interpretive dancer with a wreath of gold laurel leaves around my head.

I don't remember Florence at all, but I remember Venice—where Mother's book says we went next—very well. I especially remember the little tramcar over on the Lido that was pulled by mules. I got the croup there twice and was pretty sick. This brought out an interesting fact about the laws of Venice at the time.

Father had come over to take us back to Chicago and when he asked the Venetian doctor how much he owed him for taking care of me, the doctor smiled and said, "Anything you like." So Father said he would appreciate it if the doctor would tell him how much because he was just a visitor there and didn't know anything about the customs of the country. The doctor explained that, by law, he was allowed to charge only two lira, or forty cents, a visit; that he had come five times; and that that was why he had said, "Anything you like." Father put a hundred dollars in his hand and the doctor stamped off in a fury, muttering rude remarks about rich stinking Americans who showed no gratitude when you saved their lousy children's lives.

Mother and I, of course, were still in our Grecian raiment when Father arrived to take us home. Father must have wondered aloud what had happened to the elegant young wife and child he had put aboard ship in New York those months and months ago, because Mother announced that these were the only kinds of clothes she intended to wear for the rest of her life. Father reminded her how awfully cold it got when the winter winds blew in off the lake in Chicago, but Mother declared that it didn't matter.

And that's how I happened to be wearing sandals and a little dress over short pants for my first day at Dr. Coulter's School in Chicago. I was used to the outfit by then, and accustomed to being, with Temple, the object of many compliments in Germany. Small children wear what their mothers and nurses put on them. In Chicago, though, I became an object of derision, and that I was not accustomed to. Getting to school on my bicycle every day, I became, of necessity, the best street fighter in Chicago. I don't remember how long this went on. Father eventually persuaded mother to confine her Grecian gowns and sandals to the house, and I must have been included in the agreement.

Around Christmastime that same year, in Berlin, Isadora met Gordon Craig and began a torturing relationship, apparently spawned in an irresistible physical attraction but nourished by their mutual adoration of the genius of Mr. Craig.

Early the next year, 1905, Isadora opened the Isadora Duncan School of the Dance in Berlin, with an impressive roster of sponsors and twenty little girls between the ages of four and eight, whose parents had agreed, at no cost to the parents, to leave them with Isadora until they reached seventeen. Temple, of course, was among them. Naturally they were all dressed in bare feet, sandals, and little Grecian dresses.

In July, the girls, bare-armed, bare-legged, and barefoot, were presented for the first time at the Kroll Opera House in Berlin doing a few little leaps across the stage as a coda to Isadora's stunning performance. More stunning was the reaction of a member of the audience, the Kaiserin Auguste Victoria, who professed herself shocked to the core at the naked limbs of the children. That was distressing enough, but when the patrons learned of Isadora's relationship with Mr. Craig—Isadora made no secret of it—the scandal shivered their high sensibilities, and they fell over each other in their rush to withdraw their support of a leader with morals so loose. The full financial burden of the school—its kapellmeister, her sister Elizabeth, who ran it when Isadora was off doing something else, its cooks, teachers, maids, nurses, gardeners, and gate-keepers, not to mention food and clothing and doctors and dentists for twenty growing girls—fell like an oak on Isadora.

I mention Gordon Craig and Isadora's school here because they became an ever larger part of the background of my boyhood as Mother's and my time in Europe grew into ever longer stretches.

About the same time that Isadora was scandalizing Germany with

stage-front defenses of her right to love without marriage, I was in
Ravinia Park, Chicago, being dragged off to see Molière in English in
the open air: *Le Malade Imaginaire, Le Bourgeois Gentilhomme.* When
Molière was finished, I squirmed through the works of Shakespeare, also
in the open air. I didn't know then that I was to suffer this kultur for
the rest of my life with Mother. We were there that season because Mr.
Donald Robertson, the actor-manager who instigated all this jollification,
was a friend of Mother and was presently to put on a play she wrote called
The Law. Father, of course, put up the money for the production. Father
always put up the money for everything.

On the day *The Law* opened in Chicago for the benefit of the
women's and children's convalescent home, I, the author's son, disappeared. Nobody was able to find me until someone reported that I was
out in front of the theatre, opening the carriage doors, bowing from the
waist in the German way and saying, "How do you do! You have probably come to see my mother's play. I hope you will enjoy it."

. . . A lovely place comes into view, a garden by a lake, a dock with
canoes, Green Lake, Wisconsin. The Morris children are having a birthday party and I have been invited up for the day by their parents, Mr.
and Mrs. Ira Nelson Morris. After stuffing the children with ice cream
and cake and putting paper hats on us, they herd us all into a big tent
with a white screen stretched in front of us. Everybody wants to know
what the screen is for. I, as a seasoned traveler and operagoer, explain
that it is for the actors to change their clothes behind, after which they
will come out and do their stuff for us. The lights go out and on the screen
comes *The Great Train Robbery,* the first movie I ever saw.

. . . A place at the edge of a lake in Canada. Aunt Mary Sunshine,
Father's sister, and I have a birchbark cabin in a birchbark grove. Aunt
Mary is always taking courses in Chicago to learn how to beat things like
small ashtrays out of copper. Here there are many pretty souvenirs with
mottos burned in birchbark. What I like best are the pillows one could
fill with pine needles oneself. On one pillow it says humorously, "I Pine
for You and Balsam." Aunt Mary has a hell of a time trying to explain
that one to me.

. . . More memories of Chicago. Our big three-cylinder Cadillac
looming amongst the gentle electric cars. One day while flying along
Lake Shore Drive, we are overtaken by a mounted policeman, who gives
us a ticket for speeding.

Mother's six months in Chicago must have been up, because there we were on that wonderful train, the Twentieth Century, on the way to the Hotel Wolcott in New York to spend a few days there before sailing for France. How exciting it was to sit out on the observation platform and to see the rails clicking by. How I loved the porters and the dining-car waiters. How kind they were to little boys. Mother always let me have the upper berth so I could peek out over the top or slide down inside the green curtain to visit her, then climb up again like a monkey. Years later I make a picture called *The Palm Beach Story* using just such sleeping-car berths in a scene where Claudette Colbert steps on Rudy Vallee's face.

But suddenly, with half of our stuff already on the loading dock at the port, Mother and I were back on the Twentieth Century, and then back in Chicago. Everybody was very grave. Father had had a terrible automobile accident.

While out being driven around by his oldest friend, Jim Heyworth, who had a new automobile, Father had been in a head-on collision. He was thrown forty feet into the air, suffering a fracture of the skull and a very bad concussion. He was unconscious for eleven days and then slowly, very slowly, he began to get better. When he came home from the hospital, there were nurses for the day and nurses for the night to attend him. Our Swedish cook sat by my bed every night until I fell asleep.

It was about this time that Father's reaction to sad things and funny things got mixed up. He couldn't shave himself for a while, so his barber used to come over to our house every day to do it for him. One day the barber started telling Father a hard-luck story with the intention of borrowing some money from him. It was a very sad story, and although Father didn't want to, and didn't feel that way, he started to laugh. The barber thought Father hadn't got the point of the story so he made it sadder, and Father laughed harder. The barber got desperate and made the story so sad that tears of laughter were rolling down Father's cheeks and he was fighting for breath. He gave the barber the five hundred dollars, more to have a moment to catch his breath than because he was convinced by the barber's story.

When finally Father was well enough to go for a walk, he took me with him into Lincoln Park. Suddenly something made him laugh very hard and he threw his very heavy ivory-handled cane at me. It just missed my head, and I was terribly frightened. But I loved him so and was so sure of his love for me that I was certain he didn't mean me any harm. The expression of his emotions still got badly mixed up for two or three years afterwards, and slightly mixed up for the rest of his life.

I don't remember how long a time after the accident Father and Mother and I were in Coronado Beach, part of San Diego. Here I *really* learned to swim, in an indoor hot seawater pool, with all kinds of slides down into it and white barrels with horses' heads on them that one tried to ride and fell off of, where one spent whole days yelling and having a wonderful time. Other times, I climbed all the way out on the breakwater made of rocks piled on each other to where, at the end, there were seals waiting hungrily, hoping there was fish for them in a pocket.

Our neighbor on one side was L. Frank Baum, who wrote the wonderful *Wizard of Oz* stories. His sons were my playmates, although they were a little older than I. On the other side of us lived a stout old Christian Science practitioner, whose name I've forgotten. Contact was established, and pretty soon, though not for the first time, Mother was dabbling in religion again. On the way back East, we went through Los Angeles, but it was just another city then. Moving pictures were still being made in New York, up around Fort Lee, I think.

From Chicago we went back to the Hotel Wolcott and then to Paris. Father was with us, but very despondent. (Did that mean he was actually pleased?) One night at the Hotel Meurice in Paris, Father climbed out the window, then moved over on to a ledge about nine inches wide between the windows. The ledge was four flights up, and Father stayed there for about an hour, laughing and saying he was going to jump. Mother finally succeeded in coaxing him back into the room, and presently he went back to his business in Chicago.

I think it was about this time, around 1905 or 1906, that Mother and I had an apartment in Paris, a furnished one, on the rue Villarette de Joyeuse. I remember that we had a parrot who chewed the edges off the furniture, besides doing his business on the carpets, and that Mother had some words with the proprietress about all this when we left.

In the salon of the apartment there was an earphone hanging beside the fireplace. I had listened to this idly once or twice, but it was completely dead and I had not the faintest idea what it was for. Then one night after dinner, Dr. Max Mertz, the kapellmeister of Isadora's school, who was visiting us, unhooked the earphone and listened to it. His face took on a beatific expression. I asked him what he was listening to and he immediately waved me down, telling me in my own house, with perfect German manners, to shut up. He now resumed his listening and his expression varied between deep puzzlement and that of someone listening to celestial music. As a matter of fact, he *was* listening to celestial music. The earphone was connected directly with a microphone in the proscenium of the Paris opera house and was a service supplied for a very reasonable fee by the telephone company. It was called the Opéraphone, and I mention it only to show that there were some fairly bright people in the world around 1900, and that the whole idea of wired shows for which one pays is not a new idea.

I remember riding horseback with a friend of my mother's and a groom, and crossing the avenue du Bois just where the avenue disappears into the Bois itself. I was trying to ride like the famous jockey Tod Sloan, with my head way forward over the horse's neck. An early automobile went exploding by, and the frightened horse threw his head up, smashed my nose and took off out of control, streaking through the Bois at full gallop, a crying, bleeding little boy on its back and a wonderful horsewoman and a yelling groom in hot pursuit.

THE NEXT THING I KNEW, I was back in Germany. Don't ask me how I got there. We had our French maid, Anna, with us and we were living in Dresden, just next door to the relocated Duncan school. The school had been given the use of a large residence, half palace and half beer garden with open-air bowling alleys, the former residence of Germany's then largest metal polish (or putz) manufacturer. This gentleman had the brilliant idea of enclosing, in every can of putz he put out, a coin. Sometimes it was only a pfennig, one-fifth of a cent, and sometimes, of course much more rarely, a twenty-mark gold piece, but always there was a coin. As a result, Globe putz outsold all other putzes twenty to one and was used by the German Army almost exclusively. The manufacturer had a large reproduction of his Globe trademark, made out of stained glass and illuminated from within, placed on the roof of his residence, or schloss. Here the girls lived and danced, and I bowled with them in the open-air alleys across the street.

I remember going to the state opera house in Dresden, because I had to catch up on my sleep by taking naps in the afternoons instead of playing in the municipal gardens with the other children, and this poisoned my existence. One of the operas I liked was *The Flying Dutchman,* especially the "Spinning Song" and the water scenes. And I liked *Samson and Delilah* because I always hoped that von Bary, the guy who had been chasing my mother around in Bayreuth, would bring the columns he shook crashing down on his head.

One day while taking a present of some highly perfumed soap over to Temple, she said it was a good thing I had brought it because they were going away on a tour. By "they" she meant the girls, including herself, who then made up the Isadora Duncan School of the Dance. Their names were Anna, Irma, Maria-Theresa, Liesel, Gretel, Erika, Isabelle, and of course, Temple. They were lovely-looking and beautifully built little girls, in age from slightly above to slightly below me, and all wonderful dancers. I have hardly ever seen anything more thrilling than their tremendous diagonal leaps across the stage, three abreast in unison, to the thundering climax of Schubert's "Marche Militaire." Sometimes Isadora danced it with them, in a dried-blood-color chiton worn to a rag, and when she did this, it was something to see. It didn't bring the house down, it brought on mass hysteria. I've seen audiences all over the world screaming themselves hoarse, pounding each other on the back, tears of joy streaming down their cheeks. People ask me what it was like when Isadora danced. I have no words to explain. There is no basis of comparison, of course, but I couldn't describe the Dempsey-Firpo fight either, although I was there.

By the time I knew her, Isadora danced always to music produced by a first-class symphony orchestra, and perhaps it was the combination of music that reached the soul and the unutterably beautiful visual interpretation of its depth and intensity by Isadora that produced the astonishing impact.

At this time, except for Temple, who was American, Isabelle, who was Belgian, and Anna, who was Swiss, these girls were all one hundred percent growing German girls with one hundred fifty percent German appetites.

The German appetite is something that must be observed firsthand to be truly appreciated. Only someone who has seen with his naked eye a group of three or four German music-lovers rush out from the Festspiel-haus at the end of *Parsifal*, Act One, cross the street to a beer garden, and there devour an entire suckling pig with an apple in its mouth and be back in their seats in time for the first downbeat of *Parsifal*, Act Two, The Overture, can begin to comprehend it. It goes without saying that these music-lovers have already dined and made plans for a solid supper. This was just a little etwas to keep body and soul together and to help better appreciate the music. A newcomer to Germany might also be surprised, in fact, he would be electrified, by the pre-breakfasts and post-breakfasts that surround the true breakfast . . . by the eleven-thirty and three-thirty sausage breaks, the pre-lunch vorspeise, the afternoon snacks, the just-before-dinner delicacies, the after-dinner sandwiches, and, at last, the supper, thank God, and the final little fortifier in the kitchen before retiring, washed down with a bucket of beer.

I have mentioned all of this so that it will be understood that the question of feeding the predominantly German pupils of the Isadora Duncan School of the Dance was not only always pressing, but always the first thing on the mind of whosoever was running the school. At this particular period, Elizabeth Duncan, Isadora's small and dessicated sister known as Tante, with whom Isadora parked the whole school when she got bored with it or had something better to do, was in charge. Tante was helped in running the school by the bald-headed kapellmeister and gentleman friend, Dr. Mertz, a musical doctor, naturally.

The food problem must have raised its hungry head again for the Duncan School, and this no doubt was the reason for the tour Temple told me about. Dr. Mertz was to conduct and the girls to dance in any town where the opera house happened to be empty between Baden-Baden and Berlin, that is to say, Wiesbaden, Frankfurt-am-Main, Koblenz, Neuwied, Bonn, Cologne, Düsseldorf, Essen, Barmen-Elberfeld, Paderbor, Bad Piermont, Fritzlar, Kassel, Bremen, Hamburg, and Hanover, and any other place in between that the manager of an opera house would let them in.

The thought of being separated from Temple, my true love, was so unbearable to me that I whined around until a brilliant inspiration struck me: I suggested myself as a program seller and, somehow, somebody fell for this pitch. Mother's consent was secured from wherever she was, and to my great joy, I was taken along as a part of the troupe.

To this happy turn of events can be attributed the availability of the club sandwich in Germany. Where I fell so in love with this masterpiece of sandwich construction that, if it could possibly be helped, I would eat nothing else, I know not. Its introduction all over, through and into the darkest corners of pre–World War I Germany, came about in a very simple way. At each of the small towns in which we performed, I would ask the Herr Oberkellner of our hotel who was writing down our lunch or dinner orders for my dream of dreams: a club sandwich. This invariably led to a long list of questions on the part of Herr Ober, followed by an even longer and halting series of replies from me. Sooner or later, but inevitably, this discourse was terminated by Herr Ober, purple with rage, grabbing me by the hand, yanking me off my chair and out into the kitchen, where he wished me on the chef.

It was this perspiring and much put-upon individual who eventually came up with the buttered toast, the tender breast of chicken, the crumbly bacon, the crisp lettuce, the garnishments of pimiento, the mayonnaise made with authentic olive oil, the soupçon of English mustard, the pretty paprika, the fragrant, freshly ground pepper, with all of which, hot under a gleaming silver dome, I was presently and triumphantly served. Since I went through this routine at least twice a day at every single stop between Baden-Baden and Berlin, I do not feel that I am taking up too much territory in modestly laying claim to the title of Pioneer and First Introducer of the Club Sandwich into Germany.

My program vending was also remarkably successful and easily topped the combined totals of all of my predecessors. My method was simplicity itself. I merely stood immovable in front of my chosen victim and forgot my German until he bought a program. As I was quite small, I did not confine my efforts to the aisles like normal program vendors, but found that I could easily enfilade the space between the actual rows of seats, thus putting the entire audience at my mercy. This discovery paid off handsomely.

By the time the tour was over and we got back to Dresden, a new character had appeared at our apartment. I know not whence he came. He was called José Velasquez, hailed from the Yucatan, and was a serious composer. I suspect he had some idea of marrying Mother—as most of the gentlemen who came around seemed to have. He and Mother were writing an operetta together called *The Vendor of Dreams.* I remember one quite pretty song in it called "Rocked on the Bough of a Phan-han-tom Tree."

Mr. Velasquez taught me my first piece on the piano, one called "Hänschen Klein, ging allein," and, possibly because of his presence, I was presently wished on some poor professor of music, who, at my mother's request, tried to teach me harmony. This was very sad.

After a while the operetta must have been finished, because Mr. Velasquez seemed to evaporate, and the next thing I knew, Mother and Anna (the maid) and I were on a train for Paris. We had accumulated quite a lot of stuff during our stay in Dresden and the compartment was stuffed, not only with baggage of every sort, but also some canary birds, a parrot, and a couple of dogs. Don't ask me how this is possible.

When we went two cars ahead to the dining car for dinner, Mother left her bag with our tickets and her checkbook in the compartment, taking with her what German money she had left, which was just about enough for the dinner.

During the middle of this meal, a very pompous uniformed official came into the car and started bawling out some announcement which we neither understood nor paid much attention to. As he passed near our table, Mother asked him if he could get us a little more kartoffeln (potatoes). At this, he looked very vexed and departed.

The train stopped somewhere after a while, but this did not interest us. Presently we finished our dinner and started back for our compartment, carrying the bones for the dogs and some bread for the birds. Our compartment, as I have noted, was two cars to the rear, but after traversing one car, there wasn't any more train, just a long vista of tracks clickety-clacketing into the distance. The utter disbelief one feels in that situation was mirrored by Claudette Colbert years later in *The Palm Beach Story*, when she went back to the car carrying the Ale and Quail Club, only to find that it was no longer attached to the train.

Mother now remembered enough of her German to find out that we were no longer on our way to Paris but on a nonstop express to Berlin, the other part of the train having been cut off a while back and sent on its way to Paris. All this was explained to her with some satisfaction by the official whose dignity she had wounded when she had asked him for more kartoffeln.

Mother asked that a wire be sent about the baggage and the tickets and the birds and the dogs, and the official said nothing could be done before we got to Berlin.

When we got to Berlin, there was more complication because, if I remember correctly, one had to surrender one's tickets, to prove one had them, before leaving the platform. And, of course, we didn't have the tickets; they were on their way to Paris in the cut-off part of the train. This brought the head man in a red cap out of his office and over to where we were.

He listened patiently to Mother's explanation, then said the matter was very simple: he would wire Cologne to have the things and animals taken out of our compartment and held for us, and in the meanwhile, all Mother had to do was to buy three tickets from Dresden to Berlin to enable us to get off the platform, and to buy three more tickets from Berlin to Paris for the first train in the morning. She would then turn in her other tickets when we got to Cologne, her money would be refunded, and everything would be hotsy-totsy.

Mother thanked him but pointed out that she had no money to buy anything with except a few silver pieces left from dinner.

"But it will be refunded to you," said the Bahnhof chief.

"But I haven't got it," said my mother.

"But you will get it back," said the Bahnhof chief, beginning to lose his patience at a woman's density.

"Get *what* back?" said my mother. "I haven't anything to give you till I get my bag from Cologne."

"But you can't leave the platform without tickets. It's against the rules," said the Bahnhof chief.

"Well, you're certainly not going to keep us standing here all night!" said my mother, and started on a ploy which always worked very well in imperial Germany. "You let us off this platform at once or I will telephone my friend, the Ab-Princess of Meiningen, immediately, and your name will be mud!"

"You m-mean His Imp-per-perial M-majesty's s-s-sister?" began the poor man, not knowing whether Mother was bluffing or not, but not daring to find out.

"I most certainly do," said Mother, knowing she had him now. "Take me to the telephone!"

I guess the Princess wasn't home or something, but we were allowed off the platform and went on foot to the cheesiest and cheapest hotel in the neighborhood, the Central. Mother had just exactly enough money for the room, although I nearly ruined everything by demanding a hot bath.

In the morning we went to the station for the early train, and here a new problem arose. We had no tickets to get through the gates to get on the train. This, however, was child's play to a woman of my mother's acumen. Waiting till just about the last German equivalent of "All aboard," she sent me, heavily rehearsed, up to the gate first. When the ticket collector said, "Billette, bitte," I pointed to Anna, our maid, just a few paces behind me, and was allowed through. When Anna was asked for her ticket, she pointed to my mother, a few paces behind her, and was also allowed through. When it came to my mother's turn, she merely pointed to an old gentleman some distance behind her, hurried by, grabbed Anna and me and shoved us on the train, a nonstop one to Cologne. Whether the old gentleman Mother pointed to got on or not, I don't know.

There was, of course, the question of food as far as Cologne. We had had no money for breakfast at the hotel and were nearly starving to death. This was solved by an amiable American gentleman, who

thought Mother was alone because she had put us in different compart-
ments to cloud the issue at ticket time. He invited her to lunch. She
accepted with pleasure and alacrity, merely muttering something about
her baby and its nurse. "Of course," said the gentleman with a wave of
the hand. We all had a fine lunch, although I think he spent a little more
than he intended to.

There was also the question of tickets when the conductor came
around, especially as he couldn't understand how we had got on the train
without any. But since it was a nonstop train, there wasn't much he could
do about it, and everything was straightened out when we pulled into
Cologne, where a soldier with a bayonet was guarding our pile of stuff,
with the parrot insulting him in French.

We got back to Paris, but the next thing I knew, we were again at
the Wolcott in New York, with Mother warbling "Rocked on the Bough
of a Phan-han-tom Tree" into the reluctant ears of Messrs. Klaw and
Erlanger. So reluctant were their ears, in fact, that we were presently on
a German liner on our way back to Paris.

8

I'M NOT CERTAIN, but I think it was about this time that I passed a most pleasant stretch with the French family Rousseau in Joinville-le-Pont, a place a little to the east of Paris, where the Marne comes in to join the Seine, although this period may very well have been before, rather than after, I introduced the club sandwich into Germany.

Time passes very slowly for lifers and small boys, and I seem to remember that at 61, rue de Paris in Joinville-le-Pont, it came to a complete stop. I was there for so long, or what seemed so long to me, that I came nearly to believe that Monsieur Rousseau was my father, his wife, my mother, and his mother-in-law, my grandmother. Their little boy, Dédé, I thought of as my brother. Besides me, there was another, very large pupil there called Gruenwald. He was considerably older than Dédé or I, but very gentle and always willing to play whatever game I suggested. It was only many years later, when he inherited one of the largest fur houses in Paris, that I learned he had always been simpleminded.

I have mentioned that Temple was my first and desperate sweetheart. Desperate suited the situation. Once in the middle of the night in my room at the Rousseaus, I started a *Tristan and Isolde* type of love dirge, with words and music by myself, to alleviate the woe I felt and to express my tragic heartbreak at being separated from Temple. In order not to make too much noise, I stuck my head under the covers. But my groans were so powerful and so continuous that presently they worked their way out, not only through the blankets and the feather plumard on top of me, but also through the adjoining walls and floors into the rest of the house. Presently, and rather faintly through all the stuff on top of me, I heard my name called. I peeked out, and there, all holding candles and leaning over my bed worriedly, stood the entire Rousseau household, including little Dédé, and big Gruenwald in some kind of nightshirt with feet in it. I must have sounded a little like Boris Godunov at that.

In September 1906, Isadora had her first child, little Deirdre, sired by Gordon Craig without benefit of clergy, which was probably a good thing, since he was already married, or about to be married, to somebody else in England, where he had sired some earlier progeny, and Isadora had become notorious for her proclamations about women having the right to bear children without submitting to the bonds of matrimony.

In the summertime, I and all the Rousseau household went to the seashore at a wonderful place called Onival. The beach was especially wonderful. Instead of a lot of sand on it to get in one's shoes and in the sandwiches when one had picnics, this beach was made out of big round pebbles one could throw at things.

We had a lovely house at Onival in which I helped Papa Rousseau to make his own shells for the shotgun with which he shot seagulls. We also preserved a large quantity of sea snakes and other extraordinary specimens in alcohol and formaldehyde and then sealed them up in big jars. I don't know why, unless they were used in the very large school called Le Parangon that Dr. Rousseau, Papa Rousseau's father, ran next door to where we lived in Joinville-le-Pont.

In the fall, Papa Rousseau trained his hunting dogs to obey with collars that seemed to have phonograph needles inside them. He also dug in his garden, cleaned out the manure from the back where the chickens and ducks and rabbits were, and shot swallows, which were attracted to the premises by a clockwork mechanism that spun wooden wings with little mirrors on them.

Every so often a beautiful lady in furs would arrive in a shining automobile with presents for everyone. This was Mother, of course. She had usually been off with Isadora somewhere when she showed up like this. After a little while, I would be able to talk to her haltingly in English. From this time on, my English had a slight French accent, which didn't wear off until some years later, when I was sent back to America to stay. But there with the Rousseaus, who were always so kind to me, I also acquired a knowledge of French deep enough to last the rest of my life.

P RESENTLY WE WERE BACK at our house in Glencoe, Illinois, where the bottom of our garden led onto the golf course. There, one night in 1907, when I was about eight, Mother and Father had a terrible row. Mother had just brought me back from Europe, and I think the row had something to do with the length of time I had been away from Chicago, a city I adored and to which Father was chained by the necessities of his banking and brokerage business, but which my mother, having tasted of Europe, could no longer tolerate. She said that if Mrs. Potter Palmer, the acknowledged queen of society, started the season off with duck Bigarade, one never got anything else but duck Bigarade wherever one went for the rest of the season, and to hell with it.

They came into my room and woke me up. Father stood there, weaving a little because he had had a few drinks, and Mother said, "Mother is going to live in Paris, darling, and Father is going to stay here in Chicago. What do you want to do?"

I adored this big man I had just been reunited with, this ex-football player, this ex-bicycle champion of Illinois, this man who had brought home a present for me every night of my life when I was little, and whose unfailing tenderness and gentleness toward me extended back into the diffused twilight before memory began. It was heaven to sit on his lap. I loved to kiss the top of his bald head, and the perfume of my father, a mixture of maleness and the best Havana cigars, was the breath of Araby to me. So without any hesitation at all I said, "I want to stay here with Father."

And he said, "I am not your father."

I looked at him in stupefaction for a moment, then at my mother to see if he were joking, then back at Father. Then I started to cry. I remember their telling me I cried for a week, undoubtedly an exaggeration, but I know the kind of crying it was because I've seen my own little boys cry that way when they are heartbroken, and after a while the intake of breath makes a gasping hollow sound more distressing than the crying itself.

However long I cried, it was long enough to sober Father up, long enough to wake up the servants Mother had brought back from Luxembourg, long enough to start Mother crying too, long enough to throw the whole house into an uproar and to start the neighbors telephoning.

Father went downstairs to a glass case he had and trying to get me to stop crying, he gave me, one by one, all the trophies, the medals, the cups, and everything else he had ever won in school and in college and later at golf. There were honors for track and field and baseball and football, and the trophy I had always liked the best, a high bicycle made of gold with a sapphire in the hub of the big wheel and a diamond in the little wheel in back. That was an idiotic thing to give a small boy. I naturally lost it a few days later, but I think that that night he thought I was going to die of grief.

Of course he became my father again very soon. More accurately, he had never ceased being my father. Marcel Pagnol expressed it better than anyone in *Fanny*, the central play of his great trilogy. The father, he said, is not the one who gives life. Dogs give life. The father is the one who gives love.

Despite my express wish, I was not left in Chicago, but taken to Paris to live, and I did not see my father for many years. But we never stopped loving each other, and in 1940 he died in my arms in Hollywood, where he had come to be near me at the end.

10

MOTHER AND I SAILED FOR PARIS on a German liner. I remember this because Mother wanted to have the purser fired. No experienced traveler, of course, ever pays more than minimum rate or admits that any child is over six. This convention is as well known to the steamship companies as it is to experienced travelers, and is accepted by all concerned.

On this occasion, while Mother was telling him the usual lies about my age, the purser looked at me very beadily and finally allowed that I looked very large to him for a little boy under six. "Are you daring to presume to doubt my word?" began my mother, drawing herself up to her full five feet five. "Of course not, *gnädige Frau!*" said the purser.

But being a rat, he came up to me presently on the boat deck, where I was torturing the brass band with the other little boys by standing just in front of the musicians and sucking lemons, which filled their instruments with spit, and inclining his head downward, he said with a sweet smile, "My! What a fine big boy you are for under six yet!" And I said, "Who is? Me? I'm going on nine!"

With a triumphant leer, he exclaimed, "Ah hah! Just as I suspected! *Nun also!*" and hotfooted it down to Mother's cabin. But by the time she got through with him, he was sorry the idea had ever entered his head.

Beginning with remarks about Germans in general, she passed lightly over boastful little idiots pretending to be older than they were, warmed to her subject with more about chivalry through the ages and not permitting oneself to doubt a lady's word, then let him have it with the Ab-Princess of Meiningen and her celebrated brother, the Kaiser, and what they would do to him with both barrels. Like the Bahnhof chief, even if the purser didn't believe it all, he dared not take a chance on its being true, so he slunk away, a beaten man.

It was on this trip, I believe, that wishing to give a theatrical performance, I invented a method called *narratage,* for which I won a gold medal and many compliments some twenty-five years later. Having chosen "Little Miss Muffet" as a down-to-earth scenario, apt to please everybody, being full of sex, suspense, and surprise, I placed a little girl passenger on a tuffet, shoved a bowl of curds and whey (or as close an approximation of them as the deck steward could provide) into her clumsy little hands, and had my mother read this deathless poem in her finest pear-shaped tones. While she read, her son, remarkably disguised as a spider by the superimposition of a green veil that covered him like a tent, appeared hissing from behind a sofa, leapt violently upon the little girl, knocked her off the tuffet, stepped in the curds and whey, then chased her screaming out of the main salon. I need hardly add that the play was an immense success.

In Paris, Mother and I were back at the Meurice, from which I one day disappeared. I didn't know that I had disappeared, of course, but I remember being found in the basement of the Hotel Continental, across the street from the Meurice, learning to shine shoes from an American bootblack.

I also remember Mother's very wealthy suitor, Judge Priest, taking us to lunch at the Meurice, a very expensive caravansary, and Mother explaining to me afterwards that small boys are not supposed to ask for wild strawberries in midwinter at seven dollars a portion just because some gentleman might be trying to make a good impression.

I was given my first tuxedo around then, with knickerbockers, of course, and I wore it to have dinner with Mother and Judge Priest at the beautiful Hotel Majestic. I had never had a tuxedo before and wishing to look my very best, I put on my newest tie with it, a magnificent one from Charvet's on the place Vendôme.

The old judge nearly strangled on the piece of celery he was eating when I approached the table and he saw that with my tuxedo I had put on a green satin four-in-hand tie. He leapt to his feet and dragged me out of the dining room and up to his suite, where he gave me a beautiful black silk bow tie and a short lecture on what gentlemen wear after dark. He was a very nice man from St. Louis and a celebrated lawyer.

But nice or not, wealthy or not, Mother didn't want him, and he presently went away from our lives and married a very nice lady to whom eventually he left millions.

I don't think Mother had millions, however, although she had started building a rather elaborate private house with elevator and built-in garage on the lovely rue Richard Wagner, a stone's throw from La Muette in the 16th arrondissement. (During the First World War, they changed the name of the street to the rue Albéric Magnard because they decided that though Wagner was Wagner, still he was a German.)

One day somebody must have decided that it was about time that I actually learned something, because all of a sudden large quantities of haberdashery and clothing started to be assembled, and I began getting the kinds of talks it was felt would prepare me for incarceration in a large French school. I think the school had been suggested to Mother by a very handsome young French actor who had started hanging around, probably with the usual objective of marrying Mother. He had been at this school himself, and as he was of a very good family and a vicomte himself, Mother must have thought the school was good enough for me.

THE NEXT THING I KNEW, I was in La Petite Ecole, the small boys' half of the great Paris Lycée Janson de Sailly. I had been enrolled as a pensionnaire, or boarding student, in this huge, grim academy with its thousands of pupils, its enormous gravel-covered play yards, its gaslights, its block-long dormitories, and its gray walls.

On my very first day there, I made friends with a little French boy called Roger Doucède and, at this writing, we are still friends. We met while making paper airplanes. His father was one of the leading contractors of public works in France and subsequently became the mayor of the 16th arrondissement.

I discovered that the demi-pensionnaires, who only had their meals in the lycée, and the externes, who came only for lessons, could dress as they liked. They usually wore black tabliers, a sort of coverall apron that buttons up the back, and bare legs and socks.

But for the boarding pupil, the wardrobe was surprisingly elaborate. Even the smallest boys, and I was about eight, wore an everyday uniform of dark blue with long trousers, a vest with little round brass buttons, and a blue coat. Under this we wore a suit of long underwear and a shirt with attached starched collar and starched bosom, about the size of a dickey. This was held together with gilt studs. Around the neck, we wore a cache-nez, or nose-hiding muffler, and on our heads, clipped bare with a zero-zero clipper, we wore a beret.

The great and interminable joke was to grab somebody else's vest by the bottom and with a slight upward jerk, undo it to the top. As our hands didn't work very well yet and were often cold, the job of rebuttoning all those little pea-shaped brass buttons was fearful. The beret and the cache-nez made excellent weapons when loaded with a handful of gravel.

For bad weather, we had a cape with a hood; for Sundays, there was an entirely different uniform with more brass on it, a leather-visored cap bearing a gold school insignia, and an overcoat with a hood to protect the cap.

Often a hundred of us would march out to the Bois de Boulogne on a Sunday, all dressed the same, the little ones in front, the great big ones in back, the pion, or teacher, to one side carrying a football in a net. This solitary piece of equipment was for *all* of us.

Besides the two uniforms, there was a great list of required linen, black lisle socks, innumerable starched shirts, long nightshirts, bath-robes, and all kinds of towels. I always wondered what these last were for, since we never washed anything but the front end of our kissers in the icy water every morning, and only brought a single towel with us, once a week, when we were marched over to a bathing establishment half a mile away, where there were absolutely heavenly hot showers in stalls made of wood.

The meals, as I remember them, were extremely simple and never consisted of anything but beans. Sometimes there were white beans and sometimes there were pink beans. The jokes about them never varied. There was supposed to have been some kind of meat in the gravy dished over the beans, but I never saw any. There was an awful lot of bread in big baskets, and I suppose the reason I like butter so much today is that I never got any there. I think we had a big red wine though, with water. We ate in a long refectory that was full of echoes. The tables were gray-veined marble and I think the attached benches were made of iron. Even so, they got broken.

Just near the refectory there was a bitterly cold and dismal little building divided into cubicles. Here a poor little Jewish man called Professor Bloch tried to teach me to play the violin. He had a rather large, purple, dripping nose and he kept his derby hat, his muffler, and his mittens on, with just the fingers poking through, while giving me my lessons. I refer to him as "poor" because he had to listen to me play the violin. Actually, I think he was quite well-to-do, and I was surprised at the elegance of his apartment the first time I went to his end-of-the-season reception to receive what became my customary red book with gold edges.

I had been playing the violin for years, since the age of five, as a matter of fact, and it must have been obvious to a half-wit that I had no talent for this instrument. I did not have then, nor before then, nor since then, including today, a vibrato. And a violin played without a vibrato is like chicken noodle soup without the noodles and with very little chicken. Each of my violin teachers had a different method of teaching me the vibrato. One would tie me to my instrument with a string around my thumb. Another would have me push the fiddle against a wall, the scroll against a wadded handkerchief. Nothing ever worked. I was incapable of producing a vibrato.

In the cubicles adjoining mine, other miserable children under the guidance of other miserable professors were studying the cello, the piano, the flute. The noise was really awful.

Twice a day, the concierge would come out into the play yard and distribute big hunks of workingman's bread and thick black bitter chocolate, which was very good.

A short time after I entered the Lycée Janson, it was announced that we were all to be vaccinated against smallpox. We lined up outside the infirmary and, as we got near the door, we were told to pull our left arms out of our shirts. Inside the infirmary I saw a very surprising sight: a young cow, hitched to a desk, wearing a leather bandage over its eyes. When I got close enough for my turn, to my horror I saw the doctor reach into the cow's hide with his forceps, cut off one of the pustules the cow seemed to be covered with, and dip his scalpel into the severed pustule. Then he rapidly jabbed the scalpel three times into my upper arm. This procedure didn't seem to hurt the cow at all and it didn't hurt me either.

But when I described all this years later in Hollywood to my doctor and yachting companion, Bert Woolfan, he told me I was full of flit, that I must be dreaming, that no technique such as I described had been used since the beginning of the nineteenth century, that I had obviously confused a steel engraving of an early Edward Jenner experiment with a recollection of my own, that since 1850 it had been done with vaccines, that there hadn't been a live cow in a hospital since Grant took Richmond, etc. But the good doctor was wrong. Exactly what I described happened to me when I was in the thirteenth class of the Lycée Janson de Sailly on the avenue Henri Martin (now Georges Mandel) in Paris in about 1907.

What's more, the vaccination took so beautifully that presently my arm started to swell up and become inflamed, and I developed a high fever. One of my professors noticed it, and I was hustled over to the infirmary and put to bed in a long ward presided over by a couple of heavyset old nuns with red faces and big white coifs. After a while, one of them came in to take our temperatures. She started down at the far end of the ward from me, and it was only when she got closer that I noticed that the thermometer was a good deal larger than any thermometer anybody had ever put under my tongue or clasped into my armpit. I kept a very suspicious eye on that thermometer. Finally, when she reached the bed next to mine, I raised myself up a little and saw beyond question what she was doing with it. By the time she got to me and started lifting up the covers, I shot out the other side of the bed like an arrow and ran yoicking through the infirmary. The old nun picked up her skirts and started after me. A very exhilarating chase was enjoyed by all until finally I was hunted down, brought to bay and, I suppose one might say, foxed.

I don't remember what we studied in the thirteenth class, but it must have been pretty simple, because I don't think any of us were particularly bright. After classes we played for a while and then studied until suppertime. After the final beans of the day, we had another study period until it was time to go to bed.

It was usually still dark when we got up, and they gave us big bowls of hot milk with a little chicory in it called café au lait. Then we played a little and yelled a lot, then studied till classes began.

There were forty to fifty boys in each class, and the classrooms were on two levels, reached by covered balconies that surrounded the play yard. The professors were all very nice and I got along with them swimmingly, except for our professor of English.

At that time in France it was absolutely forbidden and against the law for a national of any other country to be hired to teach his own language in any French school. German had to be taught by a Frenchman; Italian had to be taught by a Frenchman; and so did every other language. For some reason that I have forgotten, I had to take English. This was obviously pretty silly, because even as a small boy, I spoke much better English than the miserable individual who had to teach it to me and my classmates. The professor knew that, of course, and loathed me for it. He would present a word like "house," for instance, and then give it to the boys phonetically, which I remember came out "ah-ooze." He would look at me bitterly, his little eyes pinpoints of hatred, and say, "No doubt, Monsieur Sturges, my pronounciation of zees word ees not pleasing you!" I wasn't looking for any trouble and I would tell him that, on the contrary, I enjoyed his "pronounciation" very much. For that, I'd get two hours of retenue for being fresh.

Two of the professors I got along very well with were our professor of gymnastics and Professor Petit, who taught me French boxing, namely, boxing with the feet. The name Petit seemed so funny to me as a small boy that I could never keep a straight face while taking my lessons from him. This caused him sometimes to punch me on the nose, but not very hard.

Our gymnasium was remarkable and had more stuff in it than one could dream up in a nightmare. Furthermore, every boy had to use every piece of it during every gymnasium class. In addition to the usual complement of wooden and iron dumbbells, Indian clubs, varnished shillelaghs, wall-pulley exercisers, parallel bars, stuffed gymnastic horses, rowing machines, wrestling mats, knotted ropes, trapezes, hanging rings, and a lot of other equipment I've forgotten, all unoccupied wall space was covered by ladders which joined still other ladders on the opposite wall so that we swarmed in that gymnasium like rats in a cage.

Somebody told me back then that all of the apparatus used at the Lycée Janson and other French gymnasiums was a lot of piffle; that some brilliant Swede named Müller had proved this by doing away with all of it, item by item, while in the process of inventing something called Swedish gymnastics. Müller determined that all the exercise a human being could possibly need could be done with nothing more cumbersome than a silk handkerchief. To prove his point, Mr. Müller was copiously photographed in the altogether, a silk handkerchief stretched high above his head, his body beautiful heavily vaselined to pick up the light and shadow of every perfectly defined muscle.

It was his theory that since his method required no equipment at all except his book, the whole world would now start exercising. His faulty logic seemed reasonable enough to me as a small boy, and it was years before I realized that it was the Swede who was full of piffle and that the French gymnasts were completely right in their approach to exercise, something I should have suspected right from the beginning, having been exposed to both races. I suppose it was completely natural that Mr. Müller, being not only Swedish but a gymnast as well, should have failed completely to understand that the complicated appurtenances of a French gymnasium were there merely as decoys to mislead and misdirect the actors in the gymnastic program and to camouflage the intended benefits as play. When we waved Indian clubs around our heads, nearly braining each other, or fought with the varnished staffs, or climbed screaming up and over and down the unending ladders, or came whistling down the knotted ropes with our pants on fire, we were just having a wonderful time and were not aware of the fact that we had been exercising our deltoids, our biceps, or our triceps. We just reveled in the routine of picking up, putting down, twirling and waving around a lot of gay objects, rather than, as Mr. Müller preached, dully exercising a dull list of muscles with Latin names while breathing through the nose and standing on the balls of the feet. In bringing what he thought was efficiency into exercise, Mr. Müller was actually *stopping* people from exercising by removing the emotional efficiency of the old French method. He changed an innocuous but useful and exhilarating routine into a bore.

CHAPTER

SOMEWHERE ALONG THE WAY, Mother discovered that the private house she was building on the rue Richard Wagner was going to cost nearly four times more than what she had planned to spend, and she sold it to a very pretty lady called the Princess Baratoff. Relieved of this monument, which later became the house of Mrs. Jay Gould, Mother took an apartment around the corner in the rue Octave Feuillet. This apartment I remember chiefly because it was here, a couple of years later, that kapellmeister Mertz shoved into an eighteen-inch-deep closet a five-foot model airplane it had taken me six months to complete, thus taking his place among those who endeared themselves to me permanently. It was undoubtedly a psychic anticipation of this event, in addition to his German manners, that caused me to loathe him on sight when he appeared as a dinner guest the night that I discovered, through him, the existence of the Operaphone.

By this time, the handsome young French actor who had been hanging around Mother—and whose recommendation of the Lycée Janson had resulted in my being ensconced in that establishment—had become nearly a fixture around the place.

His name was Jacques Gretillat. If he hadn't been fourteen years younger than Mother, although he pretended to be older, I think she would have married him at that. He was a second prize of the Conservatoire, which means that he had been taken into the repertory company at the Odéon, the state theatre on the Left Bank. The first prizes of the Conservatoire went into the company at the Théâtre Français, the state theatre on the Right Bank, known as the House of Molière, and a stuffy place indeed. The Odéon on the other hand was very gay, and recent arrivals got to play big parts right away, rather than waiting for years to appear in a significant role, as was the custom at the Théâtre Français.

Gretillat was a very good-looking and pleasant young man. He took Mother and me to wonderful restaurants in Paris, outside Paris, and even as far as the Channel towns. We frequented La Rue, Marguéry's, Foyot's, famous for its filet of sole, Prunier's for shellfish, the Corner Room of the Café de Paris for bisque of lobster, the Restaurant Volney for lamb's trotters with sauce poulette, the Tour d'Argent for wild duck finished up with the press, the Brasserie Universelle for hors d'oeuvres, Frascati's for Italian food, Le Caneton for blinis with caviar, La Perouse for any-thing, Rumplemaiers' for pastry, besides going to the big Left Bank places like La Coupole, Le Dôme, Le Panthéon, a couple of rôtisseries like La Reine Padauque, and then the lovely places in the Bois: Arme-nonville, Les Cascades, the Château de Madrid, Le Pavillon de Dau-phine.

Mother turned in her big heavy Mors town car and bought a red open Grégoire with four bucket seats which Jacques liked to drive, and in which I learned to drive.

Sometimes we went as far as Rouen to eat a duck with turnips, and I remember going all the way to the Channel to eat lobster à l'américaine at the Richard the Lion-Hearted Inn. But we ate in and frequented many more places than that, some for their food, some for their atmosphere or entertainment—places like Le Clou, which even before 1870 was already famous for its shadow plays, or Le Lapin Agile up on the roof of Paris, where one ate brandied cherries and listened to the songs.

One day we drove to the charming village of Fleurines, north of Paris between Senlis and Pont Saint-Maxence. This village is surrounded by the forest of Hallâte, where Louis XIV used to hunt, and contains two ancient inns where they held the royal hunting breakfasts. It was to one of these ancient inns, l'Hôtel du Grand Cerf, that we were going that day, because Jacques had heard that they cooked wonderfully there and had also a marvelous cellar. What he heard was right on both counts. I have not tasted any wine in my entire adult life to compare with the Pommard and the Chambertin that I drank there as a boy.

Mother fell in love with the countryside, the forest, the people of the village, l'Hôtel du Grand Cerf and with Monsieur and Madame Bruneau, who owned it. Right after our first meal, she started exploring the countryside and by the next day had found some land for sale on top of the Mont Saint-Christophe, the hill that overlooked the village and from which one could see the Eiffel Tower, fifty kilometers away. She bought the land immediately, decided to build and then was seized by a very cheesy idea.

Since all the houses in the village were perfectly lovely—two or three centuries old, built of stucco-covered rubble, roofed with mossy tile, and floored with the great red octagonal tile used in France—Mother erroneously concluded that if she dispensed with an architect and merely told the local builder to build her a house, he would build one as charming as the other old village houses. She could not possibly guess that the local builder had been dreaming for years of the advent of a rich American lady so that he could really express himself.

While the house was being constructed, I was left, often for weeks at a time, in charge of Monsieur and Madame Bruneau.

When my tenth birthday rolled around, Mother got another very cheesy idea. She decided not to give me anything, but to spend the money that otherwise would have gone for presents on a gymkhana party for the children of the village. There were quite a lot of these. The house wasn't finished, so the party was held in the village square in front of the church, and included three-legged races, spoon races, and apple duckings.

Around the time Mother was arranging the party in the village square of Fleurines, Isadora went off to perform in America under a contract that didn't include the girls.

Supporting the school solely from the money she was able to earn at performances in Paris or on tours was increasingly impossible, and Isadora was beginning to allow the unacceptable idea of disbanding what was left of the school to creep in at the edges of her mind. Her students, when grown, were to carry on her teachings, and for this reason the school had always commanded a lot of her energy and all of the money she had left after her own not inconsiderable expenses. The New York concerts might keep things together a little longer, but what she really needed, she announced, was a millionaire.

An American lady offered Isadora the use of a very large château at, I think, Issy-les-Moulineaux, where according to the American lady, her mother and a large staff were rattling around with nothing to do and would be enchanted to have the young dancers as guests while Isadora was in America. Elizabeth deposited the girls and their governess and a cook there and then left for Italy with Dr. Mertz. It turned out that the mother of the generous American lady didn't want anything as destructive as children anywhere within the walls of the château and consigned them to an outbuilding on the grounds. After a while the governess and the cook left because nobody was there to pay them, and presently the little girls were left all alone. They were able to keep themselves alive, like little wild things, by supplementing the crackers and staples they had on hand with whatever fruits, vegetables, and nuts they could find in neighboring gardens.

Who was in charge of the school from time to time was always a little vague anyway. Isadora parked it with Elizabeth when she went on tour or got bored with it or had something better to do. Then, when it got on Tante's nerves, she would park it back with Isadora. Each of them, both a little absentminded, must have thought the other had arranged for the financial sustenance of the school, its staff, and its students while Isadora was in America, because the abandoned girls weren't rescued until Isadora returned to Paris in December 1908.

I heard about all this after the fact because within a month after Isadora sailed for America, I was back behind the walls at the Lycée Janson, eating beans and thinking about the rôtis and the ducks and the poulets de Bresse that Mother and Jacques were probably wolfing down at one eatery after another.

Isadora's wish for a millionaire was granted in the spring of 1909. Paris Singer came into our lives. From the estate of his father, the founder of the sewing machine dynasty, he had started receiving at age eighteen a regular income of fifteen thousand dollars a week, which, in those pre-income-tax days, was considered quite substantial. He was a gentleman-in-waiting to King Edward VII, his eldest sister was married to the by-then-deceased Prince Edmond de Polignac, and a younger sister to the Duc de Decazes. He was a celebrated collector of antiques, a famous, although invariably seasick, yachtsman, a generous backer of Rudolf Diesel and his inventions, and an encourager and contributing supporter of the great French surgeon, Doyen. He was over six feet tall and he told me to call him Uncle Mun.

Within days of meeting Isadora, Paris Singer offered to underwrite the expenses of the school and, as a man who got things done, he had the entire school and Isadora installed nearly overnight in a beautiful villa on the sea at Beaulieu, between Nice and Cannes on the French Riviera. Deirdre, Isadora's and Gordon Craig's daughter, a little over two years old, was a part of the household too. Singer lived in his château at Nice but kept wandering over to the villa to be sure that Isadora and the girls were provided with all the luxury and comfort that he thought would allow Isadora the peace of mind to teach and to compose her dances. His no-strings-attached generosity and his great kindness to her and to the girls couldn't, and didn't, fail to stir up some very warm feelings in Isadora.

I won the first prize for drawing that year and was given a big fat red book with gold edges and a little glassful of hot champagne, but I didn't get passing marks in my other subjects. Probably my French wasn't as good as we all thought it was, or more likely, I had not yet acquired the habit of studying quite as hard as one has to in order to keep afloat in a French school. It looked as if I would be sent back to study the same damned things all over again, only this time with a bunch of boys shorter than I was. But at the last moment Mother hired a tutor, a brilliant young man from the Ecole Normale called Charles Constant, and sent us to the house she had built at Fleurines, where we worked like a couple of Senegambians. With us she also sent a sculptor called Eugene Bourgouin, a first prize Prix de Rome, to do my head.

The house at Fleurines turned out to be an abortion, badly designed, and constructed with every fault that an inexperienced workman could possibly build into it. The rooms were out of proportion, the cement terrace fell in, the cesspool cannot be discussed. Kitchen odors blew straight into the living room, the fireplace smoked, and the walls were damp for as long as we lived in it. It stuck up on top of the hill like a phallic symbol. It is still standing, unfortunately, and now belongs to the French government, which has made of it an aerium, or a place to send poor city children for a change of air, a practice which the French believe essential to the health of all persons, poor or rich.

Monsieur Bourgouin, the sculptor, was a very nice fellow with a beard and slightly crossed eyes, but the bust came out well anyway, and the French government ordered a copy of it for one of the national museums.

When my birthday rolled around this time, Mother decided that the party held in the village square the year before had established a tradition that she was somehow honor bound to continue. Again, instead of presents for me, all the children of the village were invited to the party on our lawn, with prizes for everybody, and we were served ice cream, which no one from the village had ever tasted before.

Not wishing to forget such a lovely party, all the mothers started home with our silver spoons in their aprons as souvenirs, but Mother's friend, Theresa Freeman, the wife of the jockey, who had her own opinion of the French, stationed herself by the main gate and frisked everybody who was saying good-bye. In this way she managed to get back a large amount of our silverware, except, of course, in the case of really determined women who had hidden it in their corsets or their stockings. With all of this hoopla, I very rapidly became the young lord of the manor and was called *Monsieur* Preston by everybody, including grown-ups.

The summer in the country worked out very well and I passed the exams I had flunked and went back to the Lycée Janson with boys of my own age. This time, though, I was no longer a boarder but only a day pupil, or demi-pensionnaire.

I discovered we no longer lived on the rue Octave Feuillet, but in an apartment on the avenue Elisée Reclus in the Champ de Mars, just opposite a private house that the great French actor, Lucien Guitry, was building for himself. On the floor above us lived the French actor and playwright, René Fauchois, whose first success, *Beethoven,* came out about that time; I was allowed to celebrate its opening with a glass of champagne.

The apartment was small but quite nice, and something new had been added: Jacques Gretillat now lived with us.

I went to the lycée every day on my bicycle, first through the Tour Eiffel, then across the Seine, then up the many, many steps and through the old Trocadéro, then past the graveyard and down the avenue Henri Martin to school.

That winter I had my usual bout of bronchitis and just after I was to put to bed with it, an invitation came from Paris Singer inviting Mother and me to join him, Isadora, Deirdre, and Temple on a a two- or three-month cruise on the Nile in a dahabeah. We didn't go, but Temple did. At Easter vacation that school year I had some consolation by being invited to Beaulieu, where Temple and I played on the rocks while Isadora was awaiting the birth of Paris Singer's child.

Little Patrick was born May 1, 1910.

That year at the Lycée Janson was fairly routine. I suppose I learned a little something. My boxing probably improved, if not my fiddle playing. I had a few normal fights and then a whole series of them with some Portuguese boys when I decided to stamp out the homosexuality that was rampant in the bushes around the latrines. I remember Jacques saying, "Why don't you mind your own business?" when I came home one day with a black eye after another altercation with the Portuguese.

Mother and I, 1899.

LEFT, *at age five, a couple of years after Father adopted me.* ABOVE, *my incomparable father, Solomon Sturges, around 1932.* FACING PAGE, CLOCKWISE, *with my first love, Temple Duncan, Bayreuth, 1904; with Mother in Chicago, September, 1904; at age fourteen, in Trouville, 1913.*

ABOVE, *five views for a quarter,
Broadway, 1914.* RIGHT, *reading
the* Saturday Evening Post
*backstage at the Century Theater,
1915.* FACING PAGE, *this is
the photograph the camp
photographer sent "to the friends
and relatives of Preston Sturges,"
Camp Dick, Dallas, 1918.*

11

OPPOSITE PAGE, *Estelle De Wolfe-Mudge, after Mr. Godfrey bowed out.* ABOVE LEFT, *Louise Sargent Tevis, the year we married, 1938.* ABOVE RIGHT, *a posed publicity photo for the playbill of* Strictly Dishonorable, *1929.* RIGHT, *Eleanor Post Hutton before our marriage.*

RIGHT, *my first day at Universal, 1932.* BELOW, *New York opening of* The Power and the Glory, *1933.*

After classes I painted with Marcel Lenoir, the only pupil he ever had. He wouldn't take any money for teaching me, but Mother used to buy paintings from him. He told me that I would never amount to anything as a painter because it was too easy for me.

Still later that school year, I had my first adventure with a movie star. She was, as a matter of fact, the only movie star I ever slept with, practically. Mother had run into her at Isadora's and, discovering that the girl was temporarily hard-up because she was waiting for her father to forward money for her passage back to New York, Mother invited her over to our place. She was given my bed and, since there was no place else for me to sleep, a sort of cot was put together for me in the corner. Her name was Theodosia de Coppet, although I don't think she was born with that name. She was about seventeen, very dark and snakey, and just at the end of some kind of adventure with a member of the Duncan family.

She was a mysterious girl who used to receive messages from the spirits, which she would write down with her right hand while holding her left hand over her eyes and be absolutely astonished when she looked and read what the spirits had written to her.

We used to talk practically all night. She explained to me that she was not like other women, but much more primeval. "I can smell you from here," she breathed in the dark, and when I started to remonstrate, she purred, "Oh, I don't mean anything unpleasant, you understand, I mean as a tigress, for instance, might smell her prey before leaping on him." Across the dark came the sound of Theodosia inhaling deeply.

I'm sorry to report that this passionate affair never went beyond the conversational. I was never leaped upon, and presently Theodosia's father came through with a check, and Mother and I put her on the boat train.

It was some years before I heard of her again. When I got to New York in 1914 and asked where Theodosia was, because I was older by then and anxious to see any pretty girls I could, a mutual friend said, "Oh, haven't you heard? She's out in Hollywood. She's a big movie star now!"

I remarked that it was strange that I *hadn't* heard of it. "Maybe that's because she's changed her name," the friend said. "Now she calls herself Theda Bara."

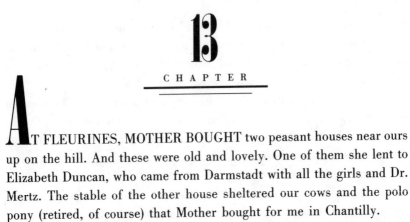

AT FLEURINES, MOTHER BOUGHT two peasant houses near ours up on the hill. And these were old and lovely. One of them she lent to Elizabeth Duncan, who came from Darmstadt with all the girls and Dr. Mertz. The stable of the other house sheltered our cows and the polo pony (retired, of course) that Mother bought for me in Chantilly.

All those summer days, I rode in the very early morning in the slanting rays of sunlight in the forest of Hallâte, and I have never seen anything lovelier. Hunting paths converged all together into what was called a carrefour, which was like the hub of a wheel, and looking down the fern-lined and leaf-covered paths was like looking into a green cathedral . . . except that instead of a priest, a deer would stick its head out and look down a trail once in a while.

I taught all the Duncan girls to ride, which they did with many squeals, and then I would carve different ones' initials with mine in the bark of different trees. This was just to teach Temple a lesson, of course, when she didn't show enough love for me.

Jack Wright, who was my age and the son of Sara Greene, the sculptress, used to come and spend the summers with me. One time when the Duncan girls had gone to dance someplace, somebody got the bright idea of sending a very pretty little English girl up from Chantilly to keep Jack and me company for the day. It was a fine idea, but nobody provided us with any means of getting the little girl from the railway station in Senlis, where Jack and I met her, out to our house, which was five miles away and up some very steep hills. I had taken Jack down to the station on the handlebars of my bicycle, but this means of transportation wasn't suitable for a little girl in a nice white starched dress, so she was forced to walk.

It was a very hot day, and I remember she got extremely waspish about the whole situation before we got to the house. Between wiping the sweat off her face, swatting the flies and trying to stamp the thick dust out of her white canvas shoes, she explained in considerable detail how in the horse-breeding-and-training circles in which she revolved in

Chantilly, a young lady arriving at the station would be met with a nice gig, a fly, a pony cart, a dog cart, or, if nothing else were available, a garbage wagon or a manure spreader, God forbid, but that certainly she would not be forced to hoof it for five miles. She had a lot of time to develop this thesis on the walk, mostly uphill, to the house, and still more time to elaborate the thesis later that afternoon, when we had to walk her back to the station. I do not remember seeing her again.

Another time when Jack and I were there alone, the house caught fire, and as the pump to fill the tank in the attic was not working, Jack and I had to rush up and down from the bottom of the garden with pails of water to put it out. This was very exhausting work and we were black in the face and had just about passed out from the frantic exertion by the time we got the last flame out. At this moment, Mother and Isadora arrived from Paris and upon being told proudly what we had done, Mother hurt out feelings considerably by saying, "Why didn't you let it burn, for heaven's sake? It's heavily insured and we'll never get another chance like this in our whole lives." She was completely right.

I don't know where Mother got the idea, but one day she ordered a lot of chicken runs to be built and then started filling them with purebred chickens of more breeds than most people have probably ever heard of. Nobody in France who has a choice ever eats anything but a chicken from Bresse, but Mother must have believed she could garner an easy fortune by introducing other fine, fat, purebred fowl to the French table. We had chickens of every size and color and condition of plumage. Some of them looked like old English sheepdogs with their feet all covered with feathers, and then there were houdans and gamecocks and a lot of kinds I've forgotten, but I have not forgotten the noise they made or how they smelled.

There were about twenty different species and, since we were breeding them, that meant twenty different roosters, who all crowed at the same time every dawn and spent the rest of the day trying to get at each other when they weren't occupied with their professional duties. We also had guinea hens, of course, who didn't stop screeching from morning till night. There were some raucous geese, too, and also some ducks.

About this time somebody gave me a Lavrock hunting dog puppy. One day, scooting around on her oversized puppy paws, she caught a chicken and amidst a fearful din dispatched it rapidly. I didn't know much about training her, but somebody told me that if the chicken the dog had killed were tied around the dog's neck until the chicken rotted off, the dog would forever avoid any chicken, dead or alive, like the burned child who forever fears the flame. Maybe the pup's olfactory sense wasn't very highly developed, or maybe she didn't make the connection between the killing and the rotting carcass trussed around her neck, or maybe she just didn't give a damn, because she kept right on chewing up all the chickens she could get her teeth into for the rest of her life. Since she was always wearing a chicken in an advanced stage of decomposition around her neck, she didn't smell very inviting either.

Nevertheless, she managed to get herself in the family way, and the next thing you know we had nine chicken murderers running around the place, all wearing dead chickens around their necks. I think we even tried a dead goose collar one time, but it didn't work any better than had the chicken collars.

I have never seen such scenes of carnage nor heard such pitiful squawkings as when those dogs got in under the fencing and went to work. Every so often, when the chickens didn't amuse them anymore, they beat it out into the forest for a few days. Then the game wardens came trailing in with long bills for what the pack of them had done to breeding pheasants and partridges and other furred or feathered game they had caught up with. Why we just didn't have them shot, I don't know. Dogs always seem to be rather sacred.

When summer was over, I got back on my bicycle and started another term at the Lycée Janson.

14

PRESENTLY MOTHER AND JACQUES must have had their final
row, because all of a sudden we weren't living on the avenue Elisée
Reclus anymore with the red Grégoire, we were living across the Champ
de Mars on the avenue Charles Floquet and we had a grey Grégoire and
a chauffeur called Marcel Bouhiron. Marcel was a stinking driver, although so fond of automobiles and so curious about them that he had
usually taken ours completely apart and spread its innards all around
him to see what made it work just when Mother needed it. He always
had a pocketful of pétards, those little bombs made by putting a tiny
amount of explosive in a tablespoonful of sand and wrapping it all in
tissue paper. These he would throw into the backs of cars we passed on
the road and as far as I could make out, Marcel was the only one in either
car who ever enjoyed the joke.

I said that we had a new apartment on the avenue Charles Floquet.
Actually we had two. Possibly still upset by her parting from Jacques,
Mother had signed a lease for a rather large apartment on the top floor
of a brand-new building, and then found another apartment on the same
street, smaller, slightly less expensive, and one that pleased her a great
deal more. Never doubting that she could get rid of the first one without
any trouble at all, as apartments in this new neighborhood were at a
premium, Mother signed a long lease for the second one.

She telephoned the first landlord and was shocked and surprised
when he told her in violent terms that she was not in America, but in
France, where people meant it when they signed leases; that she had
signed a three/six/nine/twelve year lease, without the privilege of subletting; and that was that. He didn't like Americans anyway and this
would teach them all a lesson.

He didn't know who he was threatening, of course, nor that the
object of his wrath was born with a caul on her head, but he found out
later.

The caul is a portion of the amniotic sac which, in rare cases,
emerges as a little cap, or caul, covering the head of a just-born infant.

Gaelic folklore holds that it is a mark of the Little People, assuring the infant's safe arrival and serving as a warning that the child so set apart is not one to be put upon, disturbed, or injured in any way, including the unintentional, lest the Little People's full powers of reprisal be directed at the hapless actor. The list of horrors that befell those be-nighted individuals who set out in their innocence to injure my mother includes broken bones, heart attacks, strokes, and simpler inconve-niences like splinters under the nail and falling down the stairs. Born with a caul, Mother never had to waste her energy thinking about revenge. The Little People took care of that.

Mother was quite depressed about the apartment situation when she went to see Isadora a few days later. While they were trying to figure out some way Mother could get rid of one of the apartments, preferably the first one, the Little People went to work. In walked Raymond, Isadora's charming but very strong-minded brother. I refer to him as "strong-minded" because I think you have to be strong-minded to walk around for your whole lifetime in a long toga woven by yourself, with bare feet and with your hair hanging down your back, when the rest of the world dresses a little differently.

In those days, Raymond traveled with rather large groups of his disciples, mostly of the opposite sex, often young, sometimes comely, and nearly always with recently born or about-to-be-born babies. This entou-rage required large quantities of milk, and everybody knows that there is no milk like goat's milk for raising robust babies, so attached to the entourage were a number of goats. These pleasant animals also supplied the wool with which all the disciples handwove their togas, blankets, and carpets. Spinning wheels, wool carders, and hand looms naturally accom-panied the troupe. When Raymond, followed by his apostles and disci-ples, animals, and shepherds with crooks, got off a train somewhere and started down the platform, it looked very much like the second coming of some reknowned Biblical personage.

While Mother and Isadora embraced and then rejected one solution after another for the apartment situation, a curious coincidence was revealed. It turned out that Raymond was also quite depressed by an apartment situation, not because he *had* one, but, quite to the contrary, because neither he nor any of his followers had a place to lay their heads. No landlord who saw this bedouinlike band approaching his building was even willing to allow them inside to *discuss* the matter of an apartment.

Mother said, "But, Raymond, this is extraordinary. Destiny must have planned this. It so happens that I have a large extra apartment that I am forced to pay for although I have absolutely no use for it, and I will be charmed to offer it to you for nothing for as long as you like."

To say that Raymond was also charmed is an understatement. He was absolutely delighted and departed at once to pick up his tribe where he had parked them and get a roof over their heads.

I don't know how Raymond got them all into the building, possibly when the concierge was out shopping, or he may have used guile of some kind, but the first intimation the landlord had of his new guests was when the urine from the goats, tethered out on the top-floor balcony, fell on the head of an old gentleman in a wheelchair on the balcony beneath, and the old gentleman called the landlord in a state of what used to be called high dudgeon. By the time the old gentleman was finished, there were other phone calls waiting.

As night follows day, so does number two follow number one, and in a very short time the whole front of the building was showing traces of the goat farm on the top-floor balcony. Now, besides the problem of goat droppings, which caused the other tenants to hurry in and out of the building and not to stand around in front of it, the tenants began meeting strange-looking, wild-eyed characters dressed in white in the lobby, in the elevator, or solemnly climbing the stairs. There were a good number of these characters in the top-floor apartment, which, except for the spinning wheels, wool carders, and hand looms, had no furniture of any kind. The screams of the babies and the hoofbeats of the kids trotting across the bare hardwood floors and bleating for their mothers pene-trated clearly through the whole building.

Mother was hardly able to understand what the landlord was saying, such was his rage the first time he telephoned her. But when she pointed out that she was not subletting and had a perfect right to lend her vacant apartment to distinguished friends, he was forced to calm down some-what, although at the word "distinguished" he flared up again and nearly strangled. When she told him she wouldn't do anything about the matter at all, that she had now learned her lesson, that she realized that things were different in France, and that she intended to abide by the terms of her lease to the letter, which meant keeping Raymond and company in the apartment for twelve years, the poor man nearly had a stroke. Then he begged her in a quavering voice to allow him to come over to discuss the matter. She said there was nothing at all to discuss, at which he went off the deep end again and swore he would have them all out by morning if it took the entire Paris police force and the garde républicaine to do it. Mother tried to remind him of the sweet paternalism of the French laws, which give very few rights to a landlord in the first place, and absolutely no rights when it comes to throwing young mothers and suckling babes out into the street, but the landlord was too far gone to listen to reason.

The next morning, however, when surrounded by practically all the tenants of his building, plus the commissaire of police and a couple of inspectors from the health department, the landlord began to see the light and called Mother with a voice full of sugar. Mother told him pleasantly that the matter was entirely out of her hands, that she had lent the apartment to Mr. Duncan, that she was a lady of her word, and that there was nothing more she had to say about it. If he wished and were able to make an arrangement with Mr. Duncan, that would be perfectly agreeable to her, provided, naturally, that she would be freed of her lease at the same time. And that is how the matter ended. Whether the landlord had some empty villa in the suburbs far from human habitation that he was willing to sacrifice, or some warehouse or loft that could not be injured, I never knew. But certainly Raymond moved, and Mother's lease was cancelled. She always referred to Raymond as one of the very best lease-breakers she had ever heard of.

15

I DON'T KNOW WHERE Mother heard about my new school or why she seemed to sour on the Lycée Janson, but the first thing I knew, I had been lifted bodily out of the Lycée Janson practically in the middle of a lesson and set down in the country in a very swell Anglophile school called the Ecole des Roches in Normandy. It was so swell they actually had us playing cricket. Instead of the penal format of mile-long dormitories offered by the Lycée Janson, living quarters here consisted of relatively cosy houses, each with its own housemaster. Mine was called The Pines, and my housemaster, Mr. Bernard Bell. Mr. Bernard Bell's quarters also housed his German wife, his children, and their German governess.

So British-to-the-core was the school that one of the first things the housemaster taught us, and insisted that we sing aloud each morning, was that glorious and thrilling paean that always sounded slightly ridiculous and extremely insincere when hollered out by young American, South American, Greek, German, French, Armenian, and Roumanian voices: "Rule, Britannia, Britannia rules the waves; / Britons never never never shall be slaves!"

I got off to a peculiar start at the Ecole des Roches. After a slight incident on my first day there, though, I never had any trouble again during my entire stay.

Some pal in Paris had given me what was called a couteau à cran d'arrêt, the then equivalent of a switchblade knife. I only used it to clean my fingernails and to sharpen pencils, but because it was completely illegal, I treasured it.

On my first evening at school, I was naturally surrounded and treated with contumely by young men whose distinction stemmed solely from the fact that they had arrived at the school before me. An American called Harry Morgan asked me what I could do in the way of sports, and I said I could box a little bit. He appeared to doubt this and with just a touch of derision, said that he would be very glad to take me on, if I were ready for him, of course. I made a date with him for the next day.

Adrenaline was running in our bloodstreams by then, and as anger is the most contagious of all emotions, a big boy from one of the Latin Republics, to whom I had not even spoken, became all at once very sarcastic and abusive. As he was considerably bigger and older than I was, I suddenly did a very strange thing. For the first and last time in my life, I pulled a knife on someone.

The flash of the blade was electrifying. The young man took off like a shot out of a gun and I, letting out a wild halloo, went right after him, followed by a whooping pack anxious to see the Central American carved up.

I was extremely careful never to catch up with him, contenting myself with yelling vile threats about cutting out his liver. When finally I allowed him, sobbing for breath, to disappear into a clump of bushes, he had had enough for the rest of his life, and my reputation, as least insofar as that school was concerned, was assured.

The next day Morgan came down to the boxing class conducted by a very nice English professional called Bateman and after watching me handle a very broad-shouldered Greek called Pappia without too much trouble, determined that I had not been lying to him when I told him I could box a little and decided to become my friend rather than my enemy.

Morgan used to tell us that his grandfather was J. P. Morgan, and we used to tell Morgan that he was a liar. He used to tell us he had three sisters, Conseulo and the twins, Thelma and Gloria. We believed that.

Except for briefly noting the interest my mother took in the presence of a Christian Science practitioner next door to us at Coronado Beach, I have not brought up Mother's continuous exploration of the religious faiths of the world. It is necessary to do so now.

According to my mother, she renounced the Roman Catholic faith into which she was born when, at the age of five and newly fatherless in Chicago, she walked over to the neighborhood convent to meet and accompany her mother back home. There she discovered her worshipped mother on her knees scrubbing the convent floor and was overcome with rage and humiliation. That the good sisters might actually have invented the work as an excuse to give her mother some much-needed money, there being dozens of nuns in residence willing and able to keep the convent clean, was a postulate my mother came to accept much later. But the very small girl was so infuriated at finding her mother in a servile position in the house of others that she developed an instantaneous allergy toward religion that lasted the rest of her life. I don't mean that she tried to bite clergymen on the street. On the contrary, the subject interested her, if only as a social phenomenon, and she was even willing to be convinced.

Mother never did anything by halves, and over the years we all suffered slightly, if not acutely, from her delvings into, her readings aloud of, her quotations from, and her commentaries on the Koran, the dialogues of Buddha, the *Analects* of Confucius, and Greek and Norse mythology with those exciting goddesses Freya, Frigga, Hel, Sif, Nanna, Ithunn, and Sigyn. These always made me think of our Swedish maids. We learned all about Valhalla before moving on to the beliefs held in the true land of the gods, India, and the teachings of Brahma, Vishnu, and Shiva, among others.

The study of so many conflicting theories, however, led my mother further and further away from any of the true ones. It is better and much less confusing to stick to one belief, right or wrong. It pains me to report that eventually my mother's dabblings led her into a little bout with black magic. I wish I could deny this and prevent many of her descendants from being burned at the stake, but unfortunately she not only wrote and signed a small treatise on the subject under the influence of a sinister buffoon called Aleister Crowley, but she is also mentioned either under her true name or under an alias in all books about this rancid character.

At just about the time I was becoming acclimated to the Ecole des Roches in Normandy, quite unaware, as usual, of what Mother was up to, Mother was in London acclimating herself to Aleister Crowley.

The practitioner and staunch defender of every form of vice historically known to man, generally accepted as one of the most depraved, vicious, and revolting humbugs who ever escaped from a nightmare or a lunatic asylum, universally despised and enthusiastically expelled from every country he ever tried to live in, Mr. Crowley nevertheless was considered by my mother to be not only the epitome of charm and good manners, but also the possessor of one of the very few genius-bathed brains she had been privileged to observe at work during her entire lifetime. Ask me not why! Much as I revered her, my mother was still a woman, one of that wondrous gender whose thought processes are not for male understanding.

It is possible of course that at this time, around 1910, Mr. Crowley had not yet developed the full panoply of his nefarious profession.

My mother, under the appellation of Soror Virakam and under the delusion that she was temporarily a Babylonian *uhu* or call girl, took down in spiritualistic shorthand an entire manual of black magic known as *Book Four*. This work was dictated to her from the dark blue yonder by a Babylonian pimp working under the name of Abduliz. Mother's spiritualistic shorthand turned out later to be just her ordinary handwriting, also illegible, and it further developed that Abduliz had been vibrating on the vocal chords of one Fra Perdurabo, who, it will surprise no one to learn, was Brother Crowley. The minutes of these scholarly seances are duly recorded in a book called *The Great Beast*, written by John Symonds. Herewith, quoting Mr. Crowley, a sample:

We reached Naples after two or three quarrelsome days in Rome and began house hunting. . . . Virakam's brat was to join us for the Christmas holidays, and on the day he was due to arrive we motored out as a folorn hope to Posilippo before meeting him at the station at four o'clock or thereabouts. But the previous night Virakam had a dream in which she saw the desired villa with absolute clearness. . . . After a fruitless search, we turned our automobile toward Naples, along the crest of the Posilippo. At one point there is a small side lane scarcely negotiable by motor, and indeed, hardly perceptible. . . . But Virakam sprang excitedly to her feet and told the chauffeur to drive down it. I was astonished, she being hysterically anxious to meet the train, and our time being already almost too short. But she swore passionately that the villa was down that lane. . . . "There," she cried, pointing with her finger, "there is the villa I saw in my dream!" I looked. No villa was visible. I said so. She had to agree, yet stuck to her point that she saw it. . . . The lane grew narrower, rougher, and steeper. . . . The chauffeur protested that he would be able neither to turn the car nor to back it up. . . . Virakam in a violent rage insisted on proceeding. We drove a few yards . . . then the chauffeur made up his mind to revolt and stopped the car. On the left was a wide open gate, through which we could see workmen pretending to repair a ramshackle villa. . . . Virakam called the foreman and asked in broken Italian if the place was to let. He told her no. . . . With crazy confidence, she dragged

him within and forced him to show her over the house. . . . Some
irresistible instinct compelled me to take out my notebook and pencil
and jot down the name written over the gate: Villa Caldarazzo.
. . . I added up the letters. Their sum struck me like a bullet in the
brain. It was 418, the number of the Magical Formula of the Aeon,
a numerical hyeroglyphic of the Great Work. Abduliz had made no
mistake. . . . I was entirely overwhelmed. I jumped out of the car
and ran up to the house. . . . The instant I entered I understood that
it was entirely suited for a temple, the very shape of the room seemed
somehow significant . . . as if it were filled with a peculiar emanation.
. . . Virakam, of course, was entirely certain that this was the villa
. . . to consecrate the temple and to begin the book. The idea was
as follows: I was to dictate; Virakam to transcribe. . . .

Mr. Crowley's reference to me as "the brat" doesn't bother me because,
compared to the way I refer to him, it is a compliment. I lived in the
Villa Caldarazzo for some weeks with Soror Virakam and Fra Perdurabo
and apart from its supernatural features, it had little to recommend it.
It was cold and damp, few of its windows closed properly, it was completely inaccessible and the plumbing leaked.

One of Mr. Crowley's little characteristics that I particularly loathed
was his haircut, an unpleasing variation of that nauseating style popular
with the very young set some years ago known as the Iroquois. Like some
early Yul Brynner, Mr. Crowley had his entire skull shaved except for
one small tufted square in the exact middle of his cranium. On this lawn,
or village green, he promenaded his fingers as if they were dogs one had
taken out to water.

Another of his eccentricities, which I recall with something less
than pleasure, was his repugnant reaction each time my poor mother had
so far forgotten his teachings as to utter in his hearing a singular personal
pronoun like "I" or "me" or "mine." The instant his ears were so
assaulted, he solemnly withdrew an open penknife from his robe, raised
his arm so the loose sleeve of his robe fell back to expose his bare
forearm, and then with the penknife slashed a small fresh slice under
the ladder of slices he had already incised into his forearm, cut by cut,
for each time Mother had had a similar lapse of decorum. I remember
these demonstrations well.

Reading about some of his subsequent exploits, I realize that my mother and I were lucky to escape with our lives. If I had been a little older, he might not have escaped with his.

I was glad to see the last of the Villa Caldarazzo and especially glad to see the last of Mr. Crowley and get back to school.

I don't suppose there was any connection, but in January 1911, Father filed for a divorce from Mother. I also don't suppose anybody bothered to mention it to me at the time.

Happily, when I got back to the Ecole des Roches, I was never asked to write a composition about how I spent the Christmas holidays that year.

Many of the boys at school with me were dukes and barons and marquis and all the rest of the titles so popular in France and all the other democracies since the fall of the Bastille. It was all very democratic, though, and so that no one, large or small, might appear richer than anyone else nor the faintest whiff of plutocracy infest our grove of learning, each one of us, by school regulation, received the same amount of pocket money, to wit, fifty centimes a week, a sum at that time equal to just under ten cents. This allowance really was not enough, even for boys marooned out in the country far from the fleshpots of Paris. Just as grown men will invariably find some way around an unjust or stupid rule, Prohibition, for example, or the present confiscatory taxes, so will boys, or any other group of humans, find ways to accommodate themselves to arbitrary decrees.

The town nearest to school was Verneuil-sur-Avre. Here there were a number of haberdasheries and gents' and boys' ready-made clothing emporia which extended credit to the students of the Ecole des Roches. We were not only allowed but warmly encouraged to pick out what we needed in the way of socks, handkerchiefs, underwear, mufflers, and even detached segments of the gray-green herringbone tweed knickerbocker suits that constituted the school uniform. The bills for these items were then sent to the school's accounting department, which in turn riveted them firmly to our parents' quarterly bills.

It was really too easy.

In no time at all, the enterprising merchants discovered that the boys were not only willing but absolutely eager to sign a receipt for such necessities as: one uniform complete with extra knickerbockers; one pair gloves; one pigskin belt with German silver initialed buckle; three pairs merino wool union suits with sure-close flap; one pair chrome leather soccer football shoes with patent cleats; one cablestitch sweater; one crimson satin four-in-hand necktie (the school color); one pair low black oxfords with rubber heels. The signed receipt for all of the above was exchanged for fifty francs cash or, at the then rate of exchange, about $9.80, a good deal less than the face value of the receipt. The merchandise, of course, never left the shop. This worked out beautifully for everybody except whoever had to pay the bills. The merchants were jubilant, and money flowed like water out at the school, where crap games sprang up like mushrooms.

These mountains of supposititious swag naturally had to be disposed of somehow—by theoretical loss, fictitious fire, or imaginary theft—before we went home on vacation, or our families would have expected us to arrive with trunks the size of moving vans.

Eventually, of course, somebody had to spoil the sport and blow the top off our practical arrangement. One of the shrewder parents, naturally not mine, upon receipt of his son's quarterly school bill, became so furiously incensed at his offspring's extravagance that pausing not even to put on his hat, he leapt into his car, fired up the roads all the way to Verneuil-sur-Avre and arrived at the school still gnashing his teeth and nearly speechless with rage. Controlling himself sufficiently to be understood, he waved the bill in his son's face and demanded to be shown instantly this conglomeration of haberdashery plus the rowing machine billed by a sporting-goods merchant who had joined the syndicate of swindlers.

"I lost it," whined the miserable boy. "I lost it while taking a walk."

"You took a walk with a *rowing machine,* you liar!" screamed his father, seizing him by the throat.

In no time at all, the fat was in the fire, the cat was out of the bag, and the jig was up. Professor Georges Bertier, the headmaster of the school, became properly indignant, fulminated thunderously in all directions and issued vitriolic broadsides to and concerning the merchants of Verneuil-sur-Avre. Finally he *really* wounded them by dishonoring all of their bills for the last term and refusing to pay them even one centime. This brought on pandemonium, rage, and much bitterness, but Professor Bertier ignored the yelps of pain and stood fast.

For a while it was not safe for the boys in the gray-green herringbone tweeds with the crimson satin ties to walk through the streets of

Verneuil-sur-Avre, but things were patched up eventually, and the pocket-money ceiling was raised to the equivalent of twenty cents a week.

Either that school year or the next, Mr. Bernard Bell, his wife, his children, and the governess were moved out of The Pines and given charge of a small house with very few boys. I was among the very few boys. I never knew why the Bells were moved nor why I went along with them. The grounds of the school were so enormous that at one point they were crossed by the railroad. Our small house was literally on the wrong side of the tracks, just near the splendid manual training school. A wooden overpass spanned the tracks intersecting the school grounds, and naturally there was a regulation prohibiting the boys from going down on the tracks for any reason, including laying coins on the tracks to be flattened by the passing trains. I have felt the hypnotic attraction of an approaching express locomotive. One leaves the tracks painfully, as if in slow motion.

Every once in a while a hobo would commit suicide by leaping from the overpass. When we saw one hanging around every time we went by, we knew about what to expect. The next morning his remains would be alongside the tracks.

One night I got a very bad idea. It was to stage a cat fight and wake everybody up. I and another boy stupid enough to go along with me climbed out of the window of our room onto the roof of a lean-to, jumped to the ground, crossed a little river and proceeded to a location just opposite the next residential quarters. There we set up such squealing, squalling, and snarling that, just as we had planned, everybody woke up.

What we had not planned was the number of enthusiastic pupils and professors who came out with rifles and started plugging away at the cats. With bullets zinging past our ears and splotching into the trees around us, my friend and I took off in a panic. Finding our escape blocked by a stone wall, we scrambled over it, only to find ourselves at the mercy of a farmer, also with a rifle, and a very large dog. The farmer let us off with some good advice, and we managed to get back into our room with nothing more serious than torn trousers, a few splinters, and a very bad scare.

I have played few practical jokes since then.

On the day I arrived at the Ecole des Roches I was asked automatically whether I was a Catholic or a Protestant. With a prudence splendid in one so young and completely nonreligious, I asked how long the services lasted. Told that the Catholic Mass took an hour to the Protestant service's twenty minutes, I immediately became a Protestant and eventually grew very fond of the pastor, a dear little old bearded man in a rusty frock coat with a string tie. We would meet occasionally on the road between our living quarters and the classroom building where they held the services. The Catholics had a fine separate chapel. We talked a little about religion, and I asked him one day if he really and truly believed in prayer. He said of course he did. So I asked him if he could slip me any little tips or professional secrets on the subject, as I intended to start praying for a bicycle.

He advised me to pray fervently and sincerely, but warned me not to be disappointed if God in His infinite wisdom should happen to decide that bicycle-riding was not as healthy for me as walking. I didn't care much for this interpretation as I had gathered somewhere that the success of prayer depended entirely on how much frenzy one had been able to inject into it. For about a week, therefore, I really gave it the works.

Then while out playing cricket one afternoon, who should step out of a rented car and come through a gap in the hedge but my mother, followed by a large Turkish gentlemen I had never seen before. Mother introduced me to her new husband.

His name was Vely Bey and they had just been married in London. The newlyweds were extremely nice to me and most anxious to secure my blessings and goodwill, so that I had hardly had time to mention the bicycle I was praying for before we were on our way into Verneuil-sur-Avre to buy it. It was a superb vehicle, basically vermilion, but with many nickel-plated parts. With considerable pride, I showed it to the little pastor the next Sunday morning.

He flushed with pleasure and agreed with me enthusiastically when I said I had received this marvel as the result of my prayers. He looked slightly worried, though, when I told him that it was my intention to start work on a motorcycle that very evening, that I could hardly wait to get down on my knees, and that I expected to be able to show it to him not more than three weeks hence. "It will be dark green," I announced, "with red stripes."

"My dear, dear child," he began nervously, nibbling his fingernails in his anxiety, "you *do* realize, do you not, that the reasonings of Our Lord are not always completely clear to us? In the first place, it would probably be entirely too much to hope for, and furthermore, probably most improbable, that Madame your Mother might be in the process of remarrying every time you are praying for some vehicle or other." Here he laughed toothily and continued, "In the second place, it is entirely possible, nay, even probable, that God in His infinite wisdom might not consider you quite old enough, at least yet, for such a dangerous mechanism as a motorcycle . . . which I myself would even hesitate to climb upon." Then, very gently, he concluded, "If I tell you these things, it is merely to try to spare you the kind of disappointment very young and very ardent Christians are so often heir to."

This young and ardent Christian looked at him stonily before replying, "I don't want to be rude, Pastor, but I think you have an entirely wrong slant on this whole thing. Success *must* depend exclusively on how powerfully one prays . . . and nothing else. The lives of all the saints are there to prove it. And you've got to to admit that once I get wound up, I am one hell of a pray-er." I indicated the gleaming bicycle with a wave of the hand.

Unfortunately the dear little pastor's fears were completely confirmed. I did not get a motorcycle and I have taken no further serious interest in religion from that day to this.

Among other things in that school, I learned to play soccer football. I played outside right.

On the academic side, I suppose we learned a little of everything. I remember one class I would prefer to forget. A dear little puppy was brought into the classroom and after we had been allowed to play with it and fondle it to our hearts' content, the son of a bitch who was conducting the class chloroformed it, then cheerfully dissected it right in front of us. "This, you see, is the liver. And here we have the pancreas, which feeds it. Now who can tell me what the pancreas does?" The little face of the puppy seemed still to be smiling, and one expected its tail to wag.

In the drawing class I made a caricature of the art professor that was printed in the school paper, *L'Echo des Roches.* Also foisted upon us were the regrettable crafts of pyrogravure and zinc-embossing.

Like many Englishmen, my housemaster, Mr. Bernard Bell, had been collecting stamps for years, so I started to collect stamps too. Stamp albums are very temptingly arranged with exact replicas of the stamps that are to be pasted over them printed on the pages. Naturally one never gets any of the rare stamps, but only the fairly common ones sent by relatives or acquired by trading with the other boys.

One day while looking at the facsimiles of some rare Abyssinian stamps which had been printed upside down and in black instead of red at the time of the assassination of some nobleman, it occurred to me that the idiotic convolutions and arabesques would be very easy to draw by hand. I made a few with India ink on some kind of gummed paper that was about the right thickness, and immediately my friends were drooling to get their mitts on my rare Abyssinians. Not being a crook, I did not accept any of their trading propositions, but while one of these discussions was going on, I looked around and there was Mr. Bernard Bell eyeing my Abyssinians greedily. In the catalogue the real ones were listed at some absurd figure like a thousand pounds, which was the reason Mr. Bell's eyes were bugging out of his head.

I was about to explain my pleasantry to him when he whipped out a loupe, examined them closely and exclaimed, "My God! Where did you get these?" I considered telling him the story I had made up for the boys, which was that my new grandfather-by-marriage, Ilias Pasha, Vely Bey's father, had given them to me at the time his son had become my stepfather. The only trouble with that story was that Mr. Bell would probably believe it, so I tried to brush the stamps out of sight into an envelope and said, "I don't think they're real."

"What do you mean you don't think they're real?" snarled Mr. Bell, snatching the envelope out of my hand. "I have been collecting stamps for thirty years. It was my hobby as a lad, and my father's and my grandfather's before me. Are you suggesting that I don't know the true from the false?" He picked up one of my counterfeits. "An idiot could see that this is authentic!" There was nothing left for me but to show him how I had made them, and our friendship was never quite as warm thereafter.

My violin lessons were, as usual, dismal. Monsieur Louis Bonjean, my teacher, was a jolly little Belgian known behind his back as Monsieur Jambon. Among other things, what my violin playing lacked, he said, was a vibrato. Nevertheless I sawed away while my luckier friends whooped around practicing goal-shooting at soccer.

A final musical humiliation was reserved for me. The French, very fond and proud of Molière, gave one of his allegedly hilarious comedies each year in every school. Every school naturally chose to present either

Le Malade Imaginaire or *Le Bourgeois Gentilhomme,* both considered excruciatingly funny and quite possibly so if played by a cast other than the one scraped up at my school. With these divertissements it was customary to serve up music composed by a gentleman called Lully, also cherished by the French.

As pupils of Professor Bonjean, I and some other terrible violin players were pressed into service as musicians at the court of Louis XIV, the setting chosen to enhance everybody's enjoyment of the festivities. Some fearful costumes with imitation jabots were whipped together for us by loving hands, but the important part of the whole effect was to come from the Louis XIV wigs, dripping with curls, which were ordered for us from a wig-renter in Paris. To ensure the best performances we could muster, our heads were gone over with zero-zero clippers so the wigs wouldn't itch and distract us during the performance. All of the wigs arrived the day of the recital, all of the wigs except mine. Throughout the long evening, therefore, I sat in solitary magnificence, in the middle of a veritable forest of towering Louis XIV wigs, sawing bitterly on my fiddle, looking like a boiled egg.

16

SOME TIME AFTER MOTHER MARRIED the Turkish gentleman, Vely Bey, I was snatched out of the Ecole des Roches and put down in a sort of cramming establishment located in an apartment building somewhere in Paris and run by a very nice old guy with a beard called Professor Azambré.

Professor Azambré conducted business in a couple of classrooms in a ground-floor apartment that commanded a view of a gray courtyard. The whole Azambré family and the four or five other boarders and I lived in another apartment upstairs, where all of us ate together at a long table. I cannot remember at all where I slept, but I remember the dining room because Professor Azambré's little son, sent to stand in the corner for doing something he shouldn't have done, immediately unbuttoned his pants and started doing something else against the wallpaper, his little mind confused as to what corners were for.

Professor Azambré didn't like Vely Bey for sour apples and one day confided to me (which I don't think he should have) that the reason I was never allowed to leave the school or even to go home on weekends was because Vely Bey said I was a wild child, badly in need of discipline. Even had this lie been true, I don't know how Vely Bey would have known it. Professor Azambré was very indignant about the cruelty with which I was being treated and decided on his own hook to take me along with his family one Sunday afternoon when they went to visit rich relatives in Sèvres.

Sèvres is the site of the royal porcelain works, one of the glories of France, established there at the behest of Madame de Pompadour and all of the then residents of Sèvres felt a certain obligation to have at least one magnificent set of this porcelain on display.

The Azambrés' rich relatives naturally had such a set, a very fancy one, in which they proposed to serve us some steaming hot chocolate. I was terribly glad to be there, of course, not having been off the Azambré premises in a very long time, and I suppose I was in that slightly excitable state one sees in a dog or a horse that has been locked up too long. Like the professor and his family, I was wearing my Sunday best, including the high-laced shoes worn by boys at the time.

I was also anxious to make a good impression and offered to carry the fairly heavy butler's tray around for our hostess so that she could serve each of the guests a cup of hot chocolate, little buttered sandwiches on a little sandwich plate, and a little lace-edged napkin. The hostess was charmed, shooting a look at the professor approving my presence.

As we started across the room, one long shoelace trailed behind me. I wasn't aware of it and I suppose no one else noticed it. Walking in that careful way one does when bearing a tray loaded with liquids, I must have stepped on the trailing shoelace with my other foot because all of a sudden I shot forward like a bullet out of a gun and deposited the whole tray, the set of Sèvres, the boiling chocolate, the extra hot milk, the little buttered sandwiches, the plates, and the napkins upside down in Professor Azambré's lap, exactly in that part of his Sunday trousers known as the crotch.

All hell broke loose. Everybody screamed. Professor Azambré jumped to his feet yelling and cursing, dancing on one foot and then the other, while the steaming chocolate and hot milk ran down into his high-button shoes. I don't remember exactly what he said, but the gist of it was that he was an ass not to have listened to Vely Bey, who was one hundred percent right about me, and so far as he himself was concerned, I should not only be kept in on Sundays, but also forced to wear handcuffs and be chained to the wall.

He spent the next couple of hours stamping around in a blanket like an Indian, the chocolate squirting out of his shoes, while in the other room they tried to get the mess off his trousers by pouring kettles of boiling water through them. This procedure naturally shrank them, and by the time we got on the train to go back to Paris, the professor, with his trousers all crinkled up like concertinas and not even reaching the tops of his high-button shoes anymore, didn't look very presentable and was in a very vile humor.

This was the last time I was invited to Sèvres, or any place else.

According to Vely Bey, Professor Azambré reported that with my intelligence and my total lack of discipline, I would turn out either all good or all bad. Whether this character assessment was made before or after the incident at Sèvres, I never knew.

At length Vely Bey must have decided that I was cured, or Professor

Azambré was cured of me, or Mother took a hand in the matter, or something, but however it happened, one day I was living back in our apartment on the avenue Charles Floquet.

My memories of Vely Bey are not exactly happy ones. He took the role of father dead seriously, although I don't think Mother had any intention of providing a father for me when she married him, and he gave me the signet ring with the star and crescent that he had worn as a boy as a token of my membership in this family of noble Turks.

He was convinced beyond discussion that discipline, especially self-discipline, was the only sure road to success in life, and I guess he thought Professor Azambré had not gone far enough to instill this virtue in me. I lacked, he said, a serious interest in my studies, a sure sign that self-discipline was sadly deficient, and predicted for me a future without distinction unless I managed to wrench my life away from the abyss over which I hovered. How many times had he had to order me out of the bathroom where it was discovered I was reading books like *La Main Sanglante* behind the locked door, he would demand rhetorically, citing these excursions into the literature of the unwashed as further reason for his grave doubts about how I would turn out.

One time he and Mother played a joke on me by serving my soup in a brand-new chamber pot.

Soon after my release from Professor Azambré's establishment, Vely's father and mother, presented to me as my new grandfather and grandmother, came up from Constantinople, or as they called it, Stambul, to pay us a visit.

Our apartment was relatively small, so Vely's parents stayed at the Grand Hotel. One day, by arrangement with Vely Bey, they decided to give Mother a little surprise. While she was out, they had delivered to our apartment a great deal of stuff they had brought up with them from their palace in Stambul as presents.

Mother came back from her outing and found her lovely little Louis XVI apartment with its Aubussons on the floor buried under piles of priceless Turkish carpets. All around and about stood inlaid sandalwood tabourets and screens, pierced brass braziers, precious metal narghiles with tubes and mouthpieces that looked like enema attachments, and golden bonbonnières, their tops encrusted with big, rocklike, twelfth-grade yellow diamonds with visible flaws. Silk rugs with little pieces of mirror in the shape of crescents sewn on them were nailed up all over the walls. At first Mother thought that she'd gotten off at the wrong floor, then that she was going to faint.

Instead she got hysterical and couldn't stop laughing. At each new piece Vely and his parents tried to get her to admire, she'd go off again and laugh till the tears rolled down her cheeks. Presently we got her fixed up with smelling salts, but every time she caught my eye, she started off again.

The dernier cri from the Bosphorus didn't hit it off at all with the incumbent Louis XVI, and I've always thought Mother let her marriage drift on to the rocks as much to get rid of all that Turkish delight and to see her apartment again as for anything else.

The new grandfather and grandmother were very nice though, even if they were Turks. The grandmother was enormously fat and jolly, dripping with huge yellow diamonds, and very kind to me. She used to fascinate me by putting a black powder called kohl all around the rims of her eyes, between the lashes and the eyeballs, with a little orangewood stick flattened at one end. This practice, she assured me, was most wholesome and warded off infection.

The grandfather, Ilias Pasha, was a very distinguished physician with all sorts of decorations. Among other things, he had been personal physician to Abdul-Hamid II, the last sultan of Turkey. After graduating from medical school in Heidelberg, Ilias Pasha became an assistant to the German who invented the surgical procedure for the removal of cataracts, and was thus among the very first doctors in the world to put the procedure into practice.

I liked him a lot and we got along very well. He considered me his authentic grandson, invited me along with him for walks and gave me much advice. He wore very long, but unbelievably narrow, lemon yellow shoes which turned up at the ends. One couldn't tell right from left. I asked him one day how he managed to wear shoes so narrow, and he explained that if the shoes were long enough, the width didn't matter. He was a Mohammedan, of course, but had only one wife.

17

ONE DAY DURING THE VISIT of Vely's parents, Mother got a little rash on her face. The grandfather looked at it, then made up a purple lotion with a white deposit in it. He told her the lotion was used not only by the ladies of the court of Abdul-Hamid, but by most of the women in the principal harems of Turkey. The rash disappeared almost at once, and suddenly the idea smote Mother to put it on the market under the not very original name of Le Secret du Harem. She asked the grandfather if he would tell her how to make it. At first he said he wasn't supposed to because it was a very valuable secret formula that not only cleared up the complexion but also removed wrinkles. By now Mother's tongue was hanging out. But since Mother was the wife of his son and the secret formula would not actually be leaving the family, the grandfather finally gave it to her.

Thus was born the Maison D'Este, quickly retitled the Maison Desti when the threat of the full force and effect of the law was used to persuade Mother to change the name of the shop to something other than that of the grand and vigilant family. Vely spent less and less time at his offices, where he was pursuing an interest in an aluminum-coated, semitranslucent screen for early motion pictures, and more and more time in the Secret of the Harem business.

Mother found an entresol at 4, rue de la Paix and had it decorated by the dressmaker Paul Poirét, who had just branched off into interior decoration under the name of one of his daughters, Martine. He had a tremendous talent and worldwide success, but he spent a little too freely and wound up one day tending bar in a dive belonging to one of his former mannequins.

Even before the business opened though, Mother and Vely realized that they were going to need something more to sell than the Secret of the Harem, a brand name that sounded a little corny even before the term "corny" was invented. One day a very famous manicurist called Mrs. Kantor walked in looking for a place to park herself, so Mrs. Kantor was invited into the business. A hairdresser was added, then a couple of

Chinese chiropodists, a very fine old chemist, and all at once they had a going Beauty Institute.

With all this, Mother thought she had better put in some house perfumes. She did this with the assistance of a very old French house called L. T. Piver and Company, who let her have a remarkable odor she stumbled on at their premises, not wishing themselves to launch any new perfumes, and then also sold her some of their oldest alcohol so she could recreate the perfume. She immediately named this first new perfume after her distinguished ancestor, Beatrice D'Este; then she beat it down to Venice, where she had some extraordinary glass bottles blown with a reproduction of the famous painting of the lovely Beatrice burned into the glass.

She formed an alliance with a new box firm in Paris called Tolmer, whose designs and taste in general were about seventy-five years ahead of their time. At Baccarat and Lalique some lovely crystal bottles were made for lotions based on the secret formula, and some alabaster jars were turned out for creams and unguents from the same source.

With all of these innovations, the Maison Desti began to grow very fast. Mother took a flying trip to New York, dragging me along as usual. We stayed at the Ritz, and three Ritz bellboys in blue uniforms carried her sample cases one morning when she started out on a tour to introduce and sell the Desti products. She wore her wonderful mink coat and her pearls, which were real in those days, and arriving at B. Altman's, flanked by the young men in blue with Ritz in gold letters on their collars, she made quite an entrance. A number of floorwalkers, managers, and assistant managers tumbled over each other in their anxiety to find out what she wanted. With great simplicity, Mother said, "Mr. Altman." They told her that unfortunately Mr. Altman was deceased, and asked if somebody else might do. Somebody else might do, it turned out, and whoever it was bought ten thousand dollars worth of Desti products, which was all she had brought with her.

It was during this visit, I believe, that allowed out alone one night, I wandered over to Broadway and wound up in the Winter Garden. There I saw a terribly funny vaudeville act. The Pennsylvania Station was being built at the time and its construction appeared to New Yorkers to take forever and the city was rife with jokes about it.

At the Winter Garden, the curtain went up on a set representing the minium-painted steel girders of the Pennsylvania Station reaching high into the sky. The sounds of much hammering came up from below. Now appeared Bert Williams as a Pennsylvania Railroad porter, but wearing an alpine hat with badger brush, rather than the usual porter's cap. His arms were full of bags, and he balanced himself along the narrow girder with the aid of an alpenstock. Around his waist was tied one end of a mountain rope. Presently onto the girder wobbled Leon Errol, tied to the other end of the mountain rope. He was disguised as an English tourist, complete with monocle, and the dialogue that ensued between these two great comedians was hilarious. Nor were the jokes above physical gags.

At one point Errol slipped off the girder while trying to light a cigarette. Williams laboriously hoisted him back up by the long rope that joined them at their waists. "Have you a match?" demanded Errol the instant his head reappeared. "Yassuh!" said Williams, letting go the rope to reach for his matches. We in the audience were limp with laughter. I don't know how many times Errol was dropped before Williams finally untied the rope and let him go, but it was a hell of an act.

Bert Williams was a great, great comic and I hope I don't forget to mention some of the other wonderful acts I saw him do. "Sure-Shot Dick, he seldom misses," for instance, where Williams applied for the job of assistant to Sure-Shot and, pointing to the "seldom" on the eight-sheet, said, "You couldn't make that *never,* could you?"

I enjoyed the visit very much and used to hang out the window of the Ritz and watch the switch engines shunting the cars around in the New York Central Railroad yards, which are now covered by Park Avenue.

A little while after we returned to Paris, a gentleman called upon Mother at the Maison Desti and said, "I think that what you have done, Madame Desti, in so short a time is one of the most remarkable adventures in our business that I have ever seen. Now it so happens that I do not manufacture any cosmetics, although I am the most successful perfumer in the world. I propose that you give up your several little perfumes, although they are very nice, and that you allow me to manufacture your cosmetics for you and to distribute them throughout the world. In exchange, I will give you twenty-five percent of the profits. The Desti cosmetics should make a remarkable team with my perfumes, which are called Coty."

It is with tears in my eyes even today, years and years after the event, that I am forced to report that my mother turned Mr. Coty down, believing he was trying to take advantage of her. The number of millions I would be sitting on right this minute surpasseth the imagination. On the other hand, I would probably never have written anything in my life, which would hardly have bothered anybody, and I would have had to attend a lot of sales conventions.

Nevertheless, I have never heard of a comparable act of bonehead-edness, unless it be that of her son who, in 1920, sent the head Desti manicurist out into the cold gray world because he didn't wish to be in the retail perfume business, which struck him as effeminate. The chief manicurist's name was Peggy Sage, who has since made so many millions out of her fingernail lacquers that it is horrifying to think upon. I think this proves definitely that the talent for avoidance of making money can be transmitted from generation to generation just as surely as its oppo-site, the talent for socking it away.

In a general way, I got along fairly well with Vely Bey, until one night when he took Mother and me to see *La Prise de Berg-op-Zoom,* a howlingly funny play written by Sacha Guitry and in which he was starring with his first wife, Charlotte Lyses. I howled along with every-body else in the audience until the sound of my strident boyish voice so grated on my stepfather's ears that, after telling me a couple of times to pipe down, he suddenly hauled off and slapped me in the face. Totally unaccustomed to this kind of treatment, I immediately riposted with a right to the nose, which unfortunately drew blood. After this, to the stupefaction of Mr. Guitry, his pretty wife, the other actors on stage, the prompter, who stuck his head out of his box like a turtle, and a thousand roaring spectators, we went at it. We were thrown out, of course, as quickly as possible, and the play was not interrupted for long.

When we hit the sidewalk, Vely, still holding a handkerchief to his freely bleeding nose and mortified by what had just happened in the theatre, was in a rage approaching insanity. He snarled our address on the avenue Charles Floquet to the cabdriver, pushed Mother and me into the cab and then got in himself. To say that Mother and I were apprehen-sive is to say too little. Vely had with him his walking stick with a rather heavy round gold knob and as the cab pulled away from the curb, he raised it over his head and said in a voice choked with fury, "Now I'm going to finish you!" The first blow missed braining me, but it did knock me head downwards in the cab, an excellent position for a student of

French boxing. I immediately started kicking him in the face. Mother screamed. The cabdriver pulled over to the sidewalk where a couple of French policemen were conversing, and suggested that they take a look inside his cab, because what he was hearing didn't sound too good to him.

The instant the door started to open, Vely, with a tremendous effort, regained a semblance of composure, and brushed off the whole matter to the inquiring policeman as "a little family dispute."

"Of course," said the policeman, starting to close the door, "Please excuse me."

At this moment, Mother who was really afraid for my life as, compared to me, Vely Bey was a fairly large gent, shouted, "That is a dirty lie, Monsieur l'agent, I have never seen this man before in my life!"

"Ah hah," said the policeman, "this is then an entirely different pair of detachable cuffs!" with which he reached into the cab, grabbed Vely by the back of his collar, and yanked him out on to the sidewalk. As Vely was being pulled through the door, Mother opened the other door on the traffic side of the cab, grabbed my hand, and said, "Let us go while the going is good!"

We melted into the heavy Paris traffic, got into another cab and arrived at 1 *bis,* place des Vosges, Paris Singer's house. Uncle Mun was in bed but awake and reading when his valet showed us into the enormous bedroom.

"Where did you hit him?" he asked me. He always like full details about everything. "On the nose," I replied. "That's where you made your mistake," said Uncle Mun, rising gravely and putting on his Japanese dressing gown. "You should always hit a fat man in the stomach."

He then took us to the kitchen, first to find us something to eat, in which he joined us with great pleasure, and then to find a place somewhere in the house for us to sleep.

Mother's marriage to Vely Bey was in its final stages by now. Too much anger had been released for it ever to be put back in the box, although they did try to patch things up for a while.

When Vely faded out of our lives, so did the good old grandfather, the grandmother, and all the Turkish carpets and paraphernalia of the Ottoman empire.

THE FRENCH ARE GREAT BELIEVERS in pure air. They are always saying what wonderful air there is in some particular neighborhood as opposed to some other. The non-French who live in France eventually start thinking about pure air, too.

For this reason, Paris Singer got Isadora a large and lovely place just outside of and overlooking Paris in a locality known as Bellevue. The air in Bellevue was supposed to be extra special because it was washed by the Seine at the foot of the plateau and then filtered through trees on the way up the steep hill. The house was very large, big enough not only for Isadora and her children, Deirdre and Patrick, and her normal retinue, but also with more than enough room for the girls of her school and a few guests.

Among the guests were Marguerite Namara-Toye, her mother, and her husband, Freddie Toye, who was serving as Isadora's manager. The Toyes had a one-year-old baby I sometimes used to push around in his baby carriage when I was invited out to Bellevue to fill my lungs with the remarkable air.

Besides being a most accomplished opera singer, Madame Namara-Toye played a very hot piano, and the girls and I would go stamping around in something that I fondly believed was a two-step I had learned at Miss Hinman's in Chicago when I was six or seven years old. I remembered that one had to wear gloves so as not to unstarch the little girls' dresses, but I remembered little of the dance. The girls, of course, knew nothing about American dances, but we had a fine time. Isadora was never aware of these not uncommon diversions and was not told because she would not have approved.

One day Gabriele D'Annunzio, already world-famous as a poet, playwright, and lover of Eleonora Duse, called upon Isadora at Bellevue. Isadora went into a sort of enthusiastic eulogy of her school, as she often did when talking to celebrated persons. She explained to him how the girls, when they were not dancing or exercising, would relax in splendid columned rooms, surrounded by antique fragments of statuary and beautiful drawings, reading from such elevated masters as Goethe and Schiller or Voltaire and Rousseau, while listening to the music of Bach or Brahms on the phonograph, or once in a while even something as light as Schubert. She then asked if he would like to see all this. The great man, who had always a weakness for pretty girls, said he would be delighted to. Leading the way, Isadora threw open a great door, then stopped in dismay, D'Annunzio squinting over her shoulder.

Marguerite Namara-Toye was at the piano knocking out a ragtime number, and Irma and I were whirling around doing something between a tango and a schottische.

Needless to say, I took an immediate powder and was in bad odor for some time.

19

CHAPTER

SUDDENLY AND TERRIBLY on an afternoon in April 1913, the lives of Isadora's little children ended horribly. Deirdre was just past six and half years old. Patrick, the little boy Paris Singer had fathered, was two weeks away from his third birthday.

Earlier that day, Isadora had telephoned Mother to ask if she could borrow our chauffeur, Marcel Bouhiron, to pick the children up at her studio in Neuilly and drive them out to Bellevue in her Renault town car of the type known as a bald-faced limousine. Isadora intended to stay at the studio, but the weather had turned so beautiful that she wanted the children to enjoy the wonderful air at Bellevue.

Marcel arrived at the extraordinary studio at 68, rue Chauveau, parked our open car, cranked up Isadora's Renault and was ready to go.

I must explain here that European automobiles of that period, even the very best ones like Isadora's Renault, only rarely had self-starters. These had been invented in America some time before and were in general use there, but the European manufacturers continued to consider them an unreliable novelty. The driver of a European car was obliged to exit the car, go round to the front of it, position the crank and, in effect, wind it up to get the engine started.

Isadora came out of the studio with the children and their Scottish nurse, packed them herself carefully into the car with many fur lap-robes, told the nurse to make sure that Marcel did not drive too fast, then kissed her children good-bye and stood waving after them for a moment before going back into the studio.

Marcel drove off toward the avenue bordering the Seine which cuts the rue Chauveau at right angles about three hundred yards down the street from the studio.

Reaching the avenue, Marcel was almost hit by a taxi coming down the avenue from his left and to avoid the accident, he jammed on the brakes so violently that he stalled the motor. Lacking a self-starter, he got out to crank up the engine, slamming the door behind him. What he forgot, or neglected to check, was that in his excitement he had left the car in gear.

At the very beginning of the cranking movement, the engine, being hot, started up at once, the car began to move, and Marcel threw himself to one side to avoid being run over. He ran to catch up and got a foot on the running board as he grabbed the door handle, but in this new excitement he slipped and fell, twisting his ankle, and the car, knocking badly in high gear, accelerated across the avenue straight toward the Seine.

Scrambling back on his feet, Marcel limped after it and actually caught the door handle just at the moment the car hit the far curb. The jolt dumped him off again, this time for good, and he sat where he had fallen, powerless, and watched as the heavy car rolled into the river.

The very efficient Paris firemen arrived at the scene rapidly, apparently called by someone, but it was much too late. They even had a very hard time locating the car because, due to the throttling action of a small island opposite the rue Chauveau, the current here was very swift and had moved the Renault nearly a hundred meters downstream. When they managed to lift it out with a crane, it sprinkled water from its full interior like a watering can. Finally they got it up on the bank and there, in the horror of the soaking fur robes, they found the pitiful little passengers, clutched to the breast of their nurse, whose hands still cradled their heads against her . . . quite dead, of course. There was a trace of warmth in the little boy and for a few hopeful, desperate minutes they thought maybe they could save him.

I was supposed to go with them out to Bellevue that afternoon, but was punished for some reason or other and not allowed to go. I have always thought that if I had been in the car, I probably would have been able to save them.

This pathetic tragedy shocked the world. But even more shocking was the horrid and instantaneous outburst of the professional pulpit-pounders. "How now?" they vociferated, smacking their lips. "Are you satisfied?" they thundered. "Have you learned your lesson?" they fulminated, professing to see in this devastating event the hand of God the Avenger. "So you thought you could ignore the established church, did you?" they frothed. "And bring forth your little bastards in free love, without the blessing of baptism or any of the other professional benefits.

Now are you convinced? *Now* what have you to say?" Others spoke more gently, but with no less evident satisfaction. The events, they said, spoke for themselves.

The final ceremonies were as beautiful as they were sad. Isadora's entire studio and its grounds were covered with white flowers, laid there over two days and nights by friends, acquaintances, and strangers. The expression on the nurse's face was so horror-stricken in death that her coffin was closed, but the children, so very small and still, seemed to be sleeping peacefully. Edouard Colonne's orchestra, the greatest in France and probably in Europe, which had played often for Isadora's recitals, came to Neuilly and played for her lost children. Some great actor or writer, I remember only that he had a beautiful voice, read some kind of poem, then the orchestra played again, and the three coffins were carried out.

We all went out too. The men, on foot, followed the enormous hearse with plumes and two horses to the crematory, which was way up in Montmartre. Isadora and Mother and Elizabeth and some other women rode in carriages. As we walked by on the streets, all the men we passed stopped and took their hats off, the police saluted, and the women crossed themselves.

It was a very long walk and we all got very hungry. I still remember my astonishment when we were eating afterwards at some brasserie, all with long faces and our eyes red with tears, and somebody did something very inconsequential, like sneezing, or knocking over a glass of water, and all of a sudden everybody was howling with laughter. The more we looked at each other in shocked surprise, appalled at what we were doing, the harder we laughed . . . until the tears rolled down our cheeks again and we were helpless. I refer only to the men, of course. Mother and Isadora and the other women had gone straight back to Neuilly.

But neither the tears nor the reasonless laughter could overwhelm the awful sorrow.

CHAPTER

IT'S HARD TO GO from a subject like that to the ordinary events of an autobiography, but life goes on.

The Desti business continued to prosper, and I helped a little by making posters for some of the new products and designing some boxes.

Face powders in that period came only in white, rose, and the cream color named for the celebrated actress Rachel. I don't know where Mother got the idea, but besides the three standard colors, she started putting out ochre powder, sunburn powder, and lavender powder for use under artificial light, where it appeared whiter than white. I made one very nice poster of a pretty Mexican girl with a big sombrero and very ochre-colored skin for the new powder.

Vely Bey having now completely disappeared, a new gentleman came over the horizon. Mother's new friend was a most courteous Mexican gentleman called Gabriel Elizaga, who was by profession a gambler. That is to say, having lost his not inconsiderable fortune at baccarat in the Club Haussman, the Club Haussman now had him dealing for the house, and paid him enough to get by and to eat very good lunches. His uncle had been one of the most scandalous presidents of Mexico, such a brigand that every member of his family down to the I-don't-know-how-many'th generation had had to get out of the country. But Gabriel, known as Chato to his friends, was the soul of gentleness. Like old Ilias Pasha, he used to give me advice, too, but being from a different country, his advice was different.

Never under any circumstances, he urged, was I to marry anything but a Mexican girl. Mexican girls, he assured me, would save me my money, raise me my children, prevent my servants from stealing me a peso, and be faithful unto death.

"For God's sake," he exhorted, "avoid like the pest these French women, who consider themselves the equals of men, and these American women, who consider themselves to be even their superiors!" "How about Mother?" I asked mildly. "Your mother is *really* a superior person," said Gabriel, "and I am not such a much."

The year we met Gabriel, I didn't seem to be getting over my annual bronchitis quite as fast as usual, so Mother sent me to Trouville with a very pretty Madame Moreno, who was a friend of Gabriel's and who had two lovely daughters about my age. We stayed at the Hôtel des Roches Noires, where I had a very nice month, but at the end of it, I was still coughing.

Back in Paris, Mother took me to see a lung specialist and on the way home, in the gentlest way possible to avoid frightening me, she told me that I had a tiny, tiny spot of tuberculosis. As a matter of fact, so little was made of this at the time that twenty-five years later, when a specialist was listening to my chest after a fairly severe bout with pneumonia and said, "Ah, yes, the healed lesion, . . . " I had completely forgotten that I had ever had TB and didn't know what he was talking about. As little as was made of my condition, however, it was felt that a higher altitude would expedite my recovery and it was decided to send me to school in Switzerland. Gabriel and Mother picked out a very well-spoken-of Swiss school that somebody's son had been to, and Gabriel very kindly offered to take me there. He and I entrained for Lausanne.

21

WHEN GABRIEL AND I got to the school in Lausanne that he and Mother had picked out for me, we found out that this school only took in honest-to-God, on-the-level Catholics, which I certainly was not. I don't think I was even still a Protestant after the disappointing results with the motorcycle I had prayed for.

The Catholic school was at least polite enough, after I had come all the way from Paris to enter it, to give us the name of another school down in Ouchy, the lower part of Lausanne, on the lake level. Looking down their noses, they ventured the opinion that for a non-Catholic school, La Villa was not bad. As we beat the Catholic school in every single sporting contest we had with them all the time I was there, La Villa was at least pretty good on sports.

The school was situated on both sides of the avenue down to and just before one reached Ouchy. On the left side of the avenue stood two large villas separated by some outbuildings and the gymnasium. Cement tennis courts were across the avenue, the soccer field was down by the lake, and at the lakeshore itself was the boathouse with five or six four-oared yoles, a couple of single sculls, and an eight-oared, university-type beauty, which we could use only to have our pictures taken in when the water was smooth.

The student body, like that of the Ecole des Roches, was overrun with barons and counts and marquis. One perfectly charming and beautifully mannered Spanish boy was the nephew of the Duke of Alba, and another of my great pals was Hans, Baron von Stohlterfoht, who played the piano.

The school was owned and operated by Dr. Max Aukenthaler, who was a rabid sports fan, whether because he actually liked sports or because they got a lot of publicity for the school, I don't know. We were supposed to win every time we went out, and I think we nearly always did.

Dr. Aukenthaler was not above taking every legal advantage he could to win games or cups or championships or regattas. The conference or league of Swiss schools allowed one teacher to play on each senior team. All the other schools' teams, therefore, had some professor playing who was big and that was about all. But the teacher who played on our senior soccer team was a professional soccer player disguised as a professor. I have forgotten what he was supposed to be teaching besides soccer, but since he dropped his aitches a bit, I don't think it was the classical languages.

We played our soccer matches all over Switzerland, traveling third class by train. We knocked over all the other schools, but the reason for that, aside from our professional professor, was simply that we had a large percentage of American, Canadian, and even some English and Scottish boys who were a little bigger for their ages than most of the boys in the other schools. For instance, I was fifteen, five feet eleven, and weighed almost 170 pounds.

Although we played on the senior soccer team, we were considered juniors for other purposes because we were under sixteen. Once in a while we would be sent out to play football against some other school's juniors, who were little squirts who came up to our knees.

I tried out for ice hockey, too, but the results were disastrous. When I went to buy my skates, someone—obviously a saboteur—told me to be sure to get the shoes nice and loose or my feet would freeze and I would lose my toes from gangrene. As a result of following this advice, I was skating either on one side or the other of my ankles, and one doesn't get very far in ice hockey that way.

For some wonderful reason, my fiddle had not been sent along to school with me, and I was taking piano lessons instead. My teacher was a tall, slender, disappointed-looking Swiss, whose principal job was teaching mathematics, which he did very well. The reason the piano teacher was so disappointed-looking was that he had composed a large number of études, piano solos, four-handed pieces, waltzes, quadrilles, mazurkas, gavottes, and minuets which all his friends had told him were beautiful, but which every publisher in Europe had turned down with the speed of an antelope. I mention this only so that one might understand the terrible fury with which he learned that a terrible little ragtime number that von Stohlterfoht and I had written had been accepted for immediate publication by a firm in Riga, Latvia.

The publishers in Riga didn't know any more about ragtime than von Stohlterfoht or I did. This was a fortunate happenstance; they wouldn't have touched our effusion with a ten-foot pole otherwise. My familiarity with the genre, although a little greater than it had been back at Bellevue, consisted of having danced one turkey trot, in knickerbockers, with Elsie Janis at the casino in Trouville the previous summer. Von Stohlterfoht had never even heard anybody playing such stuff and relied upon me as the expert.

He *could* play the piano, however, and write down notes, which was a lot more than I could do. I contented myself, therefore, with drawing a three-color cover allegedly in the American popular-music-style and with whistling a tune that von Stohlterfoht wrote down and arranged. This may have all seemed very authentic to the firm in Riga, although the real reason they published this musical crime was probably that von Stohlterfoht came from a very wealthy and powerful noble family in Latvia. They had already published three of his waltzes. I heard the waltzes so I know what I am talking about.

When von Stohlterfoht and I, modestly, but with pardonable pride, started scattering a few professional copies of the sheet music of "Winky" around, I believe the poor piano teacher went out and got drunk. Whether he did or not, he was certainly in a very vile humor by the time my next piano lesson came around. Muttering in that terrible language known as Schweizer Deutsch about little scheissbritches who couldn't even play the scale of C major with two hands having stuff published while men with degrees in music could sit around waiting for publication until hell froze over, he sat down at the piano and played our masterpiece over a couple of times.

The little composition made him so angry that he was practically smoking and he became speechless with rage. Then I made a mistake which made him still angrier. I told him he had not played our piece with sufficient syncopation. Suddenly he hit upon a diabolical revenge. *I* should be the one to demonstrate its proper rendition. He would make *me* learn to play it and, in order to master it, I should play nothing else until I could give recitals of my own remarkable composition.

My terrible piano playing today stems, I believe, from this punishment.

I played a little tennis too, but there were any number of boys who could beat me and who used to put me out of the tournaments regularly.

One of them, a boy called Fritz Mercur, did this to me several times, but later he became some kind of tennis champion in America so I don't feel as badly about the trouncings I got from him as otherwise I might.

One day *L'Oeuvre*, a French periodical devoted to the arts, was sent on to me from Paris; in it had been printed a caricature I had drawn of Raymond Duncan. My joy was difficult to contain, as one doesn't have many things printed as a boy. Many years later in Hollywood, I received a letter from Lugne Poe, the wonderful French actor-writer-producer-editor, who had founded *L'Oeuvre*, built the Théâtre de l'Oeuvre, and given practically everybody in France his first break. The letter asked if I needed someone to help with French versions for my motion pictures. While still wondering what to write to Mr. Poe, I received a second communication from him, this time a bright red envelope with his name and address in the upper left-hand corner. I was chagrined because I knew that he was going to bawl me out for not answering right away after his tremendous kindness to me in my boyhood.

But when I opened the envelope, I saw the letter was not in his handwriting. It was in a handwriting I knew, however, although I could not place it and could not have said whose it was had my life depended on it. The letter was in French and, translated, began, "My dear Mr. Poe, Imagine my surprise and stupefaction upon opening your wonderful magazine and finding there my drawing of Raymond Duncan . . . " I looked at the date. It was 1913, and the letter was from me. It was the old man's way of reminding me that he had done something for me, but it gave me a very strange feeling.

I thought of a boy of fifteen, without aim, without purpose, without a profession or the desire for any in particular, standing on the threshold of manhood, with no faintest idea of where that corridor on the other side of the door might lead him.

From his pocket the fifteen-year-old takes a letter he has just written and, holding it high, entrusts it to the wind. It rises gaily, timble-tumbling around the tops of the trees like a paper butterfly, then gradually becomes smaller and smaller until it disappears in the sky.

Thirty years pass, and then one day in a distant land, a man, gray at the temples, comes out of the glass doors of the great office of the great company of which he is president. Something catches his eye and looking up, he sees a white paper tumbling toward him out of the sky. It lands delicately in his hand and upon reading it, he discovers it to be his own letter, entrusted to the wind so long ago.

But *where* is the boy who wrote it?

Of course, now that I had had *two* things printed, my mathematics-music teacher looked at me with such loathing that one could practically hear him crackle. It is probably a very good thing for a boy to learn to live with enmity, as opposed to an atmosphere of love and affection, as it hardens him and gives him a taste of what he is going to run into later in life.

At Christmastime, most of the faculty and a lot of the students who lived too far away to go home were scheduled to go up into the mountains above Territet and more or less take over a little winter resort called Les Diablerets for the length of the holidays. I didn't live too far away to go home, but Mother thought the mountains would be healthy for me so I was allowed to go along.

We had a wonderful time, especially as we couldn't wash in the mornings at all because the water in the pitchers was frozen solid. This was a great relief after Lausanne, where everybody had to start the day off by passing under a shower of icy mountain water.

At Les Diablerets there were dances in the evening, which the boys in my age group did not care much about, and figure skating, skiing, and luging, but the principal sport, and the one I liked by far the best, was bobsledding. The track was really splendid, iced and well banked and with a marvelous hairpin turn banked about fifteen feet high just before the finish. Here the spectators gathered. We were pulled up to the top by a horse, and although I don't suppose we went much over ninety miles an hour on the way down, being so close to the ground made it seem almost breathlessly fast and it was quite thrilling.

I was captain and helmsman of my bob, the Greased Lightning. We won the final race and broke the track record at the same time by a rather exciting maneuver, taking the hairpin turn at full speed, without braking at all, thereby flying through the air and across a cut in the embankment left there for the horse to go through. We received much applause for this.

Nobody paid the slightest attention to the spot I was supposed to have on my lung. We ran five kilometers every day after lunch to get our wind in shape for soccer or for rowing, depending on the season. Playing outside right for two halves at soccer in which one runs forty-five minutes in each half practically without stopping, or rowing mile-and-a-quarter sprints in a four-oared yole with the tongue hanging out, at least kept one's lungs inflated with great draughts of clean mountain air, a sort of kill-or-cure regime. It's entirely possible, of course, that Mother and Gabriel had decided to forget to tell the school anything about it.

Our rowing coach was from Harvard, and I think he knew a lot more about rowing than the coaches of the other Swiss schools. Everyone had to prove that he could swim a hundred yards in the lake's icy mountain water before he was allowed to go out for crew.

We raced in yoles because squalls blew up like lightning on the lac Leman, and a scull would sink like so much pig iron. Unlike sculls, yoles were at least twenty-one inches wide and reasonably seaworthy. They had little outriggers and carried five including the coxswain, each boy handling one big oar with the school colors on the blade.

Competition was fierce. Our school's first senior crew took on all the other first senior crews; the second senior crew went up against the second senior crews of all the other schools; our first junior crew and second junior crew competed with their counterparts from all the other schools. My pals and I were on the first junior crew and we beat all the other first junior crews quite regularly.

The rowing regattas were held right down along the Ouchy shore. The finish was just about in front of the Beau Rivage Hotel. During one regatta, a pretty amazing thing happened. In one of the races, our cox brought us in outside the buoy and the school was nearly disqualified. As a result, Dr. Aukenthaler got into a terrible rage and, needing to hurt somebody, he said that I and a big South American boy called Quevedo II would be removed from the first junior crew and would row the number two and number three in the *second* junior crew. The number two and number three of the second junior crew would take our places on the first junior crew.

This terrible affront threw Quevedo II and me into the deepest depression. We wouldn't even talk to the very nice little boys we were rowing with in the second boat.

The second junior crew, as I've mentioned, is only supposed to beat the other second junior crews. Although all the boats of the first and second senior crews and the first and second junior crews of all the schools are on the water racing at the same time, each is only trying to outstrip the other crews of its class.

In the next race, Quevedo II and I went right off our heads at the pistol shot and started pulling the boat out of the water. I yelled and cursed during the entire race, threatening to murder the little boys with us if they didn't pull their guts out. Since nobody on the water pays much attention to a *second* junior crew, the final, stupefying result was that we not only beat the bejesus out of all the other second junior crews, but also all the first junior crews, all the second senior crews, and all the first senior crews, including those from our own school. Nothing like this had ever been done before, and if there were a word for sensation to the hundredth power, that's what our feat created. The strokes of our three other school crews, every one of them supposed to beat us easily, were purple with embarrassment and were razzed without mercy.

At the party that night, we were given champagne and then toasted in a speech by Dr. Aukenthaler. "Quevedo II and Sturges," he said, "are probably rotten oarsmen, but I have noticed this curious fact: whenever they are in a boat, that is the boat that wins!" It was a very pleasant vindication.

For some reason, when I left La Villa at the end of the 1913–1914 school year to go back to Paris, instead of taking everything I owned with me, I left a boxful of rowing trophies, little silver football cups, bobsled prizes, team and crew photographs, my books, my correspondence, and most of my professional copies of that remarkable piece of music called "Winky" to be sent on to me by freight. I never saw them again. They arrived in Paris all right, and the notice was mailed to me, but by then Mother had sent me to Deauville to supervise the running of the Maison Desti seaside branch. By the time I got back to Paris and found the notice, Mother's attention was on other things.

IT WAS A VERY NICE SUMMER, that summer in Deauville, the nicest one for some time, as a matter of fact. The little resort across the inlet from Trouville had been founded only the year before and was then the most fashionable playground in the world. Billionaires were ten cents a dozen. The beach and the casino and the racetrack spilled over with dukes, barons, deposed kings, maharajahs, politicians, statesmen, newspaper owners, several Rothschilds, opera stars, generals, admirals, celebrated actors, notorious actresses, vaudeville performers, gigolos, painters, professional dancers, authors, playwrights, publishers, gamblers, jewelers, perfumers, dressmakers, milliners, designers, journalists, critics, automobile manufacturers, bankers, arms manufacturers, racing-stable owners, architects, contractors, and, kept or loose, the prettiest women in the world.

Ciro's, the extraordinarily elegant and attractive Paris restaurant with a branch in London, had taken over a whole building in Deauville to open a Ciro's there for the season. The restaurant occupied the whole of the second floor of the building. On the street floor there were shops and on the floors above the restaurant there were rooms and apartments.

Mother rented one of the shops for the Maison Desti seaside branch. Her rental arrangement with Mr. Hobson, the owner of Ciro's, also included a large room and bath over the restaurant for me, plus *all* my meals thrown in. That probably makes me the only man in the world who, on a regular basis, ever ate not only his lunch and dinner at this fashionable and violently expensive restaurant, but his breakfast, tea, and occasional off-hour sandwiches.

People are often surprised at my easy familiarity with a large number of rare and sometimes precious dishes . . . little things like whole truffles boiled in champagne, or Königsberger klops, those peculiar hamburgers stuffed with chopped herring. They imagine this familiarity to be due to the fact that I once owned a large and fairly celebrated restaurant. But they are mistaken. I had already eaten all this stuff as a boy . . . at Ciro's.

Mother must have had other plans for herself that summer or it might not have occurred to her that a fifteen-year-old boy who excelled at soccer and crew was somehow ideally suited to supervising the day-to-day running of a perfumery, without himself being supervised.

However it happened, I came straight off the playing fields of La Villa and became the sole manager of a going business. Among my duties was maintaining the shop and its fixtures in a condition as glistening as its clients.

All of the beau monde—and the less beau, too—got up late in Deauville. Everybody got up late in Deauville, except me. I rose at 5:30, put on an old pair of pants and a sweater, picked up a quick cup of coffee and a croissant from Ciro's early morning cook, who was starting to build his soups, and snuck down to the shop. I dusted it, swept it out thoroughly, polished the brass, washed the windows, then hustled back upstairs and got back in bed.

At 10:30, I came down again, this time officially. Wondrously decked out in white flannel trousers, brown-and-white shoes, a tan gabardine jacket with a belt in the back, and a carnation in my buttonhole, I dropped into the shop. Assuring myself, by running a suspicious finger along the shelves, that the night porter had done his work efficiently, I retired to Ciro's to enjoy an exotic breakfast.

As an adolescent, I only knew a few of the celebrities to speak to, but I knew most of them by sight, which was useful when they came into the Desti establishment. I did know Mother's friend, Jules Bache, the banker, and Maurice and Florence Walton, the great ballroom dancers, and Elsie Janis, and Bayo, the world's greatest tango dancer, and Irene Bordoni, and Tod Sloan, and Kid McCoy, and Frank Moran, and some of the boatriders from the New York Bar who came up for weekends. (In case the profession has been forgotten, a boatrider is a man who plays cards on boats and wins.)

The darling of all these people and the uncrowned King of Deauville was the son of an Auvergnat grocer, a tiny little man who looked like a jockey. His real name was Goursat, but under the signature of Sem he had become the world's most extraordinary caricaturist. To be ridiculed by Sem was a great honor. His albums of drawings, beginning with *Tangoville-sur-Mer,* which celebrated the heyday of Deauville, are collectors' items and perfectly remarkable. Everybody who was anybody is there, instantly recognizable and hilariously drawn. It is difficult to prove how truly phenomenal he was because caricature is an evanescent pursuit, the one form of portraiture which demands of the viewer complete familiarity with the features of the victims. With the passage of time, their faces are nearly always forgotten. Sem was by far the greatest talent in this anteroom of the arts that I have ever seen during my lifetime.

One of Sem's great friends and favorite subjects was the most beautiful mannequin in France, the breathtaking Jacqueline Forzane. I couldn't take my eyes off her wherever and whenever I saw her. It didn't do me any good, though.

I made a little time, though, with another less celebrated beauty by pretending to be nineteen. Then Mother came to Deauville for a weekend and seeing me approaching the table, said to the girl, "Isn't he *big* for fifteen?" That was it for me. The girl rose, spilling her cocktail, and walked furiously away and never spoke to me again until I ran into her in New York some time later when I was *really* nineteen . . . and she wasn't anymore.

Very suddenly, on one of those last days of July 1914, an era came to an end. Nobody knew this, of course. Austria declared war on some place called Serbia, wherever that was, making the neighbors of both countries very nervous. All of us thought that if there were a war at all, it was going to be just one of those nice quick little wars that last only long enough for everybody to be decorated and for a few soldiers to appear with bandages around their heads, supported by two pals, ready to sing the theme song.

A couple of days later, France and Germany mobilized, but why this should stop all the trains from Deauville to Paris was difficult for everyone to understand. It did, however, and people without cars, I mean simple people like waiters and cooks and bartenders and croupiers and salespeople and shopkeepers, who never had cars in 1914, were pretty badly stranded. Everything in Deauville had stopped like a clock whose pendulum someone has reached in and grabbed.

Boys going on sixteen didn't have cars either in 1914. I was very relieved and grateful when Mr. Hobson appeared and told me to pack my things, that he was taking me to Paris to deliver me to my mother. Normally it took a little over two hours from Deauville to Paris in a fast car, but it took us a good deal longer. There were signs of mobilization on every road and considerable excitement in every village. A fragmentary railway service was reestablished a few days later, but on this first day, all trains went to the front.

Mother was greatly relieved to see me, but the minute I showed up, she decided to send me to America at once, reasoning that patriotic music, flag waving, and uniforms impelled very young men to look for the nearest recruiting office.

Remembering that she was practically a full-fledged physician, Mother had already offered her services and those of every other red-blooded American woman in Paris to the American ambassador through the columns of the *New York Herald.* The American ambassador, Mr. Myron T. Herrick, had asked her by telephone to please shut up and quit rocking the boat. The war was going to be a small one, of a few weeks' duration at the very most, and had nothing to do with America in general and especially nothing to do with American women living in Paris. Mother was as sore as a boil about this.

At our apartment I found the notice that the box with my cups and trophies and photographs had arrived from Switzerland, but now there was no money for nonsense.

Mother took me to the Gare Saint-Lazare and kissed me good-bye. She had given me an empty trunk which I was to take to Deauville and fill up with as many bottles of perfume and other Desti products as I could cram into it. From Deauville I was to take the little boat over to Le Havre and then board the French liner on which she had secured passage for me, and proceed to New York.

When I got into Le Havre on the little steamer from Deauville, my trunk, extraordinarily heavy with perfumery, presented a difficult problem. How was I to get it from the little quay where we had arrived over to the big sheds of the French Line quite a distance away, now that all the porters had been mobilized? I looked around to see if I could find a couple of bums, but they must have been mobilized, too. Suddenly I heard a very charming lower-class English voice, and around the corner came some British Tommies in the charge of a sergeant. The little company was halted and dismissed and then started wondering aloud where they could get some beer. I went over to them and volunteered as a guide and interpreter, adding that I would treat them to the beer if they would help me to get my trunk over to the French Line.

Lifted by six Tommies, the trunk fairly flew down the street, and they took it right aboard for me. The beers were most welcome. They were laughing, cheerful, gallant young men without an aitch among them, a part of England's little professional army of about ninety thousand at that period, every one of whom fell in France during those first days of the war to end all wars.

EVERY SHIP LEAVING EUROPE in those first days of August 1914 was packed, jammed, and overrun with passengers wanting to get out while the getting out was good. Even with much influence, Mother had been able to get me only steerage passage. I had never traveled in any class but first class before, but this was great fun.

First of all, the usual strict shipboard class distinctions were in abeyance because it was wartime, and those of us who had steerage tickets were still treated like socially acceptable passengers. Secondly, we never went near our appointed eight-to-a-cabin bunks way down in the smelly yonder except to snatch our bed pads out of them and to drag them up on the promenade deck, where we spent beautiful balmy nights in the first-class passengers' deck chairs, covered with their expensive blankets.

I was probably the youngest, but there were some students who had been studying on the Left Bank in Paris who were not much older than I. We all had a fine time with much laughter. I have no recollection of eating slops in the bowels of the ship, so that it is probable that we managed, by the use of many broad *A*'s and a super-refined manner, to so demoralize the purser and the chief steward that they allowed us to eat in the first-class dining room with the swells.

During the trip, I occasionally wondered aloud how I was going to get my trunk, filled with expensive perfumery, through customs. Mother had been able to give me very little money and, no matter how customs figured its take, I was pretty sure the sum they would demand would exceed my cash on hand.

The day before we landed, a very nice middle-aged American lady came to tell me that she had been talking over my predicament with some of the other ladies on board and that they had decided to help me. They would parcel out among themselves in small quantities the perfumes and Desti products in the trunk and then send the stuff back to me after we landed. Customs would take no interest in a few beauty products any woman might have in her baggage. She warned me, though, that if I said one word aloud about it to anyone, all of the ladies would deny it and call me a liar.

As a matter of fact, it wasn't very difficult to go through American customs at that period. All one had to do was put a ten-dollar bill under the top shirt, where the inspector always looked first. Having been trained in sleight of hand, the inspector would palm the bill and then look ferociously through one's used laundry without finding anything, and one was through customs.

It might have been more difficult with a trunk full of cut crystal bottles, all bearing the same trademark.

Within a few days, the ladies got everything back to me at 347 Fifth Avenue, the address Mother had told me to go to when I arrived in New York. It turned out that this was where a remarkably stout woman who lived on nothing but gin had established the American headquarters of the Desti business. Her name was Daisy Andrews. I have not the faintest idea how or when Daisy got in touch with Mother or when the American headquarters deal was made. Daisy was an interesting woman, and before she died of cirrhosis of the liver about ten years later, I got to know her quite well. She was one of a group of women with deep booming voices, powerful handshakes, and a fondness for mannish clothes that existed in New York at that time. Daisy stood just a little over five feet but weighed the same as Primo Carnera and, I must admit, she would have looked slightly peculiar dressed like one of the Dolly Sisters.

When I arrived in New York, unannounced and unexpected, Daisy was puzzled. She didn't know what to do with an almost sixteen-year-old boy, so she sent me to Father in Chicago, the city of my dreams.

Father hadn't seen me since I was a little boy and had no idea what I looked like. At Union Station in Chicago, where the Twentieth Century came in, he waited at the head of the platform, abreast of the locomotive, and took off his hat, hoping that I would remember what *he* looked like.

Suddenly out of the stream of strangers appeared a young man about six feet tall who seized him fondly in his arms and then, making joyful sounds, kissed him, European-style, on both cheeks. This amused Father very much. The next time I came to Chicago, having learned the American style of *not* kissing one's father, he grabbed me in *his* arms, kissed *me* on both cheeks, and said, "I've been saving that for you!"

Father hadn't seen me in so very long that he had many questions to ask me. He took me over to the University Club, got me a big room and bath and, among other things, asked if I had ever had a drink. I replied that I most certainly had. I told him that I had been drinking wine with my meals for lo these many years, and that whenever Mother had anything else on the table, I was given some of that, too. I went further and volunteered the information that, due to some peculiarity or other, alcohol did not affect me at all.

"No matter how much you drink?" asked Father in surprise.

"The quantity does not seem to have anything to do with it," I replied.

"This is very interesting," said Father. "You are apparently a very unusual young man! I presume then that I can take you to . . . I suppose you could call it a party, that this young lady I know is giving tonight, without danger of your falling on your face?"

I replied, with what must have been infuriating assurance, "If anybody falls on his face, it won't be me!"

"We'll see about that," said Father.

Our hostess was a very pretty young lady called Mrs. Chester and she had some other very pretty young ladies in the apartment when we got there. There were also some gentlemen who were not only Father's friends, but also his clients at Noyes & Jackson.

I was very nicely received and immediately given a full glass of bourbon. As this was followed by another, which was followed at once by a third, I realized that there was some sort of conspiracy afoot to teach me not to boast about my capacity. I could have stopped drinking, but that would have spoiled everyone's pleasure, the last thing I wanted to do. I loved Father dearly and wanted him to enjoy my presence, so I drank what they gave me and resisted as best I could by going into the kitchen and taking long drinks of water between what they were pouring for me. After a while I was spending most of my time in the bathroom. Even so, the time came when I started to get very sleepy. A charming young blonde took me into a bedroom and tried reviving me with cold compresses, but it was too late. She helped me take off my shoes and put me to bed.

Unless I am mistaken, however, I have a dim recollection of having helped hoist Father into some kind of bed before I passed out, so the contest may be considered to have been a standoff, without loss of face on either side.

Before the month of August 1914 was over, America announced that it wasn't taking sides in the war, which seemed to be adding new belligerents to one side or the other all month long, and I had my sixteenth birthday.

For some reason, it was decided to send me to school in New York rather than Chicago. Father may have felt there was some bitterness toward me in the Sturges family because of the family's belief that Mother had walked out on Father after his accident. The family didn't know, or thought it made no difference, that Mother had canceled our sailing and come back to Chicago immediately to help care for Father, and that she hadn't sailed away until he was much better. Or maybe New York was chosen because the Desti business was supposed to pay for my schooling.

In any case, in New York I was enrolled in the Irving Preparatory School conducted by a Dr. Ray. The school was located around Eighty-ninth and Central Park West. Daisy Andrews had procured a room-and-bath apartment for me around Thirty-second and Madison. In those days, New York still had its elevated trains and its streetcars, and it was as easy to get from one place to another as it is to get around in Paris today.

The first morning I arrived at the school, a very polite young man came up to me, bowed, introduced himself as Percy O'Gorman and offered to show me around. He also introduced me to my two great friends, Eric Dressler and Rodney Combes.

I don't think I learned anything in this school either, although I can remember the subjects I particularly loathed. One was some kind of geometry. But even more than geometry, I loathed Shakespeare. In this class, I would frankly fall asleep, and Dr. Ray, pretending to be a streetcar conductor, would wake me up and tell me it was the end of the line. If there had been a poll to guess which boy in the class was least likely to become a playwright, I would certainly have won, hands down.

The school played basketball and ice hockey. My ankles weren't any stronger than they had been in Switzerland so I only went skating once. They thought I might be pretty good at basketball, although I didn't know the game at all. At practice the first day, down under some church, I saw a fellow running toward me bouncing a ball up and down, and I said "What do I do? Stop him?" Somebody said sure, so I charged him the way we did in soccer football. My shoulder hit him right in the solar plexus and he was out for half an hour. Everybody started bawling me out, except the victim himself. "Just do that to our opponents and we'll have a good season," he said.

I never got to play basketball, though. I got the mumps, and when I went back to school, athletics were considered temporarily inadvisable.

The Desti business wasn't going very well and money was running low. Father started sending me fifteen dollars a week to live on. I gave up my apartment and asked Dr. Ray if he knew where I could find a nice, clean, inexpensive room. He did. He owned a lovely brownstone house at Fifth Avenue and 129th which he had rented to a Mrs. Naughton, who, he was certain, would rent a room in it to me.

The room was on the second-floor front and had one lightolier in the middle of the ceiling. This wasn't very helpful for reading in a bed that was over in the corner, and was the reason, if not the direct cause, for the fire.

The direct cause was one of my less successful inventions. I needed a light over the bed and the solution I came up with was a candle stuck to a round piece of cardboard about the size of a butter plate. The three suspension strings I attached to the cardboard disc joined together about two feet above the disc into a single string cord. I fastened the string cord to the ceiling with a thumbtack and at once I had a lovely reading light. I got under the covers and opened my book. The candle chandelier worked perfectly.

I must have fallen asleep and the candle must have burned down to the cardboard disc and I can only guess at the sequence of what burned next, but I woke up in the dark room and, sensing something, looked down. My bed was like a bed of coals, the cotton comforter glowing like burning charcoal. Somehow the little flames had burned over me and down on both sides into the mattress, but I was untouched. Why I didn't die like everybody else who sets his bed on fire, I don't know. I reached up, got a grip on the headboard, pulled myself up like a sword out of a scabbard, and then started running back and forth with pitchers of water from the bathroom. I was so ashamed of my stupidity that I tried to put the fire out without telling anyone in the house about it. But when the water went through the old floor and a piece of plaster ceiling below fell down on Mrs. Naughton's bed, she came upstairs and took note of the damage. I can't say that she was too disagreeable about it. If the situation had been reversed, I would have been considerably more caustic.

About this time, Mother arrived from France in a pretty despondent state.

While I had been in Deauville packing all the Desti products I could into the trunk, Mother had been with Isadora at Bellevue assisting at the birth of Isadora's last child. In her terrible grief at the deaths of her children, Isadora had mated briefly with a young Italian on the island of Corfu. Discovering that she was pregnant, she was crazily certain that the new baby would really be Deirdre or Patrick coming back to her. The death of the infant two hours after it was born was the death of hope. Isadora turned Bellevue over for use as a war hospital and accompanied Mother to Deauville.

In Deauville, Mother was the prime mover in the installation and equipping of the Hôpital Matitan within the walls of the beautiful casino at Deauville. The backbreaking job began with searching out and commandeering—from luxury hotels, barber shops, and pharmacies—all of the supplies she needed: beds, mattresses, pillows, sheets, blankets, cooking and sterilizing equipment. She had the emergency receiving station all ready in time to receive the first miserable, stinking, wounded men who had jounced three weeks in cattle cars on their way back from the front. A few weeks later, when the war seemed lost and the French government had withdrawn to Bordeaux, it was Mother who drafted a Red Cross truck and bluffed her way over the refugee-covered roads all the way down France and back up to Deauville with a load of supplies to replenish the hospital's stores. With or without a degree, Dr. Dimples did her job, and I for one am proud of her.

At the beginning of the war, everybody, including Mother, felt very sorry for the Belgian refugees created when Germany invaded their country in the middle of August 1914, and Mother lent some of them the two pretty little peasant cottages we had in Fleurines.

What Mother had forgotten though, was that, having married a Turk, she was no longer an American citizen. When the Allies, the good guys, declared war on Turkey, one of the bad guys, in November 1914,

she automatically became an enemy alien, a status unpleasantly brought
to her attention when a street mob went into the Maison Desti, broke all
the bottles, then threw the furniture out of the windows. Fortunately for
the mob, and for Mother too, Mother wasn't there.

On her arrival in New York, Mother was interviewed by the newspapers. She gave out her usual stuff about perfume suiting the personality,
and went on about freedom for women as exemplified in the bobbed hair
she, Isadora, and Irene Castle sported. A full-page article appeared in
the Sunday paper, but it didn't help business very much because Mother
couldn't get any of her products over to America. The lack of product
also caused a row with Daisy Andrews, who vanished from the concern.
Mother then took the advice of a well-intentioned lawyer called Isadore
F. Finkler and went into bankruptcy. Mr. Finkler suggested it because
with Daisy Andrews gone, Mother didn't know what the business owed
or what contracts had been entered into, and Mr. Finkler said that filing
bankruptcy would clear the air and bring everything to a head. Mother
took his advice and regretted it for the rest of her life.

I was immediately taken out of school and, as it turned out, that
was the end of my formal education.

Mother took a rotten little apartment for us on Twelfth Street, the
only banal apartment I have ever known her to take, and one afternoon
I arrived home with a big smile on my face and a peculiarly shaped
package under my arm.

"What's that?" asked my mother looking at the package apprehensively. Then in a pale gray voice, she added, "That wouldn't happen to
be a *banjo* by some remote chance, would it?"

"How did you guess?" I cried enthusiastically. "Just wait till you
see it! The pawnbroker practically gave it to me for only three dollars,
including the case, and it has real mother-of-pearl between the frets and
up around the scroll!"

"It's a curse," said my mother, putting her hand to her forehead,
"a taint."

"A what?" I asked, thinking I had misunderstood her.

"A pollution of the blood," said my mother, "like leprosy. It *has*
to be from the blood, there is no other possible explanation. With the
utmost care and during your entire life, I have refrained from giving you
even a hint about this vice of your father's. I never let your Grandmother

Biden or anyone else mention it to you for fear that it might awaken a dormant strain and encourage you to emulate him. But it has all been in vain. You may as well know now. Your father was considered, in banjo circles, to be one of the very best banjo players in America. Such was his talent that manufacturers would actually send him new models for nothing, just to get his opinion and endorsement of them.

"Your father always enjoyed playing a piece on the banjo for me, always a long one, and at the beginning of our marriage, I could stand it. Then as time passed, he was no longer satisfied with just plunking out a piece once, but immediately after finishing it, he would plunk it again in several different keys. Then I would get it with variations and countermelodies woven in . . . but still the same piece. He would wind up by plunking it behind his back in a sort of contortionist's grip. One night he actually gave the finale while swinging by his knees from a trapeze he had strung up between the sliding doors. If any more loathsome instrument than the five-string banjo has ever been invented during the entire history of music, I have yet to hear of it. I thought I had suffered from that miserable thing for the last time in my life, but you can't get away from heredity! So tune up your banjo, then go down to the corner and get me some poison."

So there we were: bankrupt, living in a rotten little apartment, trying to run a business with no inventory, and unable to afford to send me to school. Things looked quite depressing. And then . . . BOOM! In November 1914, Isadora and all the girls arrived in New York, and life speeded up again.

Mother naturally went to live with Isadora, in a large suite at the Ritz. The stinking little apartment was given up, its furniture sent back to Cowperthwaite's, and a nice room was taken for me at the Hotel Irving on the south side of Gramercy Park. The customary millionaire with more houses than he knew what to do with had come through, as usual, with a magnificent private house for the use of the Duncan School on the north side of Gramercy Park. An enormous studio was found on the northeast corner of Fourth Avenue and Twenty-third and taken, as usual, without a down payment. The studio was one flight up and very cheesy looking, but by the time the walls had been covered with Isadora's old faded blue drapes and the floor with her old faded blue carpets, and the customary magnificent black Steinway concert grand had been moved in with two dozen roses and the compliments of the house of Steinway, the place looked exactly like all of Isadora's previous studios and was ready for business.

To the studio, as usual, came many interesting people. There were painters, poets, stage designers, impresarios, journalists, photographers, musicians, and one banker. Of bankers, we never had enough. Among the photographers I knew and remember well were Arnold Genthe, Edward Steichen, and Alfred Stieglitz; among the musicians, the conductor Edward Falck, the fiddler Hugo Riesenfeld, who became Isadora's concertmaster, Sigmund Spaeth, who brought us the wonderful bald pianist, George Copeland, with his blue painted eyebrows, and my great favorite, Ossip Gabrilowitsch. His playing seemed to me extraordinary and thrilled me much more than anyone else I had ever heard . . . and I had already heard plenty.

Though we received only one banker, he was one hell of a banker. Born in Frankfurt and the head of Kuhn, Loeb and Company, his name was Otto Kahn. In early 1915, he came to offer Isadora the use of the wonderful Century Theatre at Sixtieth and Central Park West. Undoubtedly some other millionaires had put in with Mr. Kahn to build the theatre, but it was generally considered his, I presume because he had lost the most money in it.

The Century had absolutely every improvement known to mankind at the time, including a separate and smaller theatre on its roof. Its innumerable dressing rooms all had baths or showers and were like rooms at the Ritz. For the stars, there were suites. It was so copiously provided with dimmer boards that they could not be placed on the customary stage-right wall, but had to be stashed under the orchestra pit and worked by remote control. There was also a complete and enormous counterweight system, and the whole stage revolved with a noise like thunder.

Up until now, Isadora's managers had arranged her American tours for performances of one night, two nights, sometimes a week, at different theatres in different cities in America. Now, thanks to the generosity of Otto Kahn, she had a theatre of her own, and at first she didn't know what to do with it. One can give a *few* dance recitals but one can't hope for a whole season of recitals, as there are far fewer dance enthusiasts than there are baseball fans, for instance. Isadora decided to alternate the dancing with the presentation of Greek tragedy, because Greek art called for the intermingling of music, declamation, and dance. Sophocles' tragedy, *Oedipus Rex*, was selected.

Now there is nothing like a big theatrical production to put all one's friends and relatives to work. With the solitary exception of Mother, who was busy downtown every day reviving the Maison Desti, everyone we knew well, slightly, or hardly at all, went to work on *Oedipus Rex*. Gordon Craig wasn't there or he would have done the scenery, and Raymond Duncan wasn't in America, which was too bad, because he would have looked very natural in the play without any effort at all. Apart from these two and Mother, practically no one was overlooked. Temple's father, Augustin Duncan, played Oedipus the King; Margaret Wycherly played the wife who was also his mother; their unfortunate children were played by the youngest members of the Duncan School, and the rest of the girls supplied some of the various choral and wailing groups required for Greek tragedy. There was a full orchestra, of course, conducted by Edward Falck, with Hugo Riesenfeld as concertmaster. I went to work as assistant stage manager, call boy, and backstage elevator operator to bring down whole elevator-loads of additional mourners and wailers.

At the theatre on the roof I met a young French actor performing there in a French repertory company. His name was Georges Renevant, and he I became friends then and are friends still today.

Isadora made a little change in the layout of the theatre's seats by having the first fifteen rows ripped out and replaced with shrubbery growing in tubs because, she said, the seats were too close to the actors, who always looked better from a distance. I happened to be out front the afternoon Otto Kahn came by to see how things were getting along. When he took a good look at all the bushes replacing the best seats in the house, he was not a happy man. Isadora also had an idea that art should not be poisoned by commerce and wanted to charge only ten cents for the seats. Otto Kahn, although appreciating the nobility of the idea, frowned upon it. It would give the theatre a bad name, he said, and would make it difficult to extract a normal admission from subsequent audiences. Furthermore, he didn't want any ten-cent spectators sitting on what was left of his expensive seats.

During the actual performance, my job was to bring on the thunder and lightning on very precise cues, notably when Gus staggered out of the Theban palace with his eyes gouged out and hanging down on his cheeks, leaning heavily on the children he had fathered by his mother. We had a swell effect here which began with distant lightning flashes, then more vivid flashes of lightning, and culminated in a great roar of thunder interspersed with lightning, indicating Jupiter Tonans' shocked fury and indignation at what Oedipus had wrought.

Thunder and lightning are generally referred to in that order, although in nature the lightning splits the air, causing the thunder that follows it. One *thinks* of thunder and lightning, but what I had to *signal* for was lightning and thunder. All my troubles arose from this.

When one is responsible for giving an offstage cue, even the simplest ones, like the ring of a telephone or a birdcall, demand considerable sangfroid, and the job is nerve-wracking. One is very much aware that everything depends on the delivery of the cue at exactly the right microsecond. One stands there, knees slightly bent, breathing heavily and, in my case, gripping two flashlights. One of these flashed green to signal the lightning, the other flashed red for the thunder. My red and green signals were picked up by a stagehand sitting way up in the flies with one hand on a big iron thunder-sheet and the other on a knife switch that threw direct current into a sputtering arc for the lightning.

The first time Gus staggered on stage, the coagulated blood from his empty eye sockets waving below his chin, something went a little wrong. I watched Gus fascinated, repeating to myself over and over, "When he opens his mouth for the big speech, thunder and lightning, when he opens his mouth for the big speech, thunder and lightning . . ." And sure enough, when he opened his mouth for the big speech, I signaled with the red flashlight. The thunder crashed down around him, he looked over at me in startled fury, then tried to shout the thunder down. But all the audience saw was a man waving his arms and all they heard was the thunder. Recognizing my terrible error, I started flashing the green light, but all this did was to cause Gus to be enveloped in flashing lightning. The thunder increased because the stagehand in the flies was a logical man and knew one couldn't have lightning without thunder. When the final curtain fell, Gus located me and made up for what the audience hadn't heard from him by what I had to listen to. I tried to explain the extreme difficulty of the job and swore it would never happen again.

The fourth or fifth time the thunder and lightning cues went wrong, I felt that apologies would be superfluous, so I just went down under the orchestra pit with the dimmer boards and waited until everyone had gone home. Thus ended my first job in the theatre. I was sixteen and a half and didn't come back to the theatre for a long time.

I don't remember exactly how the press took our *Oedipus Rex*, but I imagine reasonably well, because it's pretty hard to get bad notices for something really deep-dish.

ISADORA'S SHOWS AT THE CENTURY went on without me, and I joined Mother at the Maison Desti. Mother had moved the remains of the business out of 347 Fifth Avenue into a little shop at 23 East Ninth Street, a couple of doors from University Place and diagonally across the street from the dear old Café Lafayette. With the Café Lafayette, and the Hotel Brevoort around the corner, and the addition of the Maison Desti, the whole neighborhood had a French flavor. The shop was down a few steps in a very prettily converted old residence. The rent was forty dollars a month.

Mother was still living with Isadora, of course, so she took a room for me at the Hotel Judson on the south side of Washington Square, and I moved out of my room at the Hotel Irving.

We fixed the little shop up as well as we could with the furniture and showcases from 347 Fifth Avenue, and then we started looking around to see what we could dig up in this country in the line of boxes and bottles and raw materials until we could get things over from France again.

Although they did not compare in any way with those from the Maison Tolmer, we had some reasonably attractive boxes made by a boxmaker called Mr. Rothschild. We bought bottles from Whitall-Tatum and Company, unfortunately a far cry from those Mother got in Venice or from Baccarat or Lalique. We also bought eau-de-cologne spirits (alcohol) to make perfumes and other things, and an assortment of essential oils and fixatives. The alcohol was not aged, although the part-time chemist we found was extremely so. The essential oils were not bad, but neither were they very good. Still, we managed to put together a sort of a line that included the ochre powder, the sunburn powder, the lavender powder, the Aurore rouge, and, of course, our famous Secret of the Harem. The Secret of the Harem was now called Youth Lotion. Since the Turks had become allies of the Germans, everything Turkish had become rather inelegant, including Vely Bey, who chose this moment to show up in New York and to come to see us.

Vely Bey had just had a pretty good idea, which was to blame all smoking troubles and throat irritations on the paper that surrounded the cigarette, a pronouncement cigar and pipe-tobacco manufacturers had been bellowing for years, and to start manufacturing a brand of Turkish cigarettes held together by a leaf of tobacco. The name he gave his cigarettes, certainly a straight-from-the-shoulder one, was Paperless. They didn't do as well as they should have, probably because of his lack of capital.

The Maison Desti lacked the funds to launch any advertising campaigns and it also lacked the French merchandise the stores in America had already bought and wished to replenish. We apologized and explained that, although they looked different, the products were really the same. We managed to do a little business, but not very much.

Along about here Mother, who didn't smoke, was inspired to put out Desti's Ambre Cigarettes. As she didn't like the taste of tobacco, she thought that cigarettes perfumed with amber might mask that unpleasant taste. She found the results delicious. I thought they stank, but a number of ladies agreed with Mother, and Desti's Ambre Cigarettes became quite a little thing.

One day Isadora decided to go back to Europe and return all the girls to their parents in Germany. A war always makes people very patriotic, and most of the girls had suddenly started remembering that they were Germans after all and had begun behaving like Prussian Army officers. American-born Isadora, who, of course, was pro-Ally, said to hell with them. She would return them to the various peasants' hovels, concierges' loges, and ragpickers' cellars where she had found them in the first place in such black poverty that their parents couldn't get rid of them fast enough, and see how the ungrateful little witches liked that. Isadora, although a great artist, was also extremely human.

It would have been impossible to get the girls to Germany from either France or England, because both those countries were at war with Germany, but Italy was still neutral, and getting the girls home from there would be simple. Passages were booked on the *Dante Alighieri*, sailing on May 6, 1915.

Mother and I were just leaving for the Italian Line docks to say good-bye to everybody when Vely Bey showed up again. He didn't like Isadora at all because he felt she had helped to break up his marriage with Mother, but he came along anyway. Down at the docks, everybody was highly emotional. Augustin and his pretty wife, Margherita, and practically everybody else from the cast of *Oedipus Rex* were there, plus Edward Falck and Hugo Riesenfeld. Also gathered were Billy Roberts, one of the editors of *The Literary Digest,* and his wife, Mary, Alissa Franck, who had been Isadora's secretary but who decided to stay on in America, Arnold Genthe, Mitchell Kennerly, the publisher and art gallery owner, Sara Greene, the sculptress, and her husband, the lawyer John S. Wise, Jr., Sara's son, Jack Wright, who had spent those summers in Fleurines with me, had just been killed in the war in France.

Finally the stewards started beating on the dishpans and hollering, "All ashore what's goin' ashore!" The siren started thundering and the dockhands began snatching back the gangplanks. When all but one of the gangplanks was down, Isadora, crying into her handkerchief, called across to Mother, who was snuffling into hers, "Mary! If you don't come with me, I don't know what I'll do!" then leaned against the stanchion, the better to sob. Mother, sobbing, too, took a step toward the gangplank.

Vely, looking the picture of indignation, turned to Mother and said, "You aren't going to fall for anything *that* stupid, are you? You have no clothes! You have no baggage and you have no money!"

"You don't understand," said Mother, then taking me in her arms, she added, "Do the best you can, darling. Keep things going. I'll send you some money as soon as I can!" She shouted to the dockhands loosening the lines on the last gangplank to hold it a moment, please, and she disappeared aboard.

The next we saw of her, she was waving good-bye to us from the ship's rail. As Mother hadn't even an overcoat, Mitchell Kennerly came through like the gentleman he was, and his overcoat made the last trip up the gangplank. At the rail, Mother and Isadora started laughing, and it turned out that what they were laughing at was the face on the purser when he discovered not only that *Mother* didn't have any money for her ticket, but that Isadora didn't have a dime either. This joke was too good to keep, so they imparted it to us who were waving goodbye. As Mitchell Kennerly was the only person there with any money on him, he again came through like a gentleman, this time with all the cash he had, which was just enough for the most modest passage. The weighted envelope containing this treasure bounced back from the side of the ship and landed on a catwalk far below and was finally sent aboard by means of a long string. The *Dante Alighieri,* her siren roaring, her decks white with fluttering handkerchiefs, backed into the Hudson.

As the ship disappeared down the river, Vely Bey removed his hat, mopped the top of his bald head, looked very worried and announced that the Desti business would have to close. "Why?" I asked. He answered the question with a question. "Who is going to run it?" I said *I* was going to run it and he looked at me as if he knew now, for the first time, that my whole family was nutty. He reminded me that that I wouldn't even be seventeen years old for another few months, that running a business was a man's job, that what I had done in Deauville was only bumblepuppy, that I was completely incapable of running a business, and he was going to close it at once.

I told him that he was going to do nothing of the kind. He reminded me that he was still my mother's husband, that by law the business probably belonged to him anyway, that, in any case, it had been founded on a formula supplied by his father. Then he repeated that we would go at once to 23 East Ninth Street, where he would lock the door. I told him that my mother had told me to keep things going and to do the best I could and that if he tried to interfere, I would have him arrested. He saw that I was very intense and serious about this, besides being a lot bigger than I had been at *La Prise de Berg-op-Zoom.* Finally he said, "All right! Be it on your own head! Don't come to me when you get in trouble!" with which he departed to take care of his own troubles, which were not few.

CHAPTER

I RODE BACK TO EAST NINTH STREET with Sara Greene and her husband. They had a lovely studio house which had been the large stables of some early resident of Fifth Avenue at Ninth Street. John S. Wise, Jr. was by way of being my guardian in New York while Mother was away, at least Mother had muttered something to this effect just before she boarded the *Dante Alighieri*. Sara Greene was very fond of me because I had been her son's best friend, and also because Mother had befriended her and her small son when Mother was rich and Sara was very poor. Now the positions were more or less reversed.

Sara and John S. used to talk about sending me to Andover, but this did not occur. Whenever I ran out of money completely, I went to John S. for help, and he always gave me some wise saying like, "Anticipation is always worse than realization." I don't think he ever gave me any money. He did give me five dollars once in exchange for painting his bathroom with a five-gallon can of white enamel paint that some paint manufacturing client had given him for nothing.

White enamel is terrible stuff to work with as no matter how thinly one spreads it out on the ceiling, it gathers together again in drops that hang down like icicles. One keeps trying to smooth the hanging drops out until the arm grows weary from being held so long in a position over the head. Standing on a board which straddled the bathtub and held the paint, I worked desperately to make these stalactites disappear—until my foot slipped. The board, the five gallons of enamel paint, and I fell into the bathtub. I hadn't thought to put the stopper in, so by the time I got out and got some of the paint off me, the rest of it had gone down through the piping of the whole house, where it hardened and brought on a considerable plumber's bill. Maybe that's why I wasn't sent to Andover. I was just as glad though, because running the shop was a lot of fun.

The very first thing I did after watching my mother sail out of sight down the Hudson River was to give up my expensive eight-dollars-a-week room at the Hotel Judson. I moved into a nice rooming house across the street from 23 East Ninth, where I got a large room in the back for three dollars a week. No extra charge was made for the bedbugs, which appeared in vast regiments, bit like hell and stank to high heaven when squashed with the thumbnail. The landlady, a very nice German woman with two beautiful blonde daughters, was always surprised and shocked when she heard about the bedbugs and swore that this was the first inkling she had had of their existence. However, the whole rooming house smelled very strongly of kerosene, squirted into cracks to get rid of the insects, so I fear she was not speaking the truth. Somewhere I had read that these sofa scorpions didn't like the bitter taste of soap and would not bite one through it. One desperate night, I rose up, lathered myself all over and walked around for a long time with my arms up in the air until the soap dried. Then, daring the beasts to bite me now, I went back to bed. But I did not go back to sleep. The bedbugs avoided me, but I discovered in misery that dried soap itches even more than bedbugs. But the landlady did have those two beautiful daughters, and trying to get them to come into my room to look at my collection of postcards was a diversion in itself. Finally, they did come, but together, so I really had to show them my postcards, of which I had very few, after all.

Mother had left a very nice young girl called Louise and a young man called William Heim to help me with the shop. I don't remember how much Louise got, but Heim, who came mostly out of kindness, got just enough to live on. At some point, my ex-classmates, Eric Dressler and Rodney Combes, came down and helped, too. I think I gave them five dollars a week.

When we had a good day, I would take everybody to dine at the Hotel Albert around the corner, where we stuffed ourselves on the dollar dinner. If the day hadn't been so good, we'd have dinner in the shop by candlelight with fine rich milk, a mountain of liverwurst, and about sixty cents-worth of spaghetti with sweet butter and black pepper from an Italian place down the street. We ate very well.

All of us would help to get out an order when one came in. They *did* come in every once in a while, because the Desti business had started out in America as a real business, and Jordan Marsh in Boston, or the City of Paris in San Francisco, or Marshall Field in Chicago, or Wannamaker's or Bonwit Teller or B. Altman in New York would send in orders to replace the Desti products they had sold.

Apart from the orders, which, if they came in at all, came in with the morning mail, we had a certain amount of drop-in business and also some carriage trade. People who have never run a shop have no idea how exciting it is. It is very much like watching a roulette wheel, except that one doesn't have to put up more money for each additional spin.

Take a rotten day: no orders, no drop-in trade, no nothing, and someone about to be sent over to the German delicatessen for some liverwurst. The imaginary roulette wheel spins, and suddenly a long, open Pierce Arrow pulls up in front of the shop, carrying, we suppose, a visitor for one of the swells who lives upstairs, like pretty little Mrs. Waldo Pierce. A liveried, colored chauffeur runs around the back of the car, comes to attention at the door, opens the tonneau, and onto the sidewalk steps a tall and very handsome young colored woman, quietly and tastefully dressed. Colored people weren't quite so rich in 1915 as they are now, so we are stupefied by this apparition, which sweeps into the shop and buys eighty dollars' worth of stuff, with a heavy emphasis on the ochre powder. The day is made! Devoured by curiosity, one wonders who *is* this statuesque bronze beauty? She is a simple soul and quite willing to identify herself. It turns out that she is the daughter of Madame Walker, who made a little invention to take the kink out of overkinked hair, and made millions with it. The daughter was delighted with the Desti products and came back quite often in her Pierce Arrow.

On another day, a rather shy but very pretty girl, who looked as though she were just a little older than I, came into the shop and seemed delighted with everything I showed her. She ordered all sorts of things, which pleased me, then sat on the desk and had a couple of cigarettes with me. After paying for everything, she said that she was on foot and couldn't very well carry all she had bought and asked if I would have it delivered.

I don't know what kind of expression came over my face when I heard her name, but it must have been quite startled because she started laughing at my discomfiture. Her name was Evelyn Nesbit, and she had come through a searing and horrendous scandal that had covered the front pages of the newspapers of the world for years. Her husband, Harry K. Thaw, had shot and killed the great American architect Stanford White in the open-air café on the roof of the beautiful Madison Square Garden, which Mr. White had designed. Mr. Thaw had been seized by a spasm of retroactive jealousy and epileptic rage over some alleged prenuptial hocus-pocus between Mr. White and the then fifteen-year-old Miss Nesbit. I suppose it was Miss Nesbit's shooting her mouth off that brought on the killing of Mr. White, and I therefore not only urge, but I beseech any poor miserable young creature who might have suffered the same fate-worse-than-death as Miss Nesbit to suffer in silence and to keep her trap shut instead of going around promoting murders.

One day a charming lady came in with her son, who was just my age. She was the widow of the great Shakespearean actor Richard Mansfield, and her son Dickie Mansfield and I became great friends. They lived at the Algonquin Hotel, and introduced me to that quite wonderful caravansary by sometimes inviting me to tea there. I started suspecting Dickie was a little off his rocker from the first time I met him. He used to come down to the shop and help to get out the orders like my other friends, reciting Shakespeare all the while. Sometimes he would make suggestions for new perfumes that were really idiotic. His mother had him in some kind of school in Massachusetts or Connecticut, where one day, probably striving to emulate the English highwayman Dick Turpin, he got a revolver from somewhere, tied a handkerchief over the lower part of his face, hired a horse and tried to hold up the local bus. He was recognized and immediately arrested, and only the absurdity of his venture saved him from serious punishment. But there wasn't much health in him, and not too much later he became ill from some silly infection and died. We all went to his funeral. He was seventeen by then.

The last of the customers who might be of some interest was a tall, slightly buxom blonde, so beautiful and so good-natured, it took one's breath away. She was considerably older than I, but had she wanted the shop, I would have given it to her for the asking. She thought all the products were lovely, bought quantities of them, asked that they be sent, gave me her address and said her name was Mrs. Moore. My face must have fallen and she asked me what the matter was. Although I don't remember exactly what I said, it was something like, "You *must* have another name! There *couldn't* be anyone as beautiful as you in the world that I have never heard of." I suppose this would have pleased any woman, and it pleased her. She laughed and said yes she did have another name, one I quite possibly *had* heard of. It was Lillian Russell. Around 1934 I wrote a motion picture called *Diamond Jim,* and the part of Lillian Russell was played by the exceptionally pretty Binnie Barnes; exceptionally pretty, but not quite up to the original.

All sorts of people came into the shop at one time or another, and the better known they were, the nicer they were.

One day in July 1915, about two months after Mother had sailed off on the *Dante Alighieri,* an unbelievable cable came to the shop. It was from Mother, announcing that through Morgan Harjes and Company in Paris and J. P. Morgan and Company in New York, she was sending me two thousand dollars, with which I was to press forward with the business and to do some advertising. This is how it happened.

On the day the *Dante Alighieri* docked in Naples, Italy entered the war. Isadora went on to Paris to see if she could scratch up some money, and Mother volunteered to get the girls back to Germany by way of Switzerland. Arriving in Zurich, naturally without any money at all, she heard that Mrs. Harold McCormick of Chicago was at a hotel there undergoing some kind of treatment. Mrs. McCormick was not only married to the son of the founder of the great McCormick Harvester Company, but was reasonably well-to-do in her own right, being the daughter of John D. Rockefeller. She was exactly the kind of friend Mother needed at that moment.

Mother's earlier described imagination-to-thought-to-probability-to-certainty syndrome overtook her.

She was seized by the feeling that she must have met Mrs. McCormick *some* place, *some* time, although exactly when or where she could not recall. It took only a very short time for this nebulous feeling to become almost a certainty, then a certainty, then an absolutely positive certainty beyond the faintest peradventure of doubt. Within five minutes, she could remember perfectly, or nearly perfectly, what Mrs. McCormick had been wearing at the time. The only question remaining was *where* she had met Mrs. McCormick. Might it have been at the Onwentsia Club? Easily, of course, unless Mrs. McCormick happened not to be a member. Might it have been at the van Ingens? At the Ira Morrises? At Mrs. Potter Palmer's? In each instance, the answer again was easily, unless Mrs. McCormick happened not to know them. Then came an inspiration. When Caruso sang in Chicago, *everybody* went to hear him, and presently Mother remembered, again beyond any question of doubt, that *that* was where she had met Mrs. McCormick.

So Mother called on Mrs. McCormick. Rather than confuse Mrs. McCormick at the last moment with a lot of stale news about 1911 divorces and subsequent remarriages to Turks, always difficult to explain, but especially so now, and taking into consideration that the lady was taking treatment, Mother merely sent in her name as Mrs. Solomon Sturges of Chicago.

Mrs. McCormick remembered Mother, almost, though not nearly as well as she remembered Caruso. Tea was served. Mrs. McCormick enjoyed a reputation as a kind and charitable woman and she proceeded to embellish that reputation by coming first to the assistance of Isadora's poor little stranded pupils, then to the assistance of Isadora herself by helping with the arrangements for a most successful concert in Zurich, then to the assistance of her friend Mrs. Solomon Sturges of Chicago.

Mr. Harold McCormick arrived in Zurich a few days later and guaranteed Mother's account in the amount of ten thousand dollars at Morgan Harjes and Company in Paris, one-fifth of which her cable said was being sent to me.

While I stood in the middle of the shop exulting over my two thousand dollars' worth of news and wishing someone would come in so I could share it, my boxmaker, Mr. Rothschild, entered. He was happy at the news—first, because he was a very nice man and sincerely pleased by my good luck; second, because I would now be able to pay him something on the account the shop owed; and third, because if business got bigger through advertising, the shop would be that much bigger a customer. He told me that I was lucky he had dropped in at this moment because I probably knew nothing about banks or how important a first-class bank was to a business. "Thanks God, with me here to guide you, so soon you are getting your money, we are taking a little walk down to the Drovers' and Coalheavers' Trust Company, where I am introducing you personally." I don't remember the exact name of the bank he had in mind, but it was something that brought drovers and coalheavers to mind.

Very soon a letter came from J. P. Morgan and Company at 23 Wall Street, giving notice that a certain sum had been received by them for me. I took the subway down there with the letter in my hand. I was taken into an office and presented with a beautiful blue-gray cheque with J. P. Morgan and Company written all over it in wavy parallel lines. The cheque was for two thousand dollars, payable to me. I had never seen so much money before. The banker asked me what I was going to do with it and I began to tell him the things my mother had told me to spend the money for. But that was not what he meant. He asked if I had a bank account to put it in, was not surprised to learn I had never had one, and asked if I would like to bank with them. I thanked him and said I would like that very much.

Back at the shop a half hour later, Mr. Rothschild walked in. Relieved for me that I had received the money, he was ready to take me to the trust company for drovers to open the first-class bank account and appalled to learn that I had already a bank account. He squinted his eyes so he could withstand my response and asked me where, after all his advice, I had put the money. He was stunned to discover that the account was at J. P. Morgan and Company and then stupefied to hear that they had suggested I bank with them. "But why did they offer such account to you? Was the gentleman offering maybe a friend of your mother's or something?" He wasn't, of course, so Mr. Rothschild left shaking his head in wonderment.

Two thousand dollars seemed such an enormous sum to me that I didn't bother to keep any stubs. I bought half-page ads advertising the Maison Desti and its products in *Vogue* and *Vanity Fair* as my mother had told me, and wrote out a couple of other cheques for other expenses. One day I got a phone call from J. P. Morgan and Company informing me that a check of mine for $4.67 had just been presented and that I had only a balance of $4.12 left. I told them that they were insane, that I had two thousand dollars, less a few small checks, and then I hurried downtown full of righteous indignation.

They had the goods on me, however, in the form of a large pile of paid checks, not one of which I had ever bothered to write down or to subtract. I was horrified, of course. By now I had learned what it meant to have a bank account at J. P. Morgan and Company, that extraordinary bank with only six hundred depositors, of which I had been one, and six hundred million dollars on deposit. That strange and aloof institution was not even a member of the New York Clearing House, so that every check I drew had to be carried personally, by hand, from one bank to another and presented for payment by a gentleman in a derby hat. By now I knew that merely having an account in J. P. Morgan and Company was almost like walking down Wall Street with J. P. Morgan's hand on one's shoulder. The thought of losing this wonderful thing by my negligence and youthful stupidity filled me with dismay.

I told them what an idiot I had been, how much I regretted it, and promised faithfully always to fill out my stubs and to make immediate subtractions so that never again would it be possible for me to give out a check without, as the French call it, provisions. I borrowed a little money from Paris Singer which I put into the account and swore not to touch, and I didn't, until I absolutely had to. J. P. Morgan and Company kept my account for about three more years.

CHAPTER

ONE DAY VELY BEY SHOWED UP AGAIN and then so did Daisy Andrews. The next thing I knew, the two of them had promoted a sort of restaurant-cabaret with singing and tea dancing in the afternoon. For the principal attraction, they brought over from Paris a man called A. Nilsson Fysher, whose major claim to fame was that he had written the words of a very lovely song called "Pour un peu d'amour" in French and "Just a Little Love, a Little Kiss" in English. Fysher was a sharp-looking, powerfully built man of medium height from somewhere around Smyrna in Turkey or one of those places in the Levant. He sang with much charm in a warm husky whisper, after first asking the customers to forgive him for the loss of a voice . . . which he never had. He was an expert showman, since he had been running a cabaret of his own for years in Paris. Vely and Daisy called their new establishment Chez Fysher, and it had begun to do very well.

One day Daisy Andrews sent for me and offered me a job. She said that she would have two suits made for me by a first-class tailor and then pay me a hundred dollars a week to dance with the lady customers of Chez Fysher during the afternoon tea dances.

I could well have used a hundred dollars a week but I had to turn the job down. The reason was a very simple one, but one which might not be readily grasped. It had to do with the fact that the name of Sturges was not actually mine by right, but had been *given* to me. I knew that the whole Sturges family, with the exception of Father, who never had an uncharitable thought in his life, was waiting patiently for me to do something dishonorable like stealing, or giving a bad check, or something of that nature, so that it could sit back and say, "You see? Not a real Sturges." The fact that my exaggerated care of this name kept me reasonably straight and out of trouble for years may seem absurd, but it is a fact. Especially when I was young, I tried always to behave as I imagined I would have behaved had I been a *real* Sturges, and my efforts not to bring dishonor upon this name, nor to tarnish it in any way, resulted in some quixotic and occasionally very expensive decisions.

That is why I couldn't take the job Daisy Andrews offered me. I couldn't see a Sturges as a gigolo.

27

THERE WERE MANY FASCINATING NIGHTCLUBS in the city at that period which I could not afford to visit unless some wealthy friend like Paris Singer were in town. On my own, I went mostly to the Beaux Arts, a charming establishment on the ground floor of the building which at this writing still stands at Sixth Avenue and Fortieth Street. Except perhaps to the post office, the Avenue of the Americas is still Sixth Avenue to everyone else, even newcomers. The Beaux Arts was owned by one of the Bustanoby brothers; the other brother owned the Domino Club on the third floor of a little rookery just above Columbus Circle. When I was seventeen, I had a wild crush on Isabelle Rodriguez, the beautiful Spanish dancer at the Domino Club, and I would go there nearly every night and wait until five in the morning to take her home. She never even kissed me, but once a month her mother used to invite me to eat arroz con pollo, which I have not eaten since.

When Paris Singer was in town, I became a temporary millionaire and went *every* place: George Rector's, the Midnight Frolic over the Ziegfeld Follies, the Biltmore Roof, Delmonico's, Reisenweber's, Shanley's, and my favorite place of all, the Knickerbocker Grill downstairs in the Knickerbocker Hotel on the southeast corner of Broadway and Forty-second Street. The building is still there, but the glamor is gone. As a matter of fact, most of the glamor seems to have gone out of the whole damned world. Not one of the places that I knew well, New York, London, Paris, Deauville, Nice, Cannes, Monte Carlo, Berlin, or Dresden compares in any way with how it used to be. I am not an economist, but I think it has to do with our meek acceptance of confiscatory taxes. Wealth is needed to have elegance, and elegance is needed to have glamor and gaiety. The gents with the expense accounts and credit cards who do the spending these days do not seem to compare in any way with the millionaires I remember. Fat and vulgar though he may have been, Diamond Jim Brady having supper with *both* Dolly Sisters at the Domino Club was still quite a sight to behold, and I was glad to have seen it when I wrote *Diamond Jim.*

The Knickerbocker Grill was a delightful place. Arthur Kraus and his orchestra would play "Tishamingo Blues" for me, and the great maître d'hôtel Ernest Cerruti, privately persuaded that I was Paris Singer's illegitimate son, treated me like a prince. Since I looked almost exactly like one of the four sons Paris Singer *had* produced, it was impossible to disabuse Mr. Cerruti of this notion. He was a great pal of mine, and when I took a girl down to the Knickerbocker, he let me put my check on the cuff, if necessary, and sometimes even went so far as to lend me a little money to spend during the rest of the evening.

I made another wonderful friend at the Knickerbocker Grill, whose kindness probably had a lot to do with my eventually becoming a playwright. He was a little man with silver hair called Jack Welch, who was the general manager for the production firm of the marvelous George M. Cohan and his partner Sam Harris. Mr. Welch was married to the sister of Temple Duncan's mother, and when he met me and realized that I had neither money nor connections in New York, he volunteered the news that a simple phone call to his office would get me at least *one* seat at *any time* to *any* show in New York, that if the show wasn't too big a hit, I could probably have a pair, but of one seat I could be certain. The fact that I am familiar with that entire theatrical period is due entirely to him.

I joined a new association called the American Legion, which, like the Lafayette Escadrille, was one of those pro-Ally ventures in which young Americans indicated what they would like to do when and if the United States declared war on Germany. There was very little sentiment to support any such thing in this country, and the leader of minding our own business was a Senator LaFollette. A joke greatly relished at the period was to refer to these associations as "LaFollette We Are Here!" outfits. I put myself down as a motorcycle dispatch rider and received for my subscription money an identification card and a beautiful enamel button bearing a white star with a bright red center surrounded by a blue rim. Somebody down in Washington didn't like the American Legion idea while America was at peace, however, and presently our subscription money was returned to us and we heard no more about the movement. The design of the beautiful enamel button subsequently appeared on all American war planes.

I had what I suppose was my first girlfriend along about here, if girlfriend means what I think it does. She was the first girl who, instead of sending me home at the end of the evening, allowed me to wait over until the next day.

Her name was Doris and she had been a chorus girl or something like that in London. Her health was not the best and she helped me to remember this rather important night in my life by having a severe hemorrhage around three o'clock in the morning. I was immune to TB, having had it, but this dramatic eruption lent to the whole exercise a slightly Dumas fils, or *Lady of the Camellias* flavor. The role of Armand suited me quite well, I thought. Just before leaving to visit Canada with Paris Singer and his wife Joan and Temple, I became so worried about the poor little thing that I scratched up sixty dollars of hard-borrowed money and paid the rent on our little love nest on Washington Square South.

She thanked me for this, upon my return from Quebec one day early, by not being quite alone when I called on her unexpectedly as a happy surprise. I was the one who got the surprise. Uncle Mun philosophically pointed out that I would probably be getting surprises of this nature for the rest of my life, so I might as well get used to them, and hardened to them, while I was young.

I didn't have time to grieve long because Mother, who had been gone for over a year, sent for me to join her in London. By this time, the summer of 1916, the German U-boats were taking quite a toll on Allied shipping on the high seas, though they weren't sinking the ships of noncombatants. Crossing the Atlantic, even on a liner with an enormous American flag painted on each side and brilliantly illuminated at night, was still pretty exciting.

Finally the ship got to Falmouth, and then it was even more exciting because they wouldn't let me off the boat. The English authorities appeared to have just discovered that my mother had married a Turk, making her an enemy alien for the British too, and that fact tinged with suspicion my intent to enter England. At the last moment, when it looked as if I were about to have a free and disappointing trip back to America, a very high-ranking British officer poked into the group surrounding me and wanted to know why the tender was being kept waiting. When they told him it was because of me, he asked a few sharp questions. In no time at all my troubles were over, because it turned out that he knew Mother quite well. Shortly thereafter I was whizzing up the Blighty on one of those heavenly smooth English trains.

On our way from the station to see the London branch of the Maison Desti, Mother told me that she was indeed regarded as an enemy alien and had to go down to the Bow Street police station once a week to prove she wasn't sabotaging anything. They nevertheless had allowed her to reestablish the Desti perfumery business at 6, 7, and 8 Old Bond Street, upstairs over Teofani, the tobacconist's.

There were all sorts of new things at the shop, including some perfumed cigarettes with rose-petal tips dedicated to the French revue artist Alice Delysia. There was a new perfume called Whither Thou Goest. The old Secret of the Harem was still there under its new name of Youth Lotion, and, as usual, business was rotten.

Mother had a charming apartment at 7 Saint Martin's Lane and a little house at Uxbridge which she rented from Lady Mosely. She was not quite alone, of course. This time in attendance there was a certain Captain Kelly, an American flyer who had been shot down and rather badly busted-up while serving in the Royal Flying Corps.

My progress toward manhood proceeded at full gallop with a very pretty salesgirl in our shop who, though she didn't suffer from consumption like Doris, suffered from other failures of health.

On August 29, I celebrated my eighteenth birthday.

One night at dinner at Clara Weil's with Mother and some other friends, we heard the sirens and hurried out on the terrace to see the show. The sky above London was alive with the groping shafts of the great searchlights, then suddenly they all converged on one point. Out of a cloud came the tiny silver cigar that was a zeppelin. Guns went off everywhere, and far below, the fighter planes, looking like gnats, struggled to get up to it. I suppose I should remember all sorts of things about that summer and fall, political and military, but I am ashamed to say I remember nothing. I remember dining at Simpson's on the Strand and giving the carver sixpence for an extra slice of beef, and going to a place called the Cheshire Cheese, where, if one made the movements of uncorking a champagne bottle in front of its cage, an ancient parrot made the squeaking noise and the sound of the pop of the cork. Mother thought I was getting a little too interested in the Desti establishment's salesgirl, but before sending me back to America, she had a complete wardrobe made for me, including full dress and dinner jacket.

I got back to New York around October 1916 and discovered I had even less interest in the perfumery business than I had had when I left.

What I wanted to be was a stockbroker like Father and to have, eventually, a seat on the New York Stock Exchange and a close-cropped mustache. Father didn't think much of the idea when I wrote to him about it. In fact, he had a very poor opinion of stockbrokering generally and at the end of his life, characterized the profession as essentially the same as that of a betting commissioner.

, I became so persuasive in my letters to Father describing the future great killings I was going to make, that finally Father telephoned Mr. William Wainwright, a partner in F. B. Keech and Company of New York. I was sent down there, interviewed by Mr. Keech himself, who looked at me piercingly while explaining the responsibilities of my position, and then engaged me as a runner at seven dollars a week.

Looking back, I realize that I was quite an ass and had no talent for Wall Street whatsoever. I thought a runner was supposed to run, and in practically no time at all I had worn out all the expensive shoes Father and Mother separately had bought for me. When I ran back to the office in a heavy sweat, having run all the way to make my comparisons and deliveries, I imagined that somebody would notice this, the way they did in those Horatio Alger novels, and say, "Keep your eye on Sturges!" or "Do you realize that Sturges went to twenty-four places this afternoon in the same time that the other boys went to eight?" But all the running did for me was to cause me to soak my feet every night in a little chowder made with ten cents-worth of Allen's Foot Ease powder and some boiling water.

Nobody in the office gave a damn about how fast I ran because they were all busy doing other things. The rules governing the conduct of a stockbroker's employees were very strict in my time. No employee was permitted to gamble, I mean, invest, on the market under pain of instant dismissal. It need hardly be said then that not a single one of us back near the cashier's cage where the runners were supervised ever had any connection with acting on a hot tip, which we were in a very good position to hear about.

By a singular coincidence, however, all of these same employees came from sporting families. Mr. Cremerius, the cashier, for instance, was absolutely forbidden to play the market, quite obviously because he would have to do the checking up on himself to see if he had enough margin, among other things. His aged mother, however, had a very active little account with F. B. Keech and Company, and during the day her son followed the buy or sell instructions he received from her by telephone. With the solitary exception of myself, the dumbbell, everybody back near the cage had a sporting relative with an account at F. B. Keech and Company, and those were sporting days.

I remember the first time we did a million shares and I stayed until three in the morning to help the bookkeepers close their books; and the time when Bethlehem Steel B went up eighty points in one afternoon. That was the time when seats on the exchange, like Father's, were worth $750,000 and later went much higher.

One day Paris Singer wanted to buy twenty thousand dollars' worth of Anglo-French bonds, and when he put the order through me, they raised my salary to ten dollars a week.

The Desti business was running by itself; that is, it was making enough to pay the forty dollars rent, the telephone bill, and Louise's salary. Father was still sending me fifteen dollars a week and, now that my salary had been increased to ten dollars a week, I felt that prosperity had enveloped me and I envisioned a gay old time.

It is always when a man is in such a position that a woman comes along and takes it away from him.

In my case, it was my Grandmother Biden. She arrived in New York from Germany where she had been visiting her son, my uncle Sidney Biden the lieder singer, in Berlin. She announced in a quavering voice that she hadn't a place to lay her head, that, no doubt, she never would again, and that it was pretty sad to get to be seventy-four years old and feeble, and to find oneself in this position.

She was, of course, as strong as a horse, looked like a woman of fifty, with plenty of curves, played the piano wonderfully and sang extremely well, as the whole family, even I, had built-in resonance. She was such a superb cook that she had merely to announce that she would accept a few boarders in any house she might acquire in order to precipitate a riot, so she was really in no trouble at all and could have laid her head any place she pleased. But I was barely eighteen and I fell for the whole thing, hook, line, and sinker, and galloped forth on my pure white charger, the plumes of my helmet trembling with indignation over poor Grandmother's predicament.

We went to Cowperthwaite's, the famous five-dollars-down-and-five-dollars-when-you-catch-me furniture firm, and chose a fumed oak dining-room suite (pronounced to rhyme with flute at Cowperthwaite's) a vitriol blue sitting-room carpet, two blue velvet chairs with mahogany arms, a standing lamp with a pull chain, a complete bird's-eye maple bedroom suite, and a sort of studio couch I slept on with my feet shooting off the end. From a music store in the neighborhood, I got an upright piano especially for Grandmother. The owner of this music store was so touched at the prospect of a very young man furnishing a home for his aged grandmother that he made the monthly payments so small that even I was persuaded that he could not come out ahead on the deal unless he had stolen the piano in the first place.

All of this stuff was installed in a downstairs rear apartment at Broadway and 142nd Street with a view of the downstairs rear of another terrible apartment house. It was a nice long ride on the subway down to Wall Street from there. The rent was thirty-five dollars a month and included a switchboard and a telephone service. A girl who had somewhere heard and been pleased with the fairly deep growl into which my voice had changed, got hold of the service number and used to call me up every night. I would stand at the wall telephone in the hallway for a couple of hours begging her to tell me who she was, and for a couple of hours she wouldn't tell me. These vapid and unbearable conversations night after night made my grandmother furious. When the young lady, who turned out to be a pretty divorcée three or four years older than I, finally yielded and allowed me to call on her on Riverside Drive and I didn't get home until five in the mornings, my grandmother's fury increased.

Grandmother now began to act as if she were my wife rather than my grandmother, and I began to understand what my grandfather the Commodore had been through. When she wanted me to undress on a newspaper in order not to wear out the blue carpet, my grandfather got more and more of my sympathy.

Still, everything went along pretty amiably. Men have been exposed to the snapping of women for so long that I suppose they're inured to it and know by instinct how to shed it off.

Then on March 18, 1917, some German U-boats torpedoed and sank three American merchant ships. Congress approved a resolution of war, and on April 6, President Wilson declared that the United States was at war with Germany.

Now that we were really up against it, I didn't get any romantic ideas about becoming a motorcycle dispatch rider. I actually got scared to death. I became absolutely certain that I was going to be killed fighting for my country, so all I did was try to arrange for as nice a death as possible. I didn't feel like dying in the trenches with cooties crawling all over me. I wrestled with my courage for a couple of weeks and then toward the end of April 1917, I went down and volunteered as a flyer in the Aviation Section of the U.S. Signal Corps. I was just over eighteen and a half.

After a most elaborate physical exam, which included being spun dizzy on revolving chairs, I was turned down for having a larger than permissible blind spot in one eye. The blind spot is that point where the optic nerve enters the retina, and every eye has one.

I don't think I was turned down for an enlarged blind spot, but for an entirely different reason.

I was quite unaware of it at the time, but cadets, as the volunteer flyers were called, received not the thirty-three dollars a month paid to the other enlisted men, but one hundred dollars a month right off the bat, even before they had earned their commissions. This large sum of money naturally attracted a number of young men who were after the dough, rather than impelled by the chance to become heroes. Thus, whenever a young volunteer was earning less than a hundred dollars a month as a civilian, something was found to be wrong with him, and he didn't get into flying school. I was earning ten dollars a week at F. B. Keech and Company. They discovered an enlarged blind spot.

I was brokenhearted about this. I had already wrestled with my conscience and my courage, I had forgotten my fear, and now I wanted to get going and to start shooting down young German aviators as fast as possible.

I went to see Paris Singer to ask him if he knew how I could get into the Royal Flying Corps which I heard was still accepting young Americans, although this was considered not quite ethical now that America, too, was in the war. He asked if I were sure I knew what I was doing. I said that since I had already volunteered for the American air service and been turned down, I didn't know what else I could do. He warned me that the Royal Flying Corps might turn me down for the same enlarged blind spot, but gave me a letter of introduction to his friend Lady Colebrook. She had been a lady-in-waiting to Queen Alexandra at the same time that Uncle Mun had been a gentleman-in-waiting to King Edward VII. Lady Colebrook lived at the Ritz and received me charmingly, gave me a cup of tea and a letter of introduction to Major Lord Robert Innes-Kerr.

Major Lord Robert Innes-Kerr was a charmingly gotten-up gentleman with a mustache curled backwards, a beautifully fitted uniform covered with battle ribbons and pips, and the most cultured voice I had ever heard. When he found that I had not neglected to volunteer for my own country's air service first, he turned me over to a couple of sergeants for a physical exam. They didn't have quite as much apparatus as the aviation section of the U.S. Signal Corps, but they checked me over pretty thoroughly and passed me with flying colors.

I was very, very happy about this and Major Lord Robert congratulated me warmly and stood by to help me to answer the questions on a form which one of the sergeants was filling out.

"Where was you born?" asked the sergeant.

"Chicago, Illinois," I replied.

"You mean Chicago, *Ontario,*" corrected Major Lord Robert gently. "We are not allowed to take American boys."

"Chicago, Ontario," echoed the sergeant. "Occupytion?"

"Broker's runner," I said.

"Broker's *clerk,*" corrected Major Lord Robert.

"Broker's clerk," echoed the sergeant.

And so it went. I was nineteen and some weeks old, five feet eleven, and weighed twelve stone six, whatever that meant. I would be leaving for Canada as a cadet in the Royal Flying Corps within a very few weeks. I thanked them all and departed walking on air.

I wrote a happy thank-you note to Lady Colebrook and joyously called Paris Singer. Then I wrote to Father to tell him what I had done and why. At the end of the letter, I asked him please not to mention the matter to Mother in any way, as she had a silly idea that young men should serve only in the armies of their own countries and that, while I was in London, she had even complained about the rather cursory training the impatient Royal Flying Corps had given its American volunteers. This opinion she had derived from Captain Kelly. I closed my letter with my love and devotion and other such noble sentiments, then waited happily for the call from Canada.

Instead, for the first time in his life, Father double-crossed me. On receipt of my letter, he leapt to the nearest cable office, where he informed Mother full-rate and special delivery about what I was doing. He then hotfooted it back to his own office where, by the private wire to F. B. Keech and Company, he notified Colonel Keech and the Wainwright brothers that I was under age, that I could not enlist in anything without the consent of my father and my mother, neither of which I had and neither of which I was going to get. He instructed them that at the slightest move that looked like a departure for Canada, I was to be arrested and held until Father could get there from Chicago. Furthermore, he suggested to the Colonel and the Wainwright brothers, a telephone call to the Royal Flying Corps recruiting office apprising them of the facts could do no harm.

In less than twelve hours of receiving the cable, Mother was on a boat to America.

Shocked, furious, impotent, and feeling completely dishonored, I was stopped in my tracks.

28

MOTHER ARRIVED ABOUT SIX DAYS LATER on a boat so well camouflaged that I actually didn't see it when I looked out through the doorways at the pier. The protection of the big American flag on the side of the ship no longer existed, of course, as America was now in the war too, and had to take its chances with the torpedoes like any other country.

Mother didn't scold me for having joined the Royal Flying Corps; it was the other way around. My indignation at being yanked by the scruff of the neck out of something I had volunteered for was such that it was *she* who apologized. She said that if I wanted to go into the air service, she would get me into the air service of my own country. I told her this was a lot of nonsense; I had been turned down because of an overlarge blind spot in one eye. She said that an old friend of Father's and of hers, a Major General Barry, had been on the boat with her and that he had given her a letter of introduction to the proper colonel in Washington. I scornfully reminded her that she just didn't understand; it was a question of an overlarge blind spot. I asked her what she thought a letter from a major general could do about that. She said, "You might be surprised."

We stopped at the Biltmore Hotel so Mother could change her clothes and then left for Washington that same morning. When we got to a very large building in Washington, with a line about a quarter of a mile long of young men waiting to get into the army flying service, I began to understand what a letter from a major general meant. In the first place, Mother walked right to the head of the line, while I, purple with embarrassment, tried to hold her back. At the head of the line, paying no attention whatsoever to the dirty looks or audible grumblings of the waiting applicants, she sent in her letter of introduction.

I think Major General Barry was from Chicago and Mother had again forgotten that she had ever remarried, because within less than a minute a colonel came out asking for Mrs. Solomon Sturges and ushered us into his private office.

He asked me if I wanted to get into the air service and when I muttered an assent, he said, "Well, let's see what we can do about that."

Fifteen minutes later, I was taking another whack at getting into the American air service, and this time everything went like a buttered eagle. At the end of the poking, peering, prodding, and spinning in chairs, there was not the slightest mention of an overlarge blind spot.

I was taken back to the colonel's office where he was chatting with Mother and waiting for the verdict. It came very fast. He answered the telephone, hung up, then looked at me owlishly, shook his head sadly and said, "Nope."

I had been expecting this, so after a bitter look at Mother, I asked, "Why not, sir?"

He said, "Your ears are too big! They'd get in the way!" then burst out laughing at his lousy joke.

Mother took me in her arms and said, "You see?"

I had been accepted as a cadet in the Aviation Section of the U.S. Signal Corps. That was July 1917.

Back in New York, Mother wanted me to live with her until the army sent for me. This put my grandmother into such a vile humor that she departed for Chicago and I never saw her again.

Mother found a magnificent apartment right in the center of things, this time at 1 East Fifty-sixth Street over a restaurant called the Elysée. I sent part of my Cowperthwaite furniture and the upright piano to this apartment. The stuff Mother didn't want, like the bird's-eye maple bedroom suite, went back to Cowperthwaite's. Mother bought and spread around a few studio couches, then covered the floors from wall to wall with some blue carpet on credit, and we were doing fine.

Father became emotional about a very young man going off to the wars and came through with a magnificent allowance of three hundred dollars a month.

Mother attracted to herself the usual collection of mild eccentrics, forming a little society of which she was the nucleus. Sitting on our Cowperthwaite furniture I would find people like Marcel Duchamp, who had just painted his celebrated *Nude Descending a Staircase;* Jack Colton, who had not yet written *Rain* nor *The Shanghai Gesture;* Pat Leary, the millionaire lawyer, who had to drink constantly to prevent delirium tremens; Mary Fanton Roberts, who had just founded a magazine called *Touchstone;* Bob Chanler, that most wonderful combination of a true bohemian and a painter of talent with a few inherited millions; and many others.

I was still at F. B. Keech and Company earning ten dollars a week, but now that I had been accepted by the aviation service, everybody started treating me differently. Father's friend W. P. Wainwright suggested that I might like to join the Ninth Coast Regiment until I was called up. I accepted with pleasure, as I didn't know squads right from squads left, or even what constituted a squad, a poor state of affairs for someone who was about to become an officer.

I was received into the regiment in August 1917 by a Colonel Byrne and a very tall Major Delano and assigned to the First Squad. I had just turned nineteen at the end of August; the other seven men of the First Squad were between fifty-five and seventy. Since Wilson's declaration of war, the Ninth Coast Regiment was manned by members of the Home Guard, which I didn't know at the time. We all went stamping around the fine old Armory at Fourteenth Street as seriously as if the Germans were already in Brooklyn.

The soldier to my left was called Edwin Tatham. He and his brother owned what I supposed was very small company called the United Lead Company. The soldier to my right was a dear, nearsighted old man with a huge mustache called T. J. O. Rhinelander. I felt extremely sorry for him because his name suggested past glories and wealth, yet the way he dressed and had his shoes patched suggested a present painful poverty. I was enjoying enormous prosperity as a result of the three hundred dollars a month Father was sending me, and one night as we rode uptown from Fourteenth Street on the Sixth Avenue elevated, I invited him to have dinner with me in the wonderful Elysée restaurant on the ground floor of 1 East Fifty-sixth where I lived. Mr. Rhinelander thanked me for my kindness and suggested that since he lived on Fifty-second Street, a little closer, that I have dinner with him instead. I wasn't able to persuade him to come to the Elysée, so we crossed Fifty-second over to Fifth Avenue. I guess it was the patched shoes that led me to believe he lived in a run-down boarding house and I could see it quite clearly in my mind's eye as we walked along. When we got to 36 West Fifty-second, he took out a key, opened an extremely elaborate and heavy iron grill, then opened a plate-glass and wrought-iron door, and we stepped into a white marble entrance hall. From halfway up the staircase, a couple of suits of armor stared down at us. When the butler appeared to take our coats, I realized that my estimation of Mr. Rhinelander's finances had been slightly mistaken. He, his wife, and I dined in simple magnificence. They became my very dear friends both before and after my sojourn in the air service. I must have given an impression of great hunger because they extended a standing invitation to come at any time for breakfast, lunch, or dinner.

The old gentlemen of the First Squad came to consider themselves my uncles and regarded me with some envy because I was young enough to do what they all would have given anything to do: to go to war in the active service of the country.

Finally, one day in March 1918, the telegram ordering me to report for duty arrived and I entrained for Dallas, Texas, traveling for the first time in my life at the government's expense. Military policy at the time sent new men as far from home as possible. Had I been a Texan, I would have ended up on the East Coast for training. I was from the East Coast; I was sent to Texas.

Aboard the train, I met a youth of about my own age called Richard de la Chapelle, from a French family that had settled in New Jersey. We were about the same height, looked alike, and later were often mistaken for each other. On the way west, we polished our French talking to each other, but most of the time we occupied ourselves sending and receiving messages in Morse code. There were also a lot of other embryonic cadets among the passengers, practically all of whom had little buzzer sets with telegraph keys, too. The paying passengers must have had a hell of a time.

In Dallas, we were sent to a place called Camp Dick, then known as a concentration camp. In a later war, such a facility was called a boot camp. Camp Dick was actually the Dallas fairgrounds with a fence thrown around them. Most of the buildings on the fairgrounds were huge reproductions of the products for sale within them in the prewar days when the fair was open. There was a building in the shape of a gigantic Mazola bottle; another like a huge Gulden's mustard pot; an enormous Log Cabin Syrup edifice; a massive chili bowl; buildings representing almost anything edible or potable that one could think of.

There were also some horse and cattle sheds without floors. In one of those I lived. The livestock had been gone for some time, but the powerful former presence haunted the locale like a poltergeist. Finally our commandant swandangled a load of lumber and some kegs of nails from somewhere, and he and I and a few others who could wield a hammer got together and laid a pretty nice floor. This helped considerably.

In that part of the world, the temperature was 120 degrees in the shade, a little hard for Northern boys to take. At the end of twenty-mile hikes, the salt stood out in ridges on the knees of our breeches. The flat campaign hats we wore gave some shade, but the heat was still very tough on newcomers. Out on the parade ground, boys fell over from it all the time and had to be revived with cold water and a sponge. Nights we would climb up the shaky apex of the large roller coaster in the corner of the fairgrounds to try to find a breeze.

In that part of the U.S. Signal Corps known as the Aviation Section, there were two kinds of plain soldiers. Half were known as enlisted men and the other half as cadets. The differences between them were two. One was that the cadets, unless they flunked out or raised some kind of hell, would be officers; and the other was that the cadets got a hundred dollars a month, and the regular enlisted men got only thirty-three dollars a month. The differences did not sit well with the enlisted men, with the result that they loathed the cadets, although we were not really responsible for the injustice.

One of the ways in which they quenched their hatred of us to some extent was cruel, but not unfunny. Just near the parade ground on which the cadets marched around and sweated until we turned into pillars of salt, there was the machine shop, inhabited by the young men who didn't like us. In front of this shop they kept a beautiful watercooler, packed with ice and beaded with icy drops of water. At the end of a hot two hours of drilling, a desperate cadet, his tongue hanging out with thirst, would exclaim hoarsely on seeing this vision and run to it. Once there, standing on the damp ground in front of the watercooler, the cadet would fill the tin cup attached to the cooler with a chain and raise it greedily to his lips. But that is as far as it got.

From inside the machine shop, by means of a rheostat, an electric current was sent into the poor devil by way of the cup and chain. The cadet would realize at once what was happening and would try by sheer willpower to control the shaking of his hand, at least enough to toss a gulp of water into his mouth. He never succeeded. As he lifted the tin cup, the current got stronger and stronger, until finally all the icy water in it had been shaken out onto the ground. His place would then be taken by another grim-faced but eager cadet ready to fry in order to beat those bastards . . . but no one ever did. One can't beat the electric chair, either.

After a while, our colonel decided that the midday temperature of a Texas summer wasn't really intended for human beings, so they started sounding reveille at 4:30 in the morning and giving us a siesta in the middle of the day. The only trouble with this was that we had to wake up twice. I remember being very pleased with the idea of the 4:30 reveille and explaining to my buddies that we would get so accustomed to early rising that this excellent habit would stay with us for the rest of our lives. It did not, at least in my case, and I suspect that the whole theory of forcing good habits on the young is nonsense. Teaching the young to *admire* good habits is something else again and might pay off richly.

One army custom none of us had ever been exposed to, and that filled us with terror and made us shrink with embarrassment the first time, was doing what one had to do very publicly in that thoroughly democratic gathering-place known as the latrine. Ours was housed in a little wooden building without partitions of any kind. Except for the space occupied by the modestly screened door, around all the walls ran a continuous seat, or banquette, pierced at comfortable intervals with circular, well-sandpapered holes. Under these, in the continuous metal trough, ran a gurgling stream of water that added its cheerful song to the gay matitudinal conversation. Here were discussed the problems of the world, the news of the war in Europe, and here were born all the rumors that started with "I hear that . . . ," which were properly classified as latrine rumors. Here occasionally we indulged in four-part harmony to render such numbers as "Hello, Central, Give Me No-Man's-Land" and that other tearjerker about the poppies in Flanders Field. After we got over our initial embarrassment, we spent much time there with much pleasure.

In the middle of the latrine there was a sort of stand presided over by an amiable colored man in a sort of white coat. He was known as Sam. I don't think anybody had ever appointed him to the job, but rather that he had wandered onto the fairgrounds one day before they had finished with the fences, found the little square building they were building and decided the job was his by right. I don't know how lucrative the position was, none of us ever gave him more than a nickel, but he seemed highly pleased with these tips and would whisk us off with a highly commendatory "Yas, *suh.*" Besides the large quantities of the normal supplies required by a stand of this nature, Sam also carried chewing gum, toothpicks, cigarettes, cigars, chewing tobacco, the newspapers, and some ancient magazines. These last he would lend us free.

We had only been at Camp Dick for a few days when our colonel, a man who loved symmetry, decided that he couldn't bear the looks of these companies made up of extremely varied sizes of cadets. He came up with a very original idea. It was to re-form the companies and to assign all the cadets into squads according to size. The fifteen hundred of us were lined up, a boy who was six feet seven at one end of the line, and at the other end a character who had stuffed paper in his shoes to reach the minimum height requirement of five feet three. I just made the first squad and was the shortest man in it. The first time the colonel had us pass in review at a parade to which the public had been invited, he was very pleased when the big fellows were swinging by, but as the boys got shorter and shorter, some of the spectators started to snicker. When the final squad of midgets came stumping by on their short little legs, there was a howl of laughter. Without admitting he had been wrong, the colonel reassembled the companies the way they had been as quickly as possible.

This was the same colonel who, upon first organizing the camp, had lined up the first thousand enlisted men received there, excluding the cadets, and asked those who knew anything about cooking to step forward. As nobody moved, because one doesn't go into the army in wartime to become a cook, he said, "Oh, it's going to be like that, is it? All right! COUNT OFF!" When they got up to thirty, he stopped them and said, "All right, you are the cooks. Get over to the kitchens and get to work!" I don't know how true this story was, but anyone who tasted the cooking always believed it.

As a matter of fact, they had a hellish procedure there to force one to *eat* the food. When the food was first passed, one filled his plate because if the food was good, there wouldn't be any left for the second time around. Ninety-nine times out of a hundred it was lousy, and there one sat with a plateful of uneaten food. No one could leave the mess until a very sour-looking lieutenant had walked past every plate to see if anything was left on it. If there was, one had to eat for the whole next week at a special table under a huge suspended sign reading The Hogs' Table. This was intended to shame one into eating whatever the cooks came up with. After a while, everybody preferred dishonor to death by slow poisoning, and they would have had to hang The Hogs' Table signs over every table at Camp Dick. So they gave up and tried instead to improve the cooking a little.

One day the camp art photographer came around and asked me if I wanted my picture took. I said certainly not, because in the first place I didn't have any money, and in the second place I didn't think he would turn out to be a very good photographer. He was a shrewd businessman, though, with a trick not one of us could resist. First, he told me it would cost me nothing, and then showed me the flying helmet and the pair of goggles and the white silk scarf he had bought as props for the photograph. These were, of course, what we all were panting to be seen in. So far not one of us had ever been near a plane, although our families thought of us as flying cadets and sometimes addressed us thus on their envelopes, a practice which brought forth howls of derision at mail call.

To have one's picture taken in a leather helmet with a pair of goggles perched nonchalantly on the forehead was the next thing to being actually in the air. I said yes to the camp photographer, and everybody else said yes to him too.

Presently he showed up with a proof of my picture, heavily re-touched and highlighted so that I looked as if I had been gone over with vaseline. I couldn't take my eyes off the helmet and the scarf and the goggles. When he asked for my family's address, I gave him both of them, Mother's in New York and Father's in Chicago. Then he completed his trick, which was simple, awful, and always worked. He sent proofs to both the addresses I had given him, but instead of addressing them to Father and Mother by name, he addressed them "To the Friends or Relatives of Preston Sturges." Mother nearly fainted when the envelope was handed to her, and then, on reading the accompanying innocuous message, in her relief she ordered a half dozen pictures, instead of ordering me to punch the photographer in the nose. Father, being richer, ordered about a dozen shots and handed them around. I mention this merely to show that wars always do somebody some good, although practically no one speaks well of them.

Everything at Camp Dick was going along very well. The townspeo-ple were very nice to us and had begun to invite us on picnics and to dances at the Adolpus Junior Hotel when, suddenly, death struck in the guise of the worldwide 1918 influenza epidemic. Before the epidemic had run its course in this country, 20 million Americans had contracted it; 850,000 of them died.

Camp Dick was immediately closed off. Everybody was vaccinated. No one was allowed outside the camp except those on the burial squad or those who tried to help down at the hospital with boys who were going through the final delirium. I don't remember how many we lost, but the toll was dreadful. All the hospitals were completely full, and the grounds of Camp Dick were covered with tents, each housing four boys felled by the disease. Why some of us had high resistance and some had none, I don't know. Nothing happened to my close friends, Dick de la Chapelle and Frank Seested, or to me, although we were down at the hospital most of the time, on the pallbearers' detail because we were six feet tall.

My last memory of Camp Dick is of standing retreat against a hot sunset, the cadets at attention against the silhouetted background of the massively enlarged Sanka coffee pot, Bromo Quinine bottle and Coca-Cola bottle buildings, and in front of us Lieutenant Pennypacker, more or less at ease on the back of the fiery steed presented to him by the grateful citizens of Dallas.

AFTER WE HAD BEEN TORTURED into shape at Camp Dick in Dallas, we were sent to the School of Military Aeronautics in Austin, Texas, for twelve weeks of instruction. My particular class was known as the 57th Squadron.

It was a pretty tough series of courses, with examinations every Saturday. The minimum passing mark for each course was 60. A mark lower than 60 in any class resulted in being dropped back from one's own squadron to the following squadron. One more failed class resulted in being booted out of the air service altogether and sent off to who knows where as a plain enlisted man. I damn near slipped back one week.

One Saturday in the navigation class, the instructor gave us an examination paper which stated that a pilot on a reconnaissance flight started due east from Vlamertinghe to fly to Poperinghe. Nine questions based on this information followed. All of them had to do with pinpointing exactly where the pilot was, given the conditions under which he flew. After 4 minutes 12 ⅖ seconds in the air, flying at 88 miles an hour with a 20-mile-an-hour crosswind out of the west, where, *exactly,* was the pilot? Where was he 6 minutes 1⅛ seconds later, under the same flying conditions? Seven more questions of that kind were presented for solution.

Unfortunately, in my haste, I plotted the course from the starting point of Poperinghe instead of from Vlamertinghe, an easy mistake. As a result, not one of my answers jibed with the right ones worked out by the instructor, so he gave me a zero. That would have put me back into the 58th Squadron with a bunch of strangers. I tried to prove to the instructor by a tremendous feat of desperately inspired argument that I had made only *one* mistake; that all of my calculations were right on the nose if the pilot started out from Poperinghe; and that therefore I should receive a mark of 90. He wouldn't go for this, but finally he gave me a passing grade of 60 and I stayed in the 57th Squadron with my friends.

Another time in another class, I had a narrow squeak by insisting that a plane was pulled through the air by the vacuum in front of it. When the aerodynamics instructor asked me where the hell I got that idea, I used his own words to substantiate my conclusion. He had taught that a section of a propeller was an airfoil, and that an airfoil, in the shape of a wing, was kept aloft two-fifths by the pressure against its concave or under side, and three-fifths by the vacuum sucking up on its convex or upper side. Therefore, I reasoned, what was sauce for the goose was sauce for the gander; and that a plane moved forward two-fifths from the pressure behind it, and three-fifths from the vacuum in front of it. The instructor looked at me as if he would like to strangle me, but he didn't flunk me out. I am not sure to this day that the Sturgesian Theory of Flight is not the correct one.

I had one other close shave when the engineering instructor's examination asked what the clearances were in a Curtiss OX-5 motor. As I didn't remember them, I answered that the clearances were the distances separating moving objects or mechanical parts, which was the dictionary definition of clearances. Of course, that was not what the instructor wanted. He wanted to know that I knew that the clearance between the cylinder walls and the pistons of an airplane engine was two one-thousandths of an inch if the parts were cast iron, but were four one-thousandths of an inch if the parts were of the more expansile aluminum, or something like that. I contended that the question had been loosely posed and again got by.

On the whole, though, my grades were up in the nineties, and I passed quite honorably in my class.

In addition to the classroom instruction at the School of Military Aeronautics, we also had more of those long hikes, some trapshooting, machine-gun practice, the taking apart and reassembling of a machine gun in a stated number of minutes, and we learned to diagnose the trouble with an airplane motor by the appearance, smell, and sound of its exhaust.

We had quite a lot of drilling to do, taking turns acting as officers. This because General Pershing had been so displeased at the unofficer-like appearance of the first aviators they sent to him that he sent ten thousand of them back. He wanted flying *officers,* he said, not a bunch of garage hands.

We didn't have much time for fun. Besides, none of us had very much money, except for one chubby little Greek guy, a few years older than most of us, who always had a bankroll that would choke a horse.

His bunk was one removed from mine. Rumor had it that he and his brother owned a moving picture theatre, but no one believed it. It was true though, and Spyros Skouras has done quite well since those days, except in his command of English. Back there in Texas, he spoke the language reasonably well, but as the president of Twentieth Century-Fox addressing a sales convention, he is totally incomprehensible.

As we neared graduation, the 57th Squadron adopted as its motto, Up and At 'Em. Dick de la Chapelle designed the fighting cock, which together with our motto was to be painted on the sides of the war planes of the 57th Squadron when we soared into the skies over Europe to shoot down German aviators.

But first we had to learn to fly.

s

eutenant didn't
air that young
thing in aero-
vertical bank

between my
, meant that
here for the
ckpit forgot
saw a belt
ught I had
sk with a
there was
g line. To
What all
t's sake,

ned the
single-
er in a
choed,
of air
d ran

over
What
le I
me
her
ut
it,
d
y
r

th Squadron were to take place
e, about twenty miles outside of
up with earlier graduated squad-
arrival, we were told that it would
e ready for us. We were sent to work
the time.

little cadet in a flying suit asked me
had got 100 on my final examination
etter-perfect. He then asked if I were
anxious!

is radio exam twice, he explained, and if
would be kicked out of the air service. He
o prevent this catastrophe, he suggested a
me in the air and do him a little good, too.
on a flying suit, carry his flying book, report
would point out to me and say that my name
had come to take my radio test again.

?" I asked. He explained that I would be flown
und crew would ask me some stock questions by
ite panels, a method I was quite familiar with. I
ck questions by radio in international Morse code
y. It didn't sound very difficult to me or seem very
r devil, so I agreed to do it. He gave me his flying
and his helmet. I boned up a little on the answers I
on my disguise and reported to the lieutenant.

ys felt that the lieutenant was in on the deal because I
r than Bennett and my voice was quite a bit deeper. When
tly and said, "Cadet Bennett reporting for radio examina-
looked at me with considerable surprise, then nodded,
go." The lieutenant climbed into the cockpit. I followed him,
the rear cockpit, and I was in an airplane for the first time

Since I was supposed to be an old hand at this, the l

tell me what to do. I was also spared the baptism of the

men got on their first time up, being subjected to ever

acrobatics that the pilot knew, including being kept in a

until one's insides gave up.

I looked around the open cockpit, found a joystick

knees, which, since I knew *I* wasn't going to fly the plan

there were dual controls. The rear cockpit controls were

instructor to take over the flight when a student in the c

everything he knew. I put my feet on the rudder bar, the

made out of webbing hanging from the aluminum seat, and th

better attach it. In front of me there was a sort of little d

telegraph key attached to it. Outside the cockpit, on my right,

a reel about a foot in diameter, which seemed to contain fishir

the end of this line was attached a greenish fish-shaped object.

of this was for, I had not the faintest idea . . . nor, for Benne

did I dare ask.

Someone on the ground hollered, "Off?" "Off!" confir

lieutenant. The man on the ground began to twist our wooden

bladed propeller, then after a while he stopped with the propel

horizontal position and shouted, "Contact!" The lieutenant

"Contact!" An instant later came a great roar, and I got a blast

and exhaust fumes in my face, then the motor slowed down an

smoothly while it warmed up.

During this period I noticed the lieutenant putting something

his head. From somewhere a voice said, "Put on your gosport!"

the hell a gosport was, I had no faintest idea, of course, and wh

looked anxiously around the rear cockpit, the voice snarled out at

again, coming from somewhere around the little desk. I took anot

look around, picked up a piece of apparatus that seemed to be made

of some sort of vacuum-cleaner tubing with rubber bands attached to

and tried it on my face. After a moment, I found it fitted quite well a

that with this on, I could both hear and speak to the lieutenant. The on

trouble was, I couldn't see anything. I took it off and put it on the othe

way and found that I could see over it, even with my goggles in place

"All set?" yelled the lieutenant. "Yes, sir!" I answered. A ground man

pulled out the chocks in front of the wheels, the motor revved up to about

1800 on the tachometer in front of me, and the little plane started dragging and bumping out onto the rough and muddy field. A groundman grabbed a kind of handle on the outside edge of one of the lower wings and held us back until we were aimed in the proper direction, away from the *T*.

We dragged and bumped to the foot of the field and then the lieutenant gave her the gun. The joystick between my legs was pulled a way back for a period of time while we gained speed, then eased forward, which put us in a comfortable horizontal position and increased our speed considerably. A few moments later, the lieutenant pulled the stick back gently, and we were *in the air!* The little plane climbed and then we banked, I for the first time. I remember how strange it felt to have one wing dip down so very far, so that the plane was almost on its side, and still be quite comfortable in my seat, instead of leaning to one side of the cockpit. It was a new and most pleasurable feeling to look straight down the wing at the *T* below and, near it, some of my friends having coffee, and still to have no feeling of height nor any anxiety whatsoever.

We straightened out and, still climbing, flew away from Park Field. Soon I saw below us a field with a couple of shacks, some motorcycles with sidecars, and the black and white squares used for signalling. I presumed that this was where I was going to undergo the test, and the presumption was correct. Maintaining his altitude, the lieutenant started circling the field. "Let out your aerial," he yelled through the gosport tube. I dared not ask where the aerial was, and while looking around desperately, it occurred to me that the reel with the greenish fish-shaped object attached to it, mounted just outside the cockpit, might very well be it. I leaned forward, noted that the reel had a simple brake arrangement to prevent it from unwinding, and released the brake. Dragged down by the greenish fish-shaped object, the aerial started unwinding gaily, and as it spun ever faster, I felt quite proud of myself for having discovered it and turned my attention to the telegraph key. When I looked back, it was just in time to see the four or five hundred feet of aerial snap off into space. Its brake was there obviously not only to hold the wound-up aerial in place, but also to slow it down while it was unwinding, to prevent exactly what had just happened. It seemed to me that Cadet Bennett might have warned me about this.

The lieutenant turned around and, waving Bennett's flying book in his hand, shouted, "How the hell many hours are you supposed to have had in the air?" "I'm terribly sorry, sir," I began desperately, "I looked away for just one second, thinking there was plenty more line, and when I looked back, it was gone. This one must have been a lot shorter than they are as a rule."

I thought that this was a rather neat explanation and that it gave an impression of past experience. It did not impress the lieutenant, who started back to Park Field to have the aerial replaced. "I am beginning to see why you flunked out with such ease the other two times," he said meanly through his gosport tube. "You could flunk for the third time without any trouble at all!" The lieutenant was one of the ten thousand flyers sent back by General Pershing and was not in a happy frame of mind to begin with.

The mechanics who had to replace the aerial made a few snide remarks on the subject and the lieutenant did not defend me. But the mechanics were complaining about Cadet Bennett's stupidity rather than mine, so I kept my goggles down, shrugged my shoulders mentally and muttered an expression in vogue at the time, "Ish kabibble." Repairs completed, the lieutenant and I took off again and when we reached the radio field, the aerial gave me no trouble at all, nor did the test. I am happy to report that Cadet Bennett not only passed his radio examination, but did it rather brilliantly, with 88 out of a possible 100.

Park Field was surrounded by an electrified fence to protect the field from German spies, but the fence was not the only protection. Every one of us had to do guard duty, with its long hours and the accompanying nonsense of halting people one knew perfectly well for identification or the exchange of a password. It reminded me of my old millionaire friends playing at being soldiers back in the Ninth Coast Regiment Armory in New York. None of us took guard duty very seriously, and this was an error because, though there may have been very little danger from German sappers in the wilds of Tennessee, there was considerable danger attached to the United States Army rules in wartime. And it *was* wartime, even though the war seemed very far away to us. The wartime rules are the same *everywhere,* and the penalty for a soldier deserting his post in wartime is death.

One of my friends, bored with marching around a hangar full of 1914 warplanes that were kept as curiosities and that the Germans wouldn't have accepted as a gift, got so sleepy along about three o'clock one morning that he went into the hangar and climbed into a plane to catch thirty winks.

At this moment, a stupid cadet assigned to playing sergeant of the guard that night came along and found that my friend was not in sight. He marched all around the hangar to see if he was on the other side, but there was no question about it: my friend had deserted his post. Without realizing the import of what he was doing, the stupid cadet turned him in, and my friend was hauled up for court-martial, with a firing squad the only penalty if he were found guilty.

We had a hell of a time getting him off. Everybody was willing to swear on a stack of Bibles and lie, but that wouldn't have helped him any, because the sergeant of the guard had gone all around the hangar and our friend just wasn't there. Finally a young Jewish officer from Brooklyn saved his life by a simple but effective argument. The young Jewish officer contended that our friend had never left his post, but was marching solemnly around the hangar on one side, while the sergeant of the guard was marching around the other side looking for him. The sergeant of the guard said that wasn't true. "Are you trying to tell this court," queried the young officer from Brooklyn, "that you could see the four sides of this building at one and the same time?" Since nobody really wanted our friend shot, this argument got him off, but the possible death penalty made the proceedings very gruesome.

At last came the Monday morning I was to begin my flying lessons. Full of enthusiasm and with a new helmet, a pair of enormous unbreakable goggles, and the largest pair of bearskin gloves I had ever seen, which Father had sent me from Marshall Field's, I reported to my instructor, a small redheaded lieutenant known as Paprika Smith. He looked at me searchingly and then asked, "Can you keep your mouth shut?" "Yes, sir," I responded. "Then give me your flying book and get lost for a couple of hours, will you? I've got a little job to do. Go over to the YMCA hut or something."

So I had my first flying lesson hanging around the field, at least my flying book said I had one.

While I was hanging around the field, Paprika Smith was participating in an exercise not unlike that exercise in the 1950s known as the Berlin Airlift. The Park Field Airlift flew every Monday morning. It came about this way.

In addition to the electrified fence around the field and the guard duty performed by the cadets and the enlisted men, the *real* protection of Park Field was afforded by a group of large and very tough Pinkerton men, thoroughly able to handle German spies, saboteurs, or any other threat. Each Pinkerton man carried a large .44 in a shoulder holster and had no qualms about using it. None of them had any romantic ideas about going overseas with a beautiful pair of silver wings on his left bosom to shoot down Baron von Richthofen; none had any eager buddies or classmates yearning to do the same. They were there to do exactly what the colonel told them to do, to prevent *any* unlawful entry onto the field.

Most of the cadets got weekend passes to go into Memphis for a high old time, but everybody had to be back through the gates at 5:00 Monday morning. Five o'clock to the Pinkerton men meant 5:00. They laughed while slamming the gates in one's face at one second past 5:00, and said that the only way to get in was to await the arrival of the Officer of the Day. This was to be avoided at all costs. It meant being put on report, a bawling out from the colonel or the commandant of personnel, and no passes, possibly for a number of weekends.

Every Monday morning, though, there were always some cadets in Memphis who had either imbibed too heavily to get out to the field, or who had got there too late and had gone back to Memphis by car, motorcycle, or milktrain. Their problem was how to get back on the field without being shot by a Pinkerton man while trying to climb over the fence or without having to face the Officer of the Day. A solution evolved. They simply telephoned to a pal inside the field. My instructor Paprika Smith was one of the pilots who flew drunks *over* the electrified fence on Monday mornings, bypassing the Pinkerton men and the officer of the day, deplaned them, and then went back for more as fast as possible.

That is why my first recorded flying lesson actually transpired without my ever leaving the ground.

When Lieutenant Smith finally did get around to giving me my first lesson in the air, it was a hell of a lesson. First he did a terrible thing, which was forbidden, as it should have been, since it had caused some deaths from heart failure and the loss of some unborn children.

Flying out over the cotton fields a little distance from Park Field, he put the plane into a sharp dive straight toward a field of cotton pickers, pulled out of the dive at the very last split second, then fishtailed and side-slipped a few feet above the field hands as they ran terror-stricken or threw themselves yammering flat on the ground.

After this, he turned around to look at me and I could see his lips moving in what I presumed was a question about how I had liked the stunt. Since he couldn't hear my answer, he continued looking at me inquiringly, instead of looking ahead as he should have to pilot the plane. Suddenly I saw two tall poplar trees about ten feet apart immediately in front of us! Petrified, I pointed ahead and screamed a warning, but Lieutenant Smith couldn't hear me and screwed up his face in an expression that meant he hadn't understood a thing, but might, if I tried again. By now we were practically in the trees, but just as I started to squeeze my eyes shut and to hope that death wouldn't hurt too much, he flipped the joystick over to one side and we sailed between the poplars on edge with about three feet to spare on either side. He turned around again to laugh at me and I realized that the whole thing was a well-prepared joke. He knew exactly where he was while he was looking back at me and pretending not to understand my frantic pantomime. Everything depended on the timing, including our lives, but Paprika Smith was really a hell of a flyer so there wasn't much danger.

Another day, he showed me the Express-Train Jazz, which was hair-raising. He flew the plane at seventy-five miles an hour down between the telegraph poles running along both sides of the railroad tracks, and set out to catch up with the express train that passed through Millington every morning on its way to Memphis at sixty-five miles an hour. At the approach of the plane, the train's engineer and fireman indicated their displeasure with fist shakings and obscene gestures, and as we drew closer to the engineer's cab, they threw up big chunks of coal in an effort to smash the propeller and kill us. When Paprika Smith got right over the engine cab, he dipped the plane, bumped the cab roof with the plane's wheels, flew off and made another approach. The low flying and the intermittent wheel bumping were kept up all the way into the outskirts of Memphis.

The express train was subjected to this every morning without fail from one pilot or another. The stunt infuriated the engineer and the fireman, probably conjuring up visions of their being burned alive in flaming gasoline the first time somebody missed. The expressions on their faces always made me very glad that I never met them when I was in Memphis on a weekend pass.

It took a certain amount of money to spend a happy weekend in Memphis. The normal method of acquiring funds was by shooting craps cautiously all week until one had enough set aside for a room at the Hotel Chicsa and few extras. But once, for a number of weeks, we had a goldmine to draw on.

My friends Frank Seested, Dick de la Chapelle, a new friend from Mississippi, James Knox Millen, Jr., and I used to watch some of the wrestling matches the enlisted men held every Wednesday or Thursday. With us one night was another cadet we didn't know very well. He was mild-mannered, very gentlemanly, and a little older than the general run of cadets. He wasn't tall, but he was reasonably broad-shouldered and must have weighed about 165. I wish I could remember his name. He had one unique characteristic: all of his front teeth were gold. I give these details because each one was an integral part of our goldmine.

That night, the group of us watched the bouts for a while, sometimes getting quite excited. They were completely honest matches, of course, totally unlike the professional hocus-pocus of today, and the protagonists were all fine-looking, enormously big farm boys, machinists, coal heavers, baggage smashers, or whoever gets drafted into the army and instinctively volunteers for the weekly wrestling matches. On the average, they were about six feet three and weighed about 225.

Seested, de la Chapelle, and I continued to yell with enthusiasm and bellow when we thought something was especially good. Presently we noticed that our companion with the gold teeth did not seem to be sharing our admiration for the talents of the wrestlers and was looking at us with some surprise.

"You think that's *wrestling?*" he asked after a while.

"What's the matter with it?" one of us asked.

"Well, if you don't know, there's no point in my trying to tell you," he said, then added after a thoughtful pause, "but if this thing were handled right we might . . ." His voice trailed off as he watched two big slugs clumsily trying to pin each other to the mat.

"We might *what?*" somebody asked.

"Make a little money," said our friend with the auriferous smile. "Anyway enough for a few blowouts in Memphis."

"What do we have to do?" we asked eagerly. This was a fascinating subject.

"Just get me a match with one of those bums," he said, "then lay a few quiet bets at the best odds you can get."

"Which one do you think you could handle?" de la Chapelle excitedly wanted to know, "because they're kind of big . . ."

"That doesn't matter at all," said our friend quietly, "any one of them will do. You see," he added by way of explanation, "wrestling is not a matter of size, it's a matter of leverage."

"You've done some wrestling?" asked Seested, who was my partner in the crap games.

"I will not deceive you," said our friend with the gold teeth. "I have done considerable, under several names and, once or twice, with a mask on. I have also taught the subject."

"Are you absolutely sure . . ." began Millen, who was very rich and therefore loved a safe bet.

"I am *positive*. Of course, somebody could sneak up behind me and hit me with a hammer, but insofar as those guys in the ring are concerned, I will be as safe as if I were in my mother's arms. In order to make it look good, though, I will not allow it to seem as easy as it is going to be. It may even appear to you occasionally that I am about to lose, but don't let this deceive you. If this should happen, then while the farmers are whooping it up, just try to get a little more money down on me. You'll get longer odds. Steaming up the suckers is part of the profession."

Our friend with the gold teeth got into the ring that same night to voice his modest challenge for the next week's match. When his small size, compared to that of the behemoths he offered to grapple with, became apparent to the audience, their glee was unconfined; and when the hated word "cadet" was prefixed to his name, the challenge was greeted with a roar of bloodthirsty laughter. The enlisted men here loathed the cadets as much as they had at Camp Dick, and the opportunity of slamming one of them around legally, perhaps breaking his back, appealed to them enormously. Seested, de la Chapelle, and I mentioned the possibility of laying some small bets to the enlisted men around us and were assured that we would have no trouble; the sky was the limit.

The next Wednesday or Thursday, our friend with the gold teeth pulled on some black tights with leather knee-protectors and on the way over to the ring we arranged a signal, a whistled birdcall, to let our man know when the bets were down. Until he heard the whistle, he would keep everything going smoothly and interestingly.

Seested, de la Chapelle, Millen, and I were a little nervous that first night wandering through the arena looking for bets while pretending to be afraid to bet. Every time there was an explosive yell from the crowd, our hearts stopped and we froze, thinking our champion had bitten off more than he could chew. We would turn, dreading what we were going to see, but we really needn't have worried. Our man appeared quite gone at times, about to become an easy victim of the giant in front of him, but always, by some miracle, he got out of trouble and limped away painfully. While he was *in* trouble, however, we always managed to get a little more money down on him. I don't remember just what odds we averaged on that first match, but they were pretty good. Finally we ran out of betting money, so Seested, our best whistler, got as near the ring as he could, then, in a rare moment of silence, gave his imitation of a whippoorwill.

Our man nodded imperceptibly, but nothing changed in the ring for a few moments. Then suddenly, while making a grab for our man, the big farmer appeared to trip and went down heavily. Our man looked as surprised as the audience sounded. On his feet and vexed, the big farmer ran on our friend to annihilate him. Again the farmer appeared to slip, and fell heavily. After a look at the referee, as if to ask his permission, our man jumped on him and with what appeared to be much difficulty, managed to flop him over on his back. The big farmer nearly got away a couple of times, but our man got some kind of hold on his hand, and after that there was nothing for the referee to do but to slap the mat three times and proclaim our friend the winner.

A great groan went up as we started through the crowd to collect our bets. "A lucky win!" appeared to be the consensus. They dared us to bring our man back for a rematch, so we accommodated them. By skilful manipulation and the addition of some dramatic overtones, we managed to coax our little goldmine along for quite a number of weeks, during which we won and divided equally among us many an honest dollar. We went to Memphis every weekend with money in our pockets.

The citizens of Memphis were all extremely kind to us. We were invited to dances at the country club on Saturday nights and to many Sunday dinners and parties in private houses. My great friends there were the Johnsons, whom I met through Jimmy Millen. The principal attraction at the Johnsons' was their beautiful redheaded daughter, Virginia. In New York after the war, I took her to the great photographer Arnold Genthe, who did some of his first color experiments with her.

Around this time, the editor of our camp newspaper, *The Park Field Airgnat,* asked me for three hundred words of humor for an upcoming issue. I don't know why. I neither looked very funny, nor, as far as I know, had I ever said anything very funny. I tried to write three hundred words of humor built around the olive drab pajamas my mother had sent to me. The pajamas were exactly the same color as our uniforms, and I had discovered that I could get in a lot of extra sleep mornings by standing reveille in them, running around the barracks in them and diving directly back into bed in them. In the early morning dark, I looked dressed.

For the piece of humor, I tried to imagine some amusing situation in which some officer would be waiting for me when I got back from the run in my pajamas, order me over to the colonel's office, and then discover, with the colonel, that I had reported in my pajamas. But after that, nothing funny came to mind, so I abandoned the idea and retold a stale anecdote about a lunatic asylum. The *Airgnat* didn't ask me for any more pieces after that one, but they did come up with another terrible idea. Having learned that I could draw, they asked me for a weekly comic strip.

I liked to draw and coming up with one funny observation a week didn't sound too hard to do. I obliged with the adventures of a flying instructor and his cadet, called "Toot and His Loot." The strip was supposed to be funny, and sometimes it was, but all of my days became gruesome from that moment on, while I tried to think of my weekly boffo.

It is my remembrance of the weight of those horrible days of anxiety that has prevented me from accepting a weekly humorous television series even today.

One of the funniest things I ever saw happened at Park Field.

After a cadet has had a certain number of hours of dual instruction in the air and has taken off and landed enough times without his instructor having had to touch the controls, the moment arrives for his first solo flight. A small ritual is observed.

The plane carrying the instructor and the cadet lands, taxis down to the end of the field, and the instructor climbs out. He wishes the cadet a happy landing, goes to the tail assembly, ties a white handkerchief to the rudder and waves the cadet off.

Outside of a crack-up, a first solo is about the only dramatic thing that ever happens on an airfield, and news of one travels like wildfire.

One never knew what a guy was going to do his first time alone in the air. Some beginners, even with their instructors aboard, have panicked in the air and have either crashed and killed themselves and their instructors, or have had to be hit over the head with a monkey wrench by the instructor to unfreeze the controls.

A plane with a handkerchief tied to its rudder has the right of way over everything, without exception. When a first solo comes in for his first landing, everybody scatters, and he has an empty field. If he lands right smack on top of a plane sitting quietly on the runway, it is the fault of the fellow underneath.

On this particular morning, we saw the instructor tie on the handkerchief and wave his charge forward. "First solo!" someone yelled, and this went down and across and around the field in nothing flat. Two or three planes came taxiing onto the sidelines and everybody watched as the plane with the handkerchief on its tail came roaring toward us. It quickly became apparent that instead of passing by the *T,* he was coming right into the coffee stand and the parked planes. Somebody shouted to look out and we all started scattering right and left. At the very last fraction of a second, the poor misguided youth pulled straight back on his joystick, and such was his speed that he shot vertically into the air.

We all watched horrified as he held this dangerous angle for so long that we were sure he would lose his momentum and fall back on his tail, in a mishap that when it happens higher up is called a whipstall and is very dangerous even then. But again, at the very last fraction of a second, his plane tilted forward, and he flew unsteadily away toward the big hangar at the end of the field. He cleared this by inches, then, with the whole field watching, he skidded around without banking and started back toward the end of the field, where we could see his instructor desperately waving him down to a landing.

He again skidded around horizontally and started for the *T,* but instead of aiming down for a landing, he gained altitude. As he got near the *T,* he slowed his motor down to idling speed and started pancaking in. This is the most dangerous thing that can be done because, at any moment, the plane can plunge backward rather than forward, and it's all over. By now it was perfectly obvious that the boy was hysterical, that he had forgotten everything he had been taught, and that a bad crack-up was the least we could expect.

The major in charge of the field telephoned for the ambulances, and as these came howling out, the colonel in command followed right behind them in a sidecar and started bellowing orders to everyone.

At the last moment of the last pancake, the paralyzed cadet dove the plane toward the *T,* then pulled out in a kind of ground loop and started round again. As he came in once more, high and wobbly, we watched with our hearts in our mouths as he pancaked down clumsily toward the *T.* At the last moment he dove, pulled out of the dive a couple of feet off the ground and climbed straight up.

Having gained sufficient altitude, he suddenly went into a series of perfect barrel rolls, changed direction with a wonderfully executed Immelmann, shot down over the end of the field, came around in a vertical bank, dove for the strip, missing the fence by inches, roared down toward us, fishtailing to reduce his speed, then made a perfect three-point landing and rolled to a stop precisely opposite the crossarm of the *T.*

It was the instructor, of course, one of the best acrobatic flyers on the field, and it was his pupil, dressed exactly like him except for the little gold bars at the collar, who came running in from the end of the field laughing like a hyena.

It was pretty funny, and I don't think the colonel was too severe about it.

My friends and I were getting along pretty well with our flying instruction when a terrible disaster overtook us all: on the eleventh of November, 1918, the war ended.

I'm sure it sounds awful to characterize the end of the war as a terrible disaster, but when all of one's waking moments, for a long time, have been directed at the one single objective of becoming a first-class pilot and then a first-class officer in the army of one's country, and then, suddenly, one is no longer needed, or wanted, the feeling is like what the English describe as stepping on a bus that isn't there. We should have been grateful that it was all over and that not one more soldier would die in the trenches, but in 1918 we felt very differently. I wanted to take some shots at some Germans, engage some German ace in single combat, and what happened to the *poilus* in the trenches, or even our own doughboys, interested me damned little. Much time has passed since that war, and my feelings about the end of it are now quite correct.

The government decided to let us finish our flying training and at least get our reserve commissions and wings before they sent us home. The avowed reason was that we had cost so much already that it might as well spend a little more and at least get *something* for its money. But I think the real reason was a much more kindly one. It was to avoid breaking our hearts. Most of the fields, of course, including Park Field, were to be closed and dismantled, but some few, like Carlstrom Field in a place called Arcadia, Florida, were to be kept going, and it was here that I was to finish my flying training.

First, however, I was given a furlough and I went by way of Chicago to see Father.

Things began rather badly when Father asked me at the station why I had shaved off the mustache I had written to him about before showing it to him. As I *hadn't* shaved it off and had trimmed it only that morning, this hurt my feelings a little. I was so happy to see Father, though, that it was soon forgotten.

At dinner at the University Club, he asked me what I would like to do when I got out of the army, which would be fairly soon now. I said I didn't know, but that I thought I had some talent for mechanics, having just invented and drawn up a multiple-speed planetary gear arrangement for automobiles. I had just discovered that Louis Chevrolet had patented the same idea in 1900, but that only proved that I was working in the right direction.

Father asked why I didn't go out to Hollywood, California, and engage in the motion picture business.

"You mean as an *actor?*" I asked, horrified.

"Of course not," said Father, who loathed the few actors he had met. "I mean in the business end of the . . . business, or whatever you call it."

"I wouldn't know just how to start," I said.

"We'll talk it over some other time," Father told me.

The next morning he took me to his offices at Noyes & Jackson, where I had always loved to go. I watched Father and his partners all bumping their bald heads together to read the tape with the stock quotations on it as it came out of the ticker. The ticker apparatus was about the size of a Sparkletts bottled-water container. Inside, a paper tape about the size of wide adding-machine tape picked up and printed the teletyped market quotations and then advanced out of the front of the ticker. Father and his partners let the tape run through their eager fingers as they checked the figures, and then let it gather in rolls around their feet on the floor. There were several tickers in the offices, but even so, only a limited number of men at a time could see what the stocks were doing until a boy chalked the prices up on a big blackboard.

After watching this activity for some time and noting its shortcomings, I asked Father, who was freer now that the first rush was over, if he would like me to project his ticker tape onto a screen on the wall so that everybody could see it at once. "How would you do that?" he asked me solemnly, because, to the best of my knowledge and belief, no such thing had ever been done before. "Very simply. I could do it immediately with a postcard projector to show you how it would work, and perfect it later," I replied. Father asked if the demonstration would be very expensive, and was assured that it would not.

He gave me fifty dollars. I went out and bought what I needed, blew all the lights on the seventh floor of the University Club a few times, then finally projected the tape perfectly on the wall of my bedroom. I took the apparatus over to Noyes & Jackson and showed it to everybody. They all pronounced it most ingenious and complimented Father on having such a bright son, but when I asked Father if he wanted me to build a real one for him, he demurred. And he did it in the same words with which every invention I have ever made has been greeted. "Of course, it's fine," he said, "and it might be very nice to have the quotations coming out on the wall where everybody could see them, but we're getting along all right. We've always done it this way; we like the *feel* of the tape in our hands. Why not leave well enough alone?"

I thanked him for letting me make my experiment, put my apparatus on top of one of the office phone booths, moved on to see Mother in New York and missed the Trans-Lux patents by a measly ten years.

In New York I stayed a few days with Mother. She had moved the Desti business from 23 East Ninth Street to 4 West Fifty-seventh Street and was running it with manicurists again, the way we had in Paris. The manicurists were not quite young enough to amuse me, so I fooled around in the laboratory in the back, starting work on a formula for a lip rouge that would stay on for twenty-four hours. I hadn't quite worked it out when my furlough was over and I had to leave for Arcadia, Florida.

Arcadia was right smack in the middle of the Everglades, halfway between Palm Beach and Fort Myers. To reach Carlstrom Field, we climbed into a wonderful Model T Ford that had been outfitted with flanged railroad wheels. Every time I got into the contraption, it provided the most exhilarating rides I have had in my life. Track had been laid from Arcadia to the field, and over this track we zipped in our Ford, through alligator swamps, under cypress trees heavy with Spanish moss and every variety of snake, including the deadly water moccasin. At least, we imagined the trees were full of deadly snakes ready to drop down on our necks, although I never actually saw any overhead. We saw plenty of them underfoot, however, on our way to the latrine every morning, and it would have been suicidal to go there without a forked stick and a heavy club. Big cottonmouths were everywhere and we papered our walls with their skins.

Life in the army in peacetime began to exert its insidious and soporific charm. We were fed for nothing, housed for nothing, clothed for nothing, insured for nothing and given free medical and dental care. We had absolutely nothing to do but to fly through the air and do stunts, which was glorious fun. For this we received a high base pay, plus flying pay. Besides all this, as one of the artists of the now defunct *Park Field Airgnat,* I got a share of the spoils on its dissolution.

On weekends we went to Arcadia or Fort Myers, and I began to understand how easily young men could be sucked into this trap and laze away their best years working for retirement pay and security, the enemies of intelligence and initiative.

We even began *thinking* like professional soldiers and tried various versions of the old army game. Our pay telephone, for instance, a battered instrument screwed to the wall, had a hammer on a chain hanging beside it. We got the operator by dropping in a nickel, which we then retrieved by the thin wire soldered to it. When the operator told us to drop in fifty cents for three minutes (it was fifty cents to practically anyplace from Arcadia) we responded with three heavy wallops of the hammer on the side of the instrument. This naturally rattled all the gongs in the machine and sounded to the operator as though we had deposited at least a dollar and a half.

Another example of how our minds were working as soldiers in peacetime is that of the clock raffle. Needing some money to go into Fort Myers, a pal and I bought a clock that an enlisted man had artistically encased in the hub of a broken propeller. There was never any shortage of broken propellers, and we gave him five dollars for it. We then wrote up some beautiful blue tickets numbered from one to twenty-five and sold the tickets at fifty cents apiece for chances on the clock. We sold out so rapidly that it seemed a shame to let such a beautiful clock go for a gross of $12.50. Since the buyers of the blue tickets were told that the numbers went only from one to twenty-five, we didn't think it would be right to put out any more blue tickets. We made some red tickets numbered from one to twenty-five. These sold out at once, and we were considering a set of green tickets, possibly followed by yellow ones, when the purchaser of one of the original blue tickets happened to fall into conversation with the purchaser of a red ticket. They came together to pay us a call. We denied any evil intentions and pointed out that all *we* had ever said was that the tickets were fifty cents apiece and numbered from one to twenty-five, but they kept talking about the two colors, and finally we gave them their money back. I think they were unaccustomed to the same numbers being issued in different series, but all the French national lotteries are done that way to this day, so it must be perfectly honest.

We finally had the drawing, and I was slightly embarrassed when my partner, who was pulling the numbers out of the hat, won the clock himself. I suggested that it might look better if he threw the number back in the hat, but he was adamant, saying that he had won it perfectly honorably, and he refused to do it.

Fate very nearly punished him a few days later during a flight we flew in formation from Carlstrom Field to Fort Myers. Before takeoff we were briefed about one very unpleasant fact. If anything went wrong with our motors during the flight, there would be no place to put down except right in the middle of the Everglades. If we had to glide in to a landing without a motor, we were advised to pick the best opening we could see between the trees and, once beneath their foliage, to try to choose the widest alley between the trunks, to keep on going for as long as possible, then, if we still had any momentum left, to run the plane into a big tree and climb out as fast as possible. All of this was announced in the same cheerful tones airline hostesses use today in telling one just before a transoceanic flight "how to ditch without a hitch."

Ten of us climbed into our planes and took off from Carlstrom Field. After a while, flying in formation, we went into some clouds and when we got through them, there were only nine planes; my raffle partner was missing. We flew around for a while looking for signs of him, but saw nothing and resumed our flight to Fort Myers. The disappearance put a damper on everything and we didn't enjoy ourselves much in town.

The Seminoles brought him out about three weeks later; a short distance in the air was a very long walk through the swamps. The plane was lost, of course, but he was all right.

I almost got killed at Carlstrom Field, too. Just in front of the medical bungalow, where a friend of mine was standing looking out the window with a thermometer in his mouth, a cadet who wasn't a very good flyer had choked his motor and stalled it while warming up. I was passing and asked if he wanted me to crank him up. He thanked me for the offer, and I put a couple of chocks in front of the wheels and called, "Off?" The cadet confirmed, "Off." I stepped into the propeller and started twisting it around to bring it on compression. On the second twist, the motor started up and the propeller hit me with a very dull and sickening crunch, but fortunately in so many places and so near the start of the revolution that the motor stalled again.

I collapsed on the ground. My friend with the thermometer in his mouth bit right through it. The doctor who was examining him jumped right through the fly screening in the window. The cadet in the plane who had said "Off" when the contact was on, stuck his head over the side of the cockpit and vomited. A couple of mechanics got to me first and stood me on my feet. The running doctor hollered, "Leave him alone, you stupid sons . . ." so they released me and I went down again like a limp dishcloth. I was only badly bruised and not in the hospital for very long, but I am probably one of the few men ever hit by a propeller who lived to tell about it.

Another time I tore a plane to hell because I failed to notice a drainage ditch in front of me while taxiing in. One is not supposed to wreck a plane after a safe landing, so the colonel sent for me. Before tearing my hide off, he asked how many hours I'd had in the air, and after I told him, he decided to save his breath. It was just one of those things.

I heard somewhere that the government was selling its huge surplus of brand-new Martin bombers for a very modest price and wrote to Paris Singer suggesting that we start a little airline to get people to Palm Beach from New York and vice versa. The flight would take a lot less time than the dismal train trip. He replied that the idea was a good one, but that the time was not yet ripe, whatever that meant. And there went another business in which I did not pioneer.

Finally, having learned everything about flying that they were going to teach me in peacetime—in wartime the training would have gone much further—it came time for final examinations. It turned out that my examinations were to be given to me by my friend and associate, the ex-editor of the ex-*Park Field Airgnat,* and the gentleman who had shared in the division of the spoils at the publication's dissolution. I put the plane through its paces on command, and my friend and associate passed me brilliantly, with the highest rating a beginning flyer can earn: pursuit pilot.

Immediately afterwards, I was entitled to sew a pair of magnificent embroidered wings of silver and golden thread on the bosom of my beautiful officer's uniform that had been waiting in mothballs for so very, very long, entitled also to pin the little gold-plated second lieutenant bars on the shoulders and the insignia of the U.S. Signal Corps at the neck. I climbed into my magnificent uniform, pulled on the pair of too-small boots I had bought from a five-feet-six cadet who had flunked out, changed the enlisted man's cord on my campaign hat for an officer's cord, wished my mustache showed a little more and then, at government expense, departed for New York.

I was allowed to wear all this magnificence for another two weeks while I paraded up and down Fifth Avenue. My commission arrived in the mail from Washington and I had it framed and hung it on my wall. It was May 1919, and I was twenty years old. Thus ended my military career.

31

BACK IN CIVILIAN LIFE, I didn't care much for it. This may have had something to do with the fact that compared to army life, it was like being forced to swim briskly in chilly waters after floating languidly in the Gulf Stream.

Principally, though, I didn't like it because Mother had turned the Desti business once again into a sort of beauty parlor. One has to be a ladies' hairdresser to be happy in a beauty parlor. It is not that the manicurists were not perfectly charming, nor that I was not fond of them all, but one is as one is, and the perfumed atmosphere of the place did not suit me. Plenty of the customers were amusing, though.

One was a very amiable bald-headed man called Donahue, who had married one of Frank Hutton's daughters. Mr. Donahue banked at the New York Trust Company across the street and usually stopped there before coming into Desti's to have his nails done. He was a man who liked to bet, and Mother would play Odds and Evens with him, she calling out the odds or evens on the two-inch wad of new ten-dollar bills he had always just picked up at the bank. Since these were not long out of the Treasury, Mother would quickly find the proper sequence and astonish him by calling them correctly. Often she won enough for the rent. I don't think this hurt Mr. Donahue much, and it was a godsend to us because the business, as usual, just did not make any money . . . except once, for a little while.

Mother had taken on a very pretty young girl called Biddy Kleitz to help with the selling. This youngster had inherited from her Dutch or Frisian ancestors one of the tenderest and loveliest complexions ever seen on land or sea. One day a *Vogue* shopper came around to see the products and while talking to Biddy, asked her how she had come by such stupefying skin. Biddy, who was not without a sense of humor and who wanted to help business too, told the *Vogue* shopper that had the *Vogue* shopper seen her only three months before when she had started at Desti's, she would be utterly amazed now. On her arrival, Biddy went on, she had been a disaster: a walking exhibit of acne, pimples, boils, moth-patches, blackheads, and a neck like sandpaper. Her present complexion, Biddy revealed, was due solely and entirely to Desti's Youth Lotion.

The *Vogue* shopper departed in a tizzy and wrote such a glowing piece about Youth Lotion, formerly the Secret of the Harem, that the mail orders started coming in like reservations for a World Series.

A rush of business is perfectly fine when one is prepared for it, but disastrous when one is not; and we were not prepared. Every envelope the mailman hauled in contained a money order or a check for the cost of an eight-ounce bottle of Youth Lotion. One can hardly conceive of the difficulties arising when an eight-ounce bottle is to be sent through the mails to Terre Haute, Indiana, for instance. The difficulties are magnified when one really doesn't know *how* to send the bottle through the mails, and it is not *one* bottle but *one hundred* of them a day. We ran out of bottles; we ran out of alcohol; we ran out of labels; we ran out of baudruche to seal the bottles; we ran out of ribbon; we ran out of gold cord. What we did manage to get mailed sometimes got broken on the way. The spilled Youth Lotion made the customer's address unreadable, so one could not even acknowledge receipt of the damaged goods returned by the post office, much less replace them. The next thing one knew, the customer had written to *Vogue* to complain. *Vogue* gave us hell and wrote that it was returning the customer's money from its own funds, which made us feel like crooks. And it continued. More broken bottles came back, interspersed with furious letters from customers accusing us of being thieves; phone calls came in from *Vogue* suggesting about the same thing. We lived to rue the day Biddy attributed her genetic treasures to a formula in a bottle.

I remembered this experience years later when it came time to sell a wonderful gimbal candelabrum I had discovered on a Swedish sailing ship and had copied in solid brass at an engineering company I had put together in Wilmington, California. Before placing advertisements for the candelabrum in yachting magazines, I prepared for a flood of orders. I designed and had manufactured fifteen hundred shipping boxes, labels, and everything. The ads were placed. At the end of several months, I had received exactly two orders.

The philosophers are right, if it's not one thing, it's another.

Finally, I perfected the lip rouge that would stay on all day and all night and called it, after the red, red rose, Desti's Red Red Rouge. I designed a pretty box for it and some advertising displays for drugstores, and it began to sell fairly well. I visited all of the buyers of the great New York department stores, who were very kind to me and gave me orders. I remember one day talking to the buyer at B. Altman's about the selling price, telling him that if he just added fifty percent to the purchase price, it would give him a thirty-three and a third percent profit on the sale. He said, "Sonny, they never built this building on thirty-three and a third percent!"

I also visited all the drugstores, the hairdressers, and the beauty parlors I could find in New York and made selling tours out to Long Island. Again, everybody was very nice to me, and I was so innocent of any selling technique whatsoever that the buyers used to help me. "You shouldn't put it that way, Preston; you should say something like this!" After which they sold themselves a bill of goods. Commercial callowness soon became my technique.

In most of the biographies I have read, practically everything the protagonists did, even in their extreme youth, had some bearing on their later pursuits and could be cleverly woven in as a sort of object lesson. But if there is any connection between trying to sell Red Red Rouge, Youth Lotion, and sunburn powder to Miss Ferilla of Bonwit Teller's and my eventual work in the theatre and the movies, the thread escapes me.

Not many months after I took off my uniform, Mother took off for Europe, leaving me in charge of the business. She also left me with her apartment at 1 East Fifty-sixth, and when I had got rid of the six or eight unhousebroken Japanese spaniels that Mother had acquired somewhere, I settled in.

One day an old, broken-down, but remarkably talented photographer called Rochlitz wandered into the Desti place and told me that he was the best photographer in the world. To prove it, he took the best picture of me I have ever had taken. He then suggested that if I would take him in and give him a place to hang his hat, he would make a fortune for us. He turned out to be wrong about the fortune part, but I took him in because we had plenty of room in the old building. A room at the back made a sort of studio, and I built a darkroom still further back in the establishment. He knew his lighting and profession thoroughly, and I could not help but learn something. Often I made the enlargements and have had a bowing acquaintance with portrait photography ever since. He had a few business practices I couldn't tolerate and eventually we had to part. But he was one hell of a photographer, and the few things I learned from him, and the few things I had learned earlier from the painter Marcel Lenoir, were of definite help to me after I got on to a motion picture set.

At this period, I knew one of the prettiest girls I've ever seen in my life. She was a model at a millinery establishment called Tappe's whom I had met when I went in there with Mother during my furlough. Her name was Laura Grove. When I had the price, Laura used to go dancing with me.

One day Paris Singer's son, Cecil, discharged from the service too, showed up in New York, knowing nobody. I told him we'd soon fix that, I'd introduce him to the prettiest girl in New York. That night, I took him with Laura and me to the Biltmore Roof. That is how I lost Laura. She married Cecil very shortly thereafter, over the violent objections of Paris Singer, and they went off to Palm Beach, to the Everglades Club, to London, Paris, Saint-Jean-Cap-Ferrat, and the customary millionaire stopovers and sojourns. They had twin girls and a boy called David, who is now six feet three and loves to talk to me about his family, one I knew so much better than he.

My next ladyfriend was sent to me by a girl in London, who had told her to look me up when she got to New York. She was a tiny little thing who looked like a Dresden doll and had very small feet, which, for an English girl, was pretty unexpected. Her name was the Lady Eve Waddington-Greeley. She didn't hang around very long, but years later I called a picture *The Lady Eve* in souvenir of her.

I met my next girlfriend at Charlie Journal's Montmartre, and she drank like a fish. We had a lot of fun together, though she was a young woman of some mystery without visible means of support. I didn't have much support either, but at least one could tell where it was coming from. Dixie, on the other hand, was always taking large suites at the Savoy Hotel, where the Sherry-Netherlands now stands, and inviting bunches of us over for expensive parties. I did not get the vibrations of a family background of great wealth, and once or twice it flashed through my mind that there might be some rich old gentleman in the background, or even several of them. But I never saw the slightest trace of them, nor did she behave as girls sometimes do who are expecting the possible arrival of a sugar daddy.

Once or twice a month she took the train up to northern New York, where she said her parents lived. One day I had a headache and she said, "Oh, I'll get rid of that for you in a hurry," and took from her bag a little folded paper like the Seidlitz powders from the drugstore came in. She unwrapped the paper and when I asked what it was, she said she didn't know, someone had given it to her, and it was very good for headaches. I asked how one took it. She said, "Oh, you just hold it up to your nose and inhale it." I said, "Really?" and knocked the paper out of her hand. When the powder scattered to the floor, she became instantly furious and said, "You goddam fool! That cost sixteen dollars!" "I thought you didn't know what it was," I said. "Well, I don't exactly. But the fellow who gave it to me said it cost sixteen dollars and that it was very good for headaches. *Now* look at it!" "Do you use this stuff?" I asked her. "Of course I don't," she replied instantly.

Before jumping to the conclusion that I was an unusually stupid young man to fall for all this, it should be understood that in 1919 it was generally believed that no one used alcohol *and* drugs. Dixie's heavy drinking was practically a guarantee that she was not addicted to drugs.

A long time afterwards, this bit of folk wisdom proved to lack any foundation in fact.

One Sunday morning at the beginning of 1920, when I was twenty-one, I finally got out of the retail end of the perfumery business and, by severing our business arrangement with our head manicurist Peggy Sage, heedlessly said goodbye to a future of financial plenitude.

With the help of an amiable American Express driver, his wagon, and two plump horses, I had everything in the West Fifty-seventh Street shop, including the partitions and boxes of crystalware I couldn't even pick up, moved to 84 Boerum Street in the Williamsburg section of Brooklyn. The American Express driver moved so much stuff into that tiny shop that it was months before anybody could move around in it except by a sort of mountain climbing.

A little later that same Sunday morning, a freezing itinerant sign painter of about my own age, his blue gloveless hands clutching a box of paints, stuck his head in to ask if I wanted my name on the door. I ordered "Preston Sturges & Company, Importers and Exporters" painted on the glass in black, gold, and red. While the painter was laying on this magnificence, I asked him how much his racket was bringing in a week. He said some weeks were better than others, but on an average he knocked off about ten or twelve dollars, which took care of him, his mother, and his sister, but without luxuries. I asked if he'd like to come in out of the cold, learn the manufacture and packaging of perfumery and cosmetics, and earn fifteen dollars a week. He accepted, and we got to work right away. His name was John Wenzel and he learned quite rapidly, first how to make the stuff, then how to package and wrap it with cellophane, then how to fill orders and deliver them or send them by express.

Just as I had chosen a much lower-class neighborhood for my place of business, circumstances began, as they always will, to push me further down the scale in my way of living.

Mother's lease on 1 East Fifty-sixth came to an end, and I had to vacate the premises. Except for one studio couch, I sold all the furniture and the carpeting in the apartment to my friend Albert Veldheusen, a Dutchman in the perfumery business. My pal Georges Renevant, the actor who had become my friend while I was muffing my job as assistant stage manager for Isadora, came over to help me pull up the carpet, and as we watched Veldheusen move out the last of the furniture, he asked me where I was going to live. When I told him that I didn't expect to have any trouble finding a furnished room somewhere, he suggested that I come to Douglaston, Long Island, and live with them. Georges had just bought a little property there with a nice, lightly built house, a large kitchen garden, which appealed to his French soul, and a sort of lean-to which had some rabbit hutches and a chicken coop.

The extremely small house was already pretty full with Georges, his wife, her mother, a little Belgian girl war orphan they had adopted, some canaries, a number of dogs and cats, and a small monkey, whose little paws were always very sticky, although I hate to think with what. What Georges was offering me, absolutely rent-free, was the chicken coop. All I had to do was spray it, cover its inner walls with beaverboard, and I would be in business with a residence fit for a king.

I am a fairly good carpenter, and it was mostly the prospect of doing some pleasant carpentering that sucked me into this deal. Georges and I pounded away and sawed and painted while his wife, his mother-in-law, and the adopted child planted stuff in the garden.

It was a hard winter for Georges. He didn't get half the acting jobs he had been promised, and soon all that we had to eat were potatoes from the garden. Finally things got so desperate that George told me that I would have to go. I went away, thank God, or I would probably be there yet.

Back in New York, I found a room and bath on the fifth floor at the back of a brownstone building on the north side of Fifty-ninth Street between Madison and Park. The rent was as modest as it should have been. I moved my studio couch in and I was all set, except for the electricity. I still owed money to the Edison Company so I couldn't get the power turned on, but the problem was solved by running an extension cord in from the hallway.

Here I drew, inked, colored, cut out and assembled my displays for the Red Red Rouge, which I had not the money to have printed. The proprietors of the drugstores told me that when people noticed the displays had been done by hand, they tried to buy them.

Among my friends was Adelaide Kip Rhinelander, a niece of old T. J. O. Rhinelander, my friend since my Ninth Coast Regiment days. She was about my age and invited me over to her house once in a while, although she had no romantic interest in me, nor I in her. Her interest in me sprang from another well. She was in love with a handsome young man called Jack Schackno, who looked like the Prince of Wales, but she was not allowed to go out with him. She *was* allowed to go out with me, however. It was only a question of time, therefore, until she evolved a little plot, one I used many years later with much success in a motion picture called *The Miracle of Morgan's Creek.* In the picture, Betty Hutton, forbidden to go out with soldiers, gets Eddie Bracken to pretend to take her to the movies, then ditches him for the evening and rejoins him only when she is ready to go home.

This was the noble role I played in the life of Miss Rhinelander and her handsome young man. Sometimes, after a very late evening, I'd let Mr. Schackno stay at my place rather than return to the distant regions he inhabited, and we'd talk for the rest of the night about what we would do with our future lives. He had a lot more to speculate about than I did, because my future was well marked out in the perfumery and cosmetic game.

Mrs. T. J. O. Rhinelander suggested one day that I give a tea party to thank the many people whose hospitality I had accepted since my return to civilian life. I could not believe that any of these fashionable people would want to come to my modest, fifth-floor-back walk-up, but, to my astonishment, they all accepted. Ernest of The Colony sent over an enormous tray of canapés and a shakerful of cocktails; I bought a pound of Japanese green tea and I was ready.

Some of the older guests spent considerable time on the stairs, resting between flights, but eventually they all made it to the top. I was slightly embarrassed to have to turn off the only light in the room when it came time to plug in the electric plate to boil the water for the tea, but everybody seemed to enjoy this as a novelty, and many giggles came out of the darkness from the area of the studio couch, where everyone was sitting because there was no place else to sit. The party was pronounced a great success and since that day, I have never been ashamed to invite anyone even to the most humble abode.

Over in Europe, Mother's implicit belief in her own conclusions was illustrated again, this time in The Case of the Vanishing Vely Bey, or The Missing Turkish Husband.

Not having heard from Vely Bey in some time, Mother wondered aloud if he were dead. The thought having tiptoed into her mind, she was nearly persuaded of the matter a few days later and absolutely certain of it by the end of the month. Then, bearing up courageously under her widowhood, she married a young Englishman called Howard Perch, also known as Punch.

Inevitably, one day while walking down the Champs-Elysées on the arm of her new husband, my mother saw her old one walking up. She hoped for a moment that he might prove to be a ghost and considered ignoring him entirely, but at this instant, emitting a happy cry of recognition, the spectre hurried over, took her in his arms and bussed her on both cheeks. There being nothing else to do, she introduced everybody all around, after which they retired to the terrace of the nearest café for some refreshments and a little talk.

It all ended pleasantly, of course, since my mother, motivated by only the highest sentiments, never loused people's lives up on purpose. Helpful, too, was the fact that she never married anything but gentlemen, who usually behaved as advertised.

A few days before leaving for France to meet Mother's new husband, I received an invitation through Cecil Singer and Laura to come with them to spend the weekend with a couple they had met in Palm Beach, a Mr. and Mrs. Jonathan Godfrey. Mr. Godfrey, they told me, was an immensely successful manufacturer of cartridge boxes, and I was immediately seized with a strong desire not to spend the weekend with him. The Godfreys sounded like old poops to me, but Laura and Cecil insisted that it would be fun and as I was very fond of them, I accepted.

A white-haired gentleman of sixty-four years with a very white mustache met us at the Bridgeport, Connecticut, station with a magnificent open Packard. He turned out to be our host. He struck me immediately as new-rich, uneasy, and pretentious. We were not more than halfway to Fairfield when he mentioned his cousin Talleyrand, who, a few cursory questions later, turned out to have been a very distant relative of his now deceased first wife. After a while we turned into the standard Fairfield millionaire's abode, with the usual Greek portico and the standard number of columns with proper entasis. A standard butler admitted us and some confusion about getting the bags ensued. I had brought mine in with me, so I found myself alone in the front hall. As I started toward the living room to see what kind of Hampton House stuff it was furnished with, a very well-bred, quiet voice behind me said, "How do you do?"

I spun around and, up two or three steps of the main staircase, I saw a very handsome and very young and, as the French say, very well-rolled person of the opposite sex. Her hair was parted in the middle and coiled flatly over her ears. She had bangs. She was five feet three.

I asked, "Who are you?"

She said, "I am your hostess."

"You mean Mrs. Uh-Uh-Uh . . ."

She laughed and said, "That's right, Mrs. Godfrey."

Now I understood why Cecil and Laura had insisted upon my coming.

We had a very gay evening at the country club and later that night danced again and drank some more and finally all of us wound up in the Godfreys' enormous kitchen for the standard scrambled eggs. I do not remember my host being there, so it is possible that he had retired.

I still drew quite well in those days and the next day I made a colored wash of Mrs. Godfrey which pleased her very much. Mr. Godfrey must have been faintly irritated with my attentions to his wife because later in the day he invited me to see him shoot with a target pistol. Aiming at a frog at the far end of a patio pool, he shot and missed it. Since only recently I had been doing considerable target work in the

army, I said, "Permit me . . ." and dispatched the unfortunate batra-
chian.

That afternoon Mrs. Godfrey took Laura and me to see her horses
and talked about her family and the horses they had shown when she
was still a girl at home called Estelle de Wolfe Mudge. Estelle's mother,
crippled in a riding accident before Estelle's birth, took drugs, and at
eighteen Estelle had married a man of sixty-two principally to get away
from her mother and to have a household of her own. Now she was going
on twenty and I was approaching twenty-three.

After we toured the stables, Estelle drove us, wildly, to the country
club for tea. At the club she introduced Laura and me to the club
professional, Gene Sarazen, who told us that Estelle had the makings of
a golf champion. I took this with what Mr. Goldwyn calls a "dose of
salts," because at twenty-five dollars an hour, it pays to believe that one's
wealthy pupils are potential champions.

That night we laughed again, drank again, too much, and danced
again, too close. That was all, however; there were no meetings in the
moonlight, no surreptitious embraces, no stolen kisses, but scrambled
eggs, of course, in the big kitchen.

The next morning I had to go back to New York to pack for the
trip to Paris and to leave some business instructions with John Wenzel.
Cecil and Laura, who were sailing on the same boat, were already packed
and, as Cecil *had* no business to attend to, they weren't going in to New
York until the next day. Mrs. Godfrey took me to the station alone.
As the train pulled out, I said, so that she could just hear it, "I love
you . . ."

CHAPTER

I DON'T REMEMBER IF WE CROSSED on the *Aquitania* or the *Mauretania,* but I got off at Cherbourg, and the Singers, Cecil and Laura and Uncle Mun and his wife, Joan, went on to England. I got to Paris at about five in the morning and as I had nowhere else to go, I went directly to the Claridge Hotel and asked to see Mrs. Perch.

"At five in the morning!" exclaimed the sleepy but indignant concierge.

"In view of the fact that I've come all the way from New York to see her," I said, "I don't see why not."

"But not at five in the morning," said the concierge, whose mind seemed to be made up.

"But she's my mother," I said, "and she's naturally very anxious to see me the moment I arrive."

"Now I understand," said the concierge. "Everything is clear."

"Good," I said. "It's about time."

"What has happened," continued the concierge, "is that you are asking for the wrong Mrs. Perch. *This* Mrs. Perch is a young woman with very black hair whose husband is perhaps thirty-five, thirty-six. She is not your mother."

"That's where you're mistaken," I said. "No matter how black her hair is, or how young her husband, she is still my mother."

Then, getting an idea, I pulled out of my pocket a photograph of the two of them. I put it under the concierge's nose and asked, "Who is this?"

"Mr. and Mrs. Perch," he said.

"And still my mother!"

He took me upstairs, although very reluctantly, and we knocked.

I had never been described to the new husband as anything but "my baby," and when Mother got to the door and threw her arms around all 185 pounds and six feet two of me, cooing "my baby," he very nearly fell over in a syncope. Mother was extremely happy to see me, and I to see her. Mr. Perch, however, was too dazed to feel anything.

Mother had become a journalist of sorts, writing beauty articles about things like how restful it was to put cold slices of lemon between one's toes after a hard day at the office, or how to freshen one's face with cucumber, for which the *London Daily Sketch* paid her five pounds a week. One might sneer at five pounds a week, but if one is living on it, it's heavenly.

I don't know where Mother found the money, but she had taken a wonderful painter's studio for me at 91 *bis*, avenue de la Muette, a dead-end street that no longer exists, having been cut through and renamed the avenue Paul Doumer. It was not far from the house she had built in 1907, nor from my close friends the Doucèdes. She had also taken an apartment for herself and Mr. Perch on the rue Saint-Honoré, just off the rue Royale, which was being painted in preparation for their occupancy. I cannot remember where the Desti business was vegetating, but it must have been somewhere because we always had it around, like an old relative.

I moved into the painter's studio at once. It was really a hell of a studio, the kind one would give gold and rubies for today. It was up one flight over private garages and it had a private staircase, something as necessary to a young man as a studio couch. Of these, it had several. The ceiling was twenty-five feet up, with the standard loggia, or balcony, on which I slept. The morning noises were captivating: the high sounds of the hand-squeezed horns of the French taxis, the chirping of the birds, the hollering of the chauffeurs below stamping around in rubber boots as they washed and squeegeed their cars, and the powerful voice of Mademoiselle Emilienne Letellier, my concierge, as she told them to shut up before they woke me up.

Mademoiselle Letellier was a darling woman with a black mustache, probably more bachelor girl than old maid, who lived with her mother in the loge down in the courtyard. She kept my apartment theoretically clean and every morning brought me breakfast in bed of chocolate, crescents, sweet butter, and strawberry jam. She had her own idea of how young men occupy their nights and always approached my couch nervously, as if she expected several young females to throw back the covers and say "Boo!" She was often disappointed.

I had brought the formula for Desti's Red Red Rouge over to Paris with me, and Mother had hit on a new way of making the Aurora face rouge, halfway between a powder and a paste. I made drawings and designs for the displays of both the products, had them printed and cut out, and decided to flood the Paris market with them. I thought that the quickest way to do this was by circular, so I tried to buy a list of the department stores, perfumeries, beauty salons, pharmacies, and hairdressing establishments of Paris. I was told no such list existed. I couldn't believe it, as one can get such information in any American city, but it was a fact nonetheless. I asked then for a classified telephone book. "What for?" was the response. "In the first place, not half of these places have telephones and in the second place, the telephone books have not been corrected and brought up to date since 1914."

So, very grateful for the long hikes I had done down in Texas because they gave me confidence in my feet, I did the only thing possible. I *walked* every north and south street in Paris, beginning on the left, and ending on the right, writing down the names and addresses of the establishments I needed for my list. When I got through with the north and south streets, which wasn't overnight, I tackled the east and west streets from top to bottom. Every night while soaking my feet in Epsom salts and hot water, I crossed out the streets, avenues, boulevards, esplanades, allées, impasses and culs-de-sac I had heel-and-toed that day. The French are still surprised at my knowledge of Paris.

There are lots of things about Paris most Americans don't know. For one thing, the entire city is used twenty-four hours a day. I mean, there is no financial district, for instance, where nobody lives at night; no cloak-and-suit district where the lofts are occupied only by day; and there are no buildings of only one or two stories. As a result, there are seven times more people to the square mile in Paris than in New York, or any other American city. That is the explanation for the enormous number of little butcher shops and bakeries and fishmongers and charcuteries and wine merchants and vegetable stores and hardware stores and cafés and restaurants, each run by a single family, whose daughters are often lovely, with beautiful legs developed by bicycle riding.

When I got my list of possible customers all typed up, I started sending out literature, but the project didn't work out quite as well as I had hoped, or as the enormous expenditure of energy might have led one to expect. The store owners bought a certain amount of the rouges, but they were not accustomed to the direct-mail approach and were suspicious of it.

I also wrote long letters of instruction and advice to John Wenzel, the young itinerant painter I had hired in Brooklyn and had trained to make, package, and deliver the Desti products and whose presence and good work habits I trusted to keep the business going until I got back to America.

A young man without a profession, unless he is a jerk, keeps his eyes and ears open because he hopes that someday, somewhere, he will see or hear something that will lead him to the path which leads, in turn, to success and prosperity. If he is an optimist, he believes this will happen tomorrow. If he is a pessimist, he doubts that it will ever happen. I am, always was, and always will be violently optimistic. I knew at twenty that I was going to be a millionaire. I know it today. In between times, I have been.

We met a Professeur Gaston Sabathe, who occupied the front of a floor in the back of which I was establishing a new firm: Sturges, Perch and Company, Importers and Exporters—although I don't think I ever imported or exported anything in my life.

Professeur Sabathe, a French scientist with a beard, had recently invented a cure for tuberculosis, which, almost anyone would admit, is quite an invention even if it doesn't work one hundred percent of the time. I don't know exactly what cultures of what deceased microbes he made his stuff out of, but it wound up in the form of a very pale yellow liquid which was squirted into the lungs through a silver tube attached to a large, or horse doctor's, hypodermic syringe. The trick to its application was getting the patient to open the right aperture in the throat so that the stuff didn't get coughed back in the professeur's beard. After several misadventures along these lines, Professeur Sabathe developed a transparent mask with something like windshield wipers on it that, when donned to give somebody a treatment, looked like a snowplow.

If only, he said, he could get some prominent employer to use the cure on a few thousand of his employees and wipe out tuberculosis among them, it would prove once and for all the value of his discovery and take years off the time period normally required for the worldwide diffusion of its advent.

It happened that Mother knew a prominent employer located in London. In fact, she had known him in Chicago. He left America as Harry G. Selfridge, opened his department store in London as Gordon

H. Selfridge and knocked the conservative English for a loop. Harrods, Marshall and Snelgrove, and Swan and Edgar gasped their disapproval at his Chicago methods. What with weekly fire sales, reductions before inventory, weekend specials, spring, summer, fall, and winter clearouts, he cut a swath like Sherman cut through Georgia.

I felt that being connected in any way with the eradication of the white plague, as tuberculosis was known, would be an excellent thing for a young man, even if I went down in history only as an *assistant* Microbe Hunter. I offered my services as an emissary to Mr. Selfridge with his thousands of employees. Professeur Sabathe consulted his backers, of which he had more than a Broadway show, then agreed to pay my expenses, provided I traveled second class. I accepted with pleasure.

Armed with a letter from Mother, I presently found myself in the presence of the great man, who had a very large office, a large steam yacht, but only a very small or embryonic English accent. He received me warmly, and after some very short preliminaries, I plunged enthusiastically into my reasons for taking up his time. I quoted statistics to him, noted the prevalence of phthisis in damp countries like England, the probable percentage of TB sufferers among his innumerable employees, and all the other facts and figures with which Professeur Sabathe had provided me.

Mr Selfridge listened gravely to all I had to say, then sent me back to Paris with one surprising statement. "I have not, I am happy to say," he remarked in the fine rounded bass of the successful American businessman, "even *one* amongst my 3,862 employees who shows even the faintest *trace* of consumption."

I don't know what Mr. Selfridge died of. I suppose what I'm thinking would be too much to hope for.

I went to London one more time on a business venture during this Paris sojourn and had a narrow squeak.

A very good friend of mine called Pierre Weill, who made the metal boxes for our Aurora rouge, began to manufacture, very inexpensively, mechanical pencils very like the American Eversharp. If only, he said, he could get W. H. Smith and Sons, the great English firm with newsstands in every railway station in the British Isles, to display his pencils, the battle would be won.

Antennae humming, I had but one answer, "I will go."

My friend Weill was not vulgar enough to suggest by what class I should travel, he merely offered me an all-inclusive sum of money for the trip, a sum which automatically dictated third-class accommodations. The night before I was to leave, however, by train, boat, and train, a friend of mine called Ricci, who owned a little bar, said that he was flying to London the next day and suggested I fly over with him. I thanked him very much, but said the flight would be a little expensive for me as I had a fixed sum for the trip. He said that was nonsense and offered to pay the difference. I thought this over, but decided that I was not in enough of a hurry to put myself in debt to this very nice man.

When I reached London by train, boat, and train, I bought—from a W. H. Smith and Sons' newsstand—the evening paper, which carried news of a plane that had hit electric wires taking off from Le Bourget and had crashed in flames. Among the list of the dead passengers was the name of my kind friend, Monsieur Ricci.

Also, W. H. Smith and Sons didn't buy any pencils.

One of the great joys of this period of my life in Paris was the extraordinary piano playing of my friend Les Copeland, who performed nightly on an upright in the storm cellar beneath the New York Bar.

This establishment on the rue Daunou subsequently became internationally famous as *Harry's* New York Bar, although Harry, a dull Scottish bartender from Ciro's across the street, had less than nothing to do with its founding or its charming appointments and layout. He merely happened to be there with a sockful of his tips when someone had to sell it in a hurry, possibly around 1923 or 1924. Originally it had been converted from a small French bistro to the New York Bar by the great American jockey Tod Sloan. The convenience of its location between the avenue de l'Opéra and the rue de la Paix, near the American Express Company, the steamship agencies, and many of the great hotels, caused its almost immediate acceptance as the Paris terminal and meeting place for boatriders, prize fighters and their managers and trainers, roller-rink promoters, and other Americans with legitimate or illegitimate pursuits in Europe.

By the time I speak of, the New York Bar belonged to Nell Henry, a high-busted American woman and ex-diving champion, who had been married to the great English jockey Milton Henry. Her manager and companion was called Charlie Herrick. Between the two of them and Les Copeland, they knew exactly how to take care of a visiting American millionaire bent on whooping it up a little.

One of the millionaires I particularly remember was Charlie Hill, son of the great railroad man. When he arrived, they locked the doors and put all the champagne in the house on ice. Les would give out with a very good bagpipe imitation of "The Campbells Are Coming," and the festivities would begin with Mr. Hill tearing into a sword dance. We spent some marvelous evenings.

Les's wondrous playing exerted so much fascination for me that the New York Bar was one of the two places I had to visit each night, without fail, before going to bed.

The other was Fysher's, across the avenue de l'Opéra and about fifty yards up in the little square called Fontaine Gaillon. This was the same A. Nilsson Fysher who a couple of years earlier had vanished without notice from the Fysher's in New York, thus ruining Daisy Andrews and Vely Bey. But it was not to hear Fysher sing "Pour un peu d'amour" for the five hundredth time that I had to make a nightly pilgrimage to his trap. It was to hear a slender but magnificently proportioned little Russian wildcat sing "La Troika." She was the lady of my dreams at the moment and, I suspect, of A. Nilsson Fysher's, because he looked at me with a very sour expression the first time I took her home.

She was a fascinating girl who lived in one of the most obscene hotels I have ever been in or ever heard of. It was on the rue Bergère, across the street and a little distance up from the Folies. When something peculiarly choice or exciting was about to take place, the proprietor of the hotel would invite my little friend to watch the shenanigans through holes in the door pierced at the proper heights. The doors to all of the rooms in the hotel were so pierced, except those of my little friend, which I plugged up. Some of the semilunatics who patronized this establishment, especially those known as the Maquilleurs, followed always the same rather involved scenarios and often arrived with relatively large casts. All of these eccentricities seemed merely to add piquancy to my little girlfriend, and I couldn't see enough of her. Unfortunately, I soon ran out of money, and it *takes* money to take a girl out who finishes work at four in the morning. And if you haven't any money, there's always somebody else who has.

Mother ran out of money at this time too, and things began to look very desperate. So desperate had our affairs become in fact, that Mother, Punch, and I had a fifty-franc dinner at an *authentic* French table d'hôte called La Table d'Hôte Blond. Fifty francs was slightly less than a dollar then, and one couldn't expect much of a dinner for it, but this solitary dip into hopeless mediocrity was so horrifying that the very next day Mother came up with one of the brilliant, and rare, financial strokes of her life.

While we were still trying to forget the boiled beef and watery vegetables, Mother said suddenly, "I never paid it back, did I?"

"Probably not," we responded, Mr. Perch and I. "Paid *what* back?"

"Then it must still be good," said Mother triumphantly. "Since I didn't pay it back, it must still be *there!*"

"*What* must still be there?" Mr. Perch and I inquired.

"Don't upset my train of thought," said Mother and hurried away to dress.

It was a little later that morning that Mrs. Solomon Sturges of Chicago turned up at the magnificent offices of Morgan Harjes and Company in the place Vendôme and asked to see one of the vice-presidents. Mother was using the name of Mrs. Solomon Sturges of Chicago not because she was ashamed of Mr. Perch, but because it was the name under which Mr. Harold McCormick had guaranteed her account back there in Zurich when she was trying to get Isadora's pupils back to Germany. His guarantee, of course, had secured her the loan of ten thousand dollars.

"I was trying to remember," said Mother to the vice-president of the great bank, "whether I ever paid back that loan I got from you in 1915 . . ."

"We will soon find out," said the vice-president, rising politely and excusing himself. He returned after a few minutes with a small dossier, which, after blowing the dust off of it, he opened.

"No," he said after a very brief examination of the records, "you never paid it back." Then, with a beam, he added, "No doubt you would like to do so now."

"Well, not exactly," said Mother. "What I really wanted to find out was whether Mr. Harold McCormick's guarantee was still good . . ."

"Well, of course, it's still good," said the vice-president, laughing. "Did you think he'd gone bankrupt or something? With the McCormick

Harvester Company and the Rockefeller fortune behind him, that would be difficult to do, wouldn't it?"

"Yes," said Mother joining in the hearty laughter. "Then the guarantee is still good?"

"Of course, it's still good," said the vice-president, closing the dossier as he was a busy man. "Now if there is nothing else, Mrs Sturges . . ."

"But there *is,*" said Mother gently. "I would like the rest of my money."

"What money was that?" said the vice-president, the smile freezing on his face.

"The loan guaranteed by Mr. McCormick," said Mother, tapping the dossier. "His signed guarantee is right in there. I just saw it."

"But you've already *had* that money," said the vice-president, with the patient smile bankers have for women customers. "You see," he said, opening the dossier and putting on his pince-nez, "it is very carefully recorded here. Mr. McCormick guaranteed your account in the amount of ten thousand dollars on the 29th of August, 1915; you withdrew the amount on the same day, cabling two thousand dollars to Mr. Preston Sturges in New York and taking the balance in French francs, forty thousand of them."

"That's exactly what I'm talking about, and why I would like the balance of my money, which is to say, three hundred and sixty thousand francs."

"But, my dear Mrs. Sturges," said the vice-president, starting to mop his head, "you have already *had* all the money for which Mr. McCormick guaranteed your account. He guaranteed you up to ten thousand dollars. You had two thousand dollars sent to this Mr. Sturges in New York, plus forty thousand francs, which was, at the time, eight thousand dollars. Two plus eight is ten! You have, therefore, *had* the amount that Mr. McCormick guaranteed."

"All I had," said Mother doggedly, "was two thousand dollars and forty thousand francs! Since I never paid off the loan, the account is still *open* and the guarantee is still *good.* The franc is now fifty to the dollar instead of the five to the dollar it was. Mr. McCormick's guarantee is therefore good for five hundred thousand francs, less what I already had. I have had two thousand dollars and forty thousand francs, that is to say one hundred forty thousand francs. I would like the other three hundred sixty thousand francs that my guarantee calls for."

"But, my dear Mrs. Sturges," began the vice-president, now perspiring freely.

"I am quite sure," Mother interrupted gently, "that when you think this over, you will see that I am completely right. You must admit that I could go out and buy forty thousand francs for eight hundred dollars, which, with two thousand dollars added, would pay off my loan. Isn't that a fact?"

"Well, I suppose it is, in a way," conceded the unhappy vice-president.

"Not in a way," said Mother, "in the only *honest* and *fair* way. I am quite certain that if Mr. McCormick were here himself, he would tell you the same thing. He *wanted*, in effect, to lend me ten thousand dollars. I am sure he would be very much upset if he found he had only lent me two thousand and eight hundred dollars."

And they gave her the money, three hundred sixty thousand francs! I would not believe this story myself unless I had been there and helped her to spend it, but they passed a law to prevent such an absurdity from ever happening again. So far as I know, no one has ever been able to figure out who was the loser, although, very obviously, Mother was the gainer.

Naturally all of us were jubilant. Mother and Punch went off to Deauville to celebrate for a couple of weeks while I stayed on in Paris and took my little Russian friend out again.

When Mother and Punch got back, I was given two weeks in Deauville with a nice room and bath one entered through a quiet garden. I played tennis then, although never very well, and to celebrate further, Mother bought me twelve pair of long white duck tennis trousers. They were really glistening. I had never had twelve pair of white duck pants before. I have never had them since, and it is extremely probable that I shall never have them again. But I am very glad to have had them once in my life, in Deauville, when I was twenty-two. My mother had a true talent for doing charming things.

My two weeks were almost up when I met the girl.

She was sitting quietly in the tennis club one day with her governess when I spotted her and was instantly electrified. She was possibly eighteen. I immediately started drawing her picture and curiosity took care of the rest of the situation. The picture came out very well and I gave it to her.

We played tennis daily thereafter. In fact, I lived to play tennis with her. My heart started to beat every day when she arrived at the club with her governess in an immense old chauffeured limousine. Her name was Mabel de Forest and I saw her only a couple of hours each afternoon at the tennis club. When she left, I relapsed into catalepsis, where I remained until she came back the next day. What I did the rest of the time hardly impinged on my memory.

Soon the money my mother had given me was gone, but I couldn't leave the riveting Mabel de Forest. I moved out of my lovely room into a room over a very unstylish restaurant where I discovered, to my dismay, that her chauffeur had his meals. This would not bother me at all today, and it shouldn't have bothered me at twenty-two, but it did. I can only look back and be amazed at the degree of idiocy of this young man who subsequently became a reasonably intelligent citizen. Having assured myself that my Princesse Lointaine's chauffeur was not present, I would enter and partake of the excellent inexpensive food. Pretty soon, disaster struck again.

This time it was a question of laundry. Now without the funds to have my twelve pairs of white duck pants laundered, I spread them all out on the bed every day to choose the cleanest pair to go to play tennis in.

Once Mabel invited me to tea in the Casino with her friends the Baroness D'Erlanger and her daughter Baba, Paula Gella-Bond, the Baroness aux Champs Nesces, and a young man about my own age called Barrachin. Why do I remember these names so easily? Because I was in love. But then, one might well ask, how about the Russian girl in Paris? Or the young Mrs. Godfrey in Fairfield? All I can say is that I loved them all.

One day little Miss de Forest did not come to play tennis. Instead her chauffeur appeared to tell me that she was leaving unexpectedly for Paris. There was no further reason for me to stay in Deauville. I left my twelve pair of white duck trousers as security for what I owed for my inexpensive room and left for Paris on the same train as the object of my affections. We said goodbye as the train pulled into the Gare Saint-Lazare and I haven't seen her since.

A few days after I got back to Paris, Paris Singer showed up and scolded me for wasting my time in Europe when I should be in New York developing my business. I told him that the ticket was beyond my means at the moment. "Aha! I should have kept my mouth shut," he laughed, then became serious again and told me that he wouldn't pay my passage back to New York because he didn't wish to contribute to my becoming a bum. He said, however, that if he could discover some useful service I might render him, he would then be very glad to have me accompany them. "Them" included, among others, his wife Joan, and Cecil and Laura. About three minutes later he wondered aloud, "Why couldn't you be my secretary?"

I said that I would be delighted, but that I was not sure I had the qualifications necessary. "What would I have to do?"

"Well, you would have to call up restaurants and reserve tables for us for dinner." He thought for a moment. "And you would have to arrange for theatre tickets. Naturally, you would come, too. And make the arrangements for the railroad and steamship tickets to get us back to America. Do you think you could do all those things?"

I said I felt that I could discharge these duties with ease, so, very pleased with himself, Uncle Mun congratulated me on my new appointment as his secretary and then he said he supposed I could use a little money in advance. I said his assumption was not wrong, and he pressed the equivalent of fifty dollars into my hands. This generous gesture put him in such a good humor that he asked if my birthday were not almost upon us. It was, I told him; I would be twenty-three on the 29th of August. He asked if I had ever had a gold watch and when I said that I had not, he said that everybody should have one gold watch during his lifetime and that I should have one for my birthday.

I really didn't know how to thank him for all his kindnesses, but he said that thanks were not necessary and appeared quite satisfied with himself. He then told me that my secretarial duties were to start at 9:00 sharp the next morning, at which hour I was to report to his house at 1 *bis,* place des Vosges, the beautiful house in which Madame de Sévigné was born. On this we parted, I as happy as he.

Well, sir, that was quite a night. I had been without funds just long enough for all that money to be burning holes in my pockets. I sent a pneumatique to my little Russian friend in her awful hotel, then arrived in full evening dress with opera hat to take her to dinner. We had a splendid dinner and I got her to Fysher's on time to sing "La Troika."

It was after Fysher's that the real party began, all over and up and down Paris. I don't know at what hour it ended, but suddenly I woke up with a start and a foreboding of calamity in my little friend's lousy hotel. I looked at my watch and it said ten minutes to nine! I was due at the place des Vosges in ten minutes; there was no time to go out to the avenue de la Muette where I lived to shave and bathe and especially to change into something besides the swallowtailed outfit I had with me. I jumped into my clothes and staggered down the rue Bergère, my tie untied, my eyes looking like two holes burned in a sheet, and my opera hat on the back of my head. My overcoat I dragged behind me. Leaping into a cab, I gave the address and hoped for the best.

I arrived at 1 *bis,* place des Vosges and got to the top of the noble staircase at exactly 9:00 o'clock. From here a long and beautiful corridor extended past the great rooms to the domestic quarters in the distance. Joan Singer was standing at the far end of this corridor. My appearance—overcoat trailing, tie untied, and opera hat on the back of my head—at this hour of the morning filled her with horror.

She whispered, "What's the matter with you? Are you insane?"

I whispered back, "Tell Uncle Mun I was here at 9:00 sharp, but that I forgot my fountain pen so I went home to get it. I'll be back before he's awake."

This was a reasonably safe assumption, as the old boy was anything but an early riser. But as I turned to go, white and shaky, my appearance must have struck a maternal chord in Joan's heart, because she stage-whispered from the other end of the corridor, "Would you like a cup of coffee before you go?"

"Oh my God, yes," I said.

"Then come along to the kitchen. Be very careful passing Paris's door because he didn't sleep well last night."

I suppose we had been whispering louder than we thought because, just as I tiptoed past his door, it suddenly opened wide, revealing Uncle Mun, tall and magnificent in his Japanese dressing gown. Fixing me with an accusing finger, he said simply, *"You* are fired."

Thus ended my one and only secretarial job.

Of course, good humor was soon reestablished. The old boy joined me in his kitchen for coffee, and pretty soon we were laughing about the whole thing. He then expressed a desire to meet a girl so wondrous that a young man would sacrifice his job, a passage to America, and a gold watch for her. So we all had dinner that night and he and Joan agreed that she was lovely. But I didn't get taken back to America.

I wrote to John Wenzel to see if my business had been good enough to squeeze a steamship ticket out of it, but this was just a pipe dream. Finally, as usual, it was Father who came through and got me back to America.

And the minute I got back there, things began to happen.

33

THE FIRST SHOCK CAME when I called on the Rhinelanders, who were like a second set of parents for me. Mrs. Rhinelander always wanted to know what girls I was going out with and what adventures I was having and I had much to tell her. Before I got started, though, Mrs. Rhinelander asked, "Did you see what happened to your little friend Dixie Bliss?" "No, ma'am, I didn't," I said.

"I'm afraid she was murdered," Mrs. Rhinelander said and told me the story.

It turned out that the girl was a heroin runner from Canada, which explained the trips up north and the plentiful money. She had been drinking too much, the newspapers said, and was blabbing dangerously. It was necessary to get rid of her. In spite of her heavy drinking, which had convinced me that she was not addicted to drugs, Dixie was an addict, too. The papers explained that when the distributors want to get rid of someone, they give him the "hot charge," pure heroin, instantly lethal. Commercial heroin apparently was only ten percent pure, nine-tenths of it being plain white powder.

The newspapers reported that Dixie sent for the cab of a distributor-taxi driver and bought a dose from him while the cab was in motion. Apparently she took it, and that was it. The cab reached Fifth Avenue, pulled up in front of the Hotel Buckingham, where Saks Fifth Avenue now stands, and the driver got out and walked away. They found his cap on the seat and Dixie Bliss inside.

I don't want to sound heartless, but since I could not have helped her in any case, I have always been profoundly grateful for the luck that took me to Paris in those months of young manhood. Certainly I would have been investigated, as was everyone else who knew the poor kid. Certainly to this day there would be people to say, "He was in the drug racket, you know, as a young man," as there were people to say, quite seriously, "He's part colored, you know."

Joan Singer overheard a woman saying this about me in Palm Beach when I had a hit play running in New York. When Joan laughed and told the woman that she was pretty sure she was mistaken because Paris Singer had known me since I was a boy, the woman said, "Well, if he isn't colored, he's Turkish or something like that, which is practically the same thing." This, of course, had reference to Ilias Pasha and his son Vely Bey, but they always looked extremely white to me.

One day when John Wenzel was out delivering something for me, his mother and sister came to call on me at my factory on Boerum Street with some troubling news. They had come to ask if there were any way I could help to cure John of his terrible habit, a habit that was ruining his health and that, because of its cost, was keeping them on the verge of starvation.

I didn't know what they were talking about and was dumbfounded to learn that John was a cocaine addict who, with his new relative prosperity, had reached a point of such indifference and shamelessness that he would take his trousers down at the dinner table to stick the needle in his thigh. I couldn't believe my ears, but they had sent for a detective from the narcotics squad, who arrived at that moment and told me that it was true and that the boy had already served three sentences on Riker's Island.

I promised to do what I could but there was very little I *could* do. And once John knew that *I* knew about his vice or weakness or whatever it's called, our relationship changed and he didn't try as hard to do well as he had done before. I am not a psychiatrist and I do not pretend to know *why* things work out the way they do, I am merely reporting *how* they worked out. I eventually had to get rid of him, but I think that so long as he knew that I *didn't* know about his addiction, he was happy in the fact that, for at least one of the people who surrounded him, he was a decent, hardworking man with normal pride and self-respect.

This, coming on top of the news of poor Dixie's death, made me wonder what kind of people the world was populated with. Then I remembered Bob Chanler's friends and realized that I wasn't the only person who was pulling some strange numbers out of the bag.

Calm was just beginning to be reestablished when I received an invitation from Mrs. Godfrey, the wife of the old cartridge box manufacturer in Fairfield, asking me to have tea with her at the Ritz. This gave me considerable pause, and food for reflection. I began playing the impending scene in advance, and slowly my hair started to stand on end.

It's all very well (or is it?) to make spontaneous and impulsive declarations of love to handsome young women one hardly knows while trains are pulling out, but the possible consequences did not occur to me then. They did now. It started to dawn on me that because of the three hot little words I'd muttered at the Bridgeport station, the young woman could actually leave her husband, with the normal scandals and complications usually attendant upon these partings. Then, in all probability, I would be expected to do what is lightly known as the "honorable thing." The whole situation began to descend on me like a damp blanket and I began to realize how golden silence really is. I wished I had kept my trap shut instead of falling into one.

She came to the Ritz, looking as lovely as I had remembered her, accompanied by an impoverished lady acting as chaperone. I knew that I ought to tell her to go back to Fairfield and behave herself, that I had been still full of *spiritus frumenti* when I had muttered what I had muttered, but I just couldn't do it. We sat there instead, swooning into each other's eyes and yammering sweet nothings while the duenna kept a weather eye cocked for impending danger.

She had looked, the young lady told me, all over Brooklyn for my factory. Though she had driven from one end of Boerum Street to the other, she had somehow missed the firm of Preston Sturges & Company. This gave me an opening that I seized upon at once. I told her that she hadn't been able to find my factory because she had failed to take along a magnifying glass. I then brought out the fact that my business was very, very small. To make it doubly clear, at least insofar as any prospective marriage she might be thinking about was concerned, I compared myself to those unfortunate snakes in the Kentucky mountain story who hadn't a pit to hiss in. This made her laugh, but she didn't seem to get the point.

After a while, she and the chaperone had to take the train back to Bridgeport, but she gave me a rendezvous for later in the week. This was followed by others. In between times, and with many precautionary measures designed to keep her husband undisturbed, we wrote to each other. Finally one day she told me that she had made up her mind. She was leaving Fairfield, Connecticut, and her husband, and would go to live, at least for a while, with her Aunt Louise Mudge in Boston.

I was still years away from being a playwright, or a writer of any kind for that matter, but still I knew a cue when I heard one.

The next time the young lady came to town, I took her down to the Battery and into the aquarium where, surrounded by schools of stupid-looking fish, I made one of those honorable proposals that begin with, "When and *if* you should by any chance happen to be free some day, my dear . . ." I don't think even her husband could have objected, although he might not have liked it. The young lady cried gently while accepting me, and I think I snuffled a couple of times myself. I wish I could say that the fish cried also, but their expressions did not vary in the slightest.

Why the aquarium? I wonder myself. It stemmed undoubtedly from some idea that seemed brilliant at the time, but for the life of me, I can't recall it now. I don't think it had anything to do with going to visit the other poor fish.

34

IN EUROPE, OF COURSE, situations like Estelle's and mine would have been handled quite differently and with a minimum of complications. But we were young Americans and, in our own eyes at least, clean and honorable. Looking back upon it now, I think we were a pair of numbskulls, she as idiotic as I, who probably deserved a long stretch of unhappiness.

We had, instead, five years of bliss.

Not that it wasn't slightly complicated at first; it was. We saw little of each other for a long time. The young lady had left her husband, but he had not agreed to the divorce she wanted. The separation itself had created enough of a scandal that reporters could be found on the doorstep at Fairfield and even at her family home in Bristol, Rhode Island. Until her husband agreed to let her go, Estelle was very anxious to keep our troth absolutely secret; our meetings were few and always under cover of a trip to town for doctors or dentists or shopping in the company of a woman friend. An embargo was placed on even a mention of our great happiness to anyone, lest Mr. Godfrey become aware of the true nature of things.

I took a very modest apartment on Lexington Avenue in the Sixties and showed it to Estelle one day when she was able to come to New York. I told her that I hoped she would not be too unhappy living in such modest surroundings after the opulence to which she was accustomed. She said that the opulence had not made her happy and that wealth meant less than nothing to her. Then, noticing the very beautiful suit she was wearing, I said I hoped she wouldn't mind the change that would have to occur in her wardrobe either. She said she wouldn't mind, and then that maybe she wouldn't have to change it . . . because she had a little money of her own.

I said, "You mean enough for hats and things?"

And she said, "Oh, yes, quite enough for hats . . . and for some dresses, too."

It then transpired that from her deceased father's estate she had a trust income of eleven thousand dollars a year. I was stupefied. One doesn't think of a girl of eighteen with a comfortable income marrying a man over sixty, as she had done. Yet I suppose it happens every once in while. There was the Vanderbilt girl and old man Stokowski, for instance, not to mention the little Nagle girl who became old man Sturges' fourth wife when old man Sturges was entering his fifties.

Much as I disliked the un-American idea of marrying a lady with a dowry, I must admit that little Mrs. Godfrey's little private income put everything in a faintly different light. She would not, for instance, be limited to meat only once a week as my Grandmother Biden and I had been, nor would she have to dress exclusively in hand-me-downs, gifts from friends, or costumes purchased at a fire sale.

Estelle came back from the extended visit with her aunt in Boston and the first thing she did was to sublet a little country place with a pool near Hackensack, New Jersey. Then she bought a Stutz open car to get back and forth in. I continued to run my business out in Brooklyn with reasonable application, but presently found myself spending more and more time out near Hackensack. I suppose it was the pool, but it might have been William and Mary, the Negro couple Estelle had engaged, who put out some very fine dinners. Everything was going along happily and smoothly and then . . . RED ALERT!

Mr. Godfrey had become aware of and much irritated by the whole situation, and suddenly we were tipped off, I think by a housemaid at the Fairfield place who had been very fond of her young mistress, that Mr. Godfrey was on his way to the house near Hackensack to revenge himself upon us both. Whether he intended to catch us in a compromising position or whether he intended to arrive with a shooting iron, we did not know.

We hopped into the Stutz and headed west.

Greeley's advice seemed to me as good as when he first gave it. My objective, of course, was Chicago, where the homing instinct always took me when I was in trouble. I never thought the Stutz was particularly heavy to drive, and possibly I should have oiled it before taking off, but I remember that ride as one of the worst I have had in my life.

Father was his usual charming and courteous self, of course, and made us feel most welcome. He took a lovely apartment for Estelle and bought her a lot of furniture down on Clark Street. We sent for William and Mary to provide a secure household for Estelle. The theory was that Estelle should have her own quarters and that I should live in our family apartment on Goethe Street with Father. But until the arrival of William and Mary, Estelle was frightened alone at night. And after they got out there, I had so little to do in Chicago, being far away from my business, that I found myself in Estelle's apartment a good portion of the time. After a while, everything sort of settled down and was going along as smoothly and peacefully as one might hope and then . . . RED ALERT!

This time there was no tip-off. Suddenly, fairly late at night, the doorbell rang and when William went to open it, some men pushed by him, apparently looking for something. By a fortunate circumstance— one has to be lucky in this world—by the time they penetrated the apartment, I was in another apartment two floors up, whither I had gone by the back stairs. One of our neighbors, who had also had some romantic complications in his youth, had left his kitchen door unlocked. But the whole thing was a nerve-wracking nuisance, so we said to hell with it, sent the furniture back to Clark Street, the servants back to New York, thanked Father profoundly and took off in the Stutz for the East.

Father had told me since I was a little boy, "Always face the music." I had obviously forgotten this. And now that I went back to face the music, there wasn't any. It had almost stopped playing.

There was one more contretemps back in New York, during which I retired for a day with a detective to a suite in the old Waldorf Astoria on Thirty-fourth Street. (It was during this day that I learned everything about detectives that I now know, including, among other things, the *real* reason for the house dick in the hotel. He is supposed to know all the other detectives by sight and to prevent them, if necessary with a blackjack, from getting upstairs and staging a raid involving one of *his* clients.) A day or so later, the lawyers for both sides finally agreed on all of the things lawyers of separating clients have to agree to.

I wanted Mother, who was still in Paris, to meet Estelle as soon as possible, so a French divorce was decided upon. We booked passage on some Cunard liner and went over with all the Singers, who were on board too.

Mother met us at the station and, to my masculine eye, the two ladies in my life appeared to love each other at first sight. So much for the masculine eye.

Estelle and I went to the beautiful Hotel Meurice on the rue de Rivoli where I had lived as a boy, and after a late visit to Les Copeland and his piano, went back there to sleep. But one is too excited to sleep on a first night in Paris. From the balcony I showed Estelle the dawn procession of great two-wheeled farmers' carts bringing a day's supplies into the Halles, the huge central markets—the drivers asleep, the horses wagging their heads mechanically as they plodded along the well-known course. These are replaced now by large diesel trucks which are noisy and stink. Also, their drivers have to stay awake.

The next day, Freddie Singer's wife, Simone, who had known Estelle in Palm Beach, recommended to us a very nice sort of rooming house on the rue de Pergolèse. It was a large and handsome house with a garden in front. The proprietress was a large, heavy, and amiable woman and it was some time after we had moved in there that we overheard her bawling out one of the young woman tenants and realized that we were living in a house of assignation. The young woman was being scolded for coming home full of champagne and not alone, because she might have awakened the "respectable young American married couple" on the second floor. The respectable young American couple were not as married as all that, so the incident struck us as funny. We did not move, of course, but watched the comings and goings around us with new interest.

When I look back over the years and think upon the number of idiotic things that I have caused the people around me to do because of some sort of inherited persuasive gift, I grow purple with embarrassment.

At this particular juncture, I pointed out to Estelle that since the French, like many Europeans, moved around mostly on bicycles, the only way to see France through French eyes was on a bicycle. This was especially true of Paris. Although Estelle was a fine horsewoman, she had never been on a bicycle in her life and had a strong desire to keep it that way, being scared to death of the things. This cut no ice with me. Talking all the while about the beauties of cycling, I took her down to the Bazaar de l'Hôtel de Ville, one of the great department stores of the world, and there purchased two magnificent bicycles, each with three speeds, a horn, and powerful handbrakes.

All the way back to the rue de Pergolèse in an open taxi, being careful not to get a brake handle in the eye, I expounded upon the beauties of cycling in Paris and its environs. I told her about the heavenly asphalt pistes cyclistes in the Bois de Boulogne and in all the other parks, reserved for cyclists alone, and asked her to picture herself whizzing along them in the morning breeze, the leaves dripping with dew. I told her about the pistes cyclistes a few feet removed to one side of all the national roads, smooth and protected, and asked her to picture herself pedaling gaily along them against a background of châteaux and sunsets. Framed by the intricacies of her bicycle, she just stared back at me balefully.

Our return to the rue de Pergolèse with the gleaming bicycles caused much excitement. Madame herself came down into the gravel-covered front yard, followed by the felt-slippered domestics, the husband in the classical black-sleeved, black-and-yellow-striped vest and apron, the wife dressed like any other slavey. A couple of the handsome young ladies who had got in late and were still in their wrappers timidly joined the festivities, the purpose of which was to teach Estelle to ride a bicycle.

My theory was that somebody is put on the bicycle, held upright for a few feet, after which nature and the instinctive sense of balance take over. I did not subscribe at all to the theory of the teacher hanging on desperately to the underside of the seat and galloping up and down all afternoon with his tongue hanging out until his pupil got the hang of it. Madame, who said that she had done a great deal of bicycling before putting on the extra hundred pounds she was now burdened with, did not subscribe to my theory; it struck her as severe and Spartan. The first time Estelle shot into a clump of bushes and landed on her face, Madame took over the teaching.

She clucked and cackled at me disapprovingly while wiping Estelle off, astonished that I could be so cruel to such a darling little wife. Estelle got back on the bicycle and Madame, pulling her skirt up above her knees where it stayed by itself, took a powerful hold on the saddle and pushed the bicycle off toward the other end of the little garden. This time both Madame and Estelle disappeared into the bushes. For the rest of the afternoon, with many screams and hoarse yells, my bride-to-be was kept in a more or less vertical position racing around a more or less elliptical path with the breathless Madame bouncing after her like an attached balloon. I use the term "more or less" about these things because next to a hog on ice, a young woman on her first bicycle in a yard covered with loose gravel is one of the most independent things in the world.

Madame herself took a number of Brodies, landing twice on her aspidistra, the chamber valet in the striped vest was hit and run over three times, and one of the young ladies in a kimono was edged from the rear, whooping like a calliope, straight into the bushes. All in all, it was a breathless afternoon. When Estelle managed finally to wobble once around the whole yard, unsteadily, but alone, the applause was deafening. Madame invited us all in for a drink, and we limped after her into the cool kitchen. To celebrate the event, she opened a bottle of Blanc de Blanc, which tastes exactly like champagne if one has never had champagne.

Presently Estelle and I were spinning along the cyclists' paths in the Bois and she said that she enjoyed it very much. Encouraged by this, I became more ambitious and took the two bicycles by train to Senlis so that we could bicycle to the village of Fleurines and then up the hill to the house I had lived in as a boy. The project wound up in disaster. It was the hills. Hills are never pleasant to the bicyclist, but if one has been bicycling all one's life, one can at least push up them. The beginning cyclist does not have the muscles for this and just cannot manage it. Estelle burst into tears at the first long hill, and though I tied her bicycle to mine with a rope and did most of the work from then on, she didn't stop talking for the rest of the day about how much she loathed bicycles. If we hadn't been sincerely and thoroughly in love with each other, our marriage plans would have blown up right then and there.

This would not have displeased my mother, who already, long before I married the lady, had found things to dislike about her. The matter did not come to a head until a couple of years later, but when it did, it was extremely disagreeable, and had long-lasting results.

Estelle, having maintained residence in France long enough, was granted a divorce by the courts in July 1923. There must have been some kind of interdiction about the period of time before a remarriage or we would have been married at once. With the divorce secured, we packed our bags, had a farewell luncheon of chicken supreme with Mother and Isadora and Isadora's one and only husband, the mad Russian poet Serge

Essenin. A year or so thereafter, Mr. Essenin cut the veins of his wrist and wrote a farewell poem with his blood. We sold our beautiful bicycles to the chamber valet and his wife, who had been coveting them since the day we first got them, kissed Madame goodbye, waved to the young girls in the windows and took off for America.

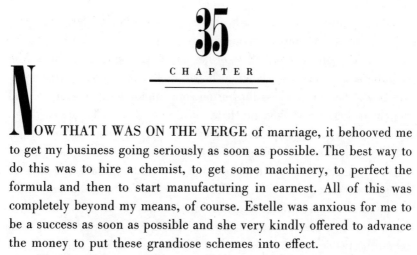

NOW THAT I WAS ON THE VERGE of marriage, it behooved me to get my business going seriously as soon as possible. The best way to do this was to hire a chemist, to get some machinery, to perfect the formula and then to start manufacturing in earnest. All of this was completely beyond my means, of course. Estelle was anxious for me to be a success as soon as possible and she very kindly offered to advance the money to put these grandiose schemes into effect.

The first thing we did was to look around for a store that was big enough to house a small cosmetics factory and we found one at 33 Throop Avenue in Brooklyn. We pulled the old partitions out of 84 Boerum Street, then moved the stuff over bit by bit to the new store. We bought some grinding and sifting machinery and ended up with a very nice laboratory and a place to package and to wrap the finished products. Then I bought a printing press and started printing labels and brochures. I invented a way of printing on curved porcelain jars and rounded aluminum tops with cuts made as rubber stamps are made. I see a great number of bottles with printing on them now, but I had never seen any then. Possibly the method had been used a long time before, but certainly I invented it for my own needs.

Upstairs over our cosmetics factory there was a very noisy billiard hall, which gave way to a sweatshop that was noisier still. One day the sweatshop went out of business and while the heavy sewing machines were being carried out, Estelle and I looked at each other and said, "This is a chance that may never come again; they may put a boilerworks up there next." Hurriedly we found Mr. Jacob Saperstein, the proprietor, and added to our lease the second floor.

I told Estelle about the thrifty French, who are very serious about their businesses and live in the backs of them or over them. I asked her if she would come to live with me there after we were married if I built her a nice apartment with my own hands. She said that she would come to live with me there even if I hired a carpenter to do it. I did build it myself and also installed a bathroom and a hot-water heater, and when we married in December 1923, we moved there and had a lot of fun.

We learned to cook and I got her an electric sewing machine. She couldn't sew on it, so to show her how easy it was, I took her measurements and laid out a dress for her on some almond-green linen we had bought in Paris, and then ran it up on the machine. The dress was in one piece and the only mistake I made, never having been a ladies' tailor, was not to realize that the great differences in a girl's measurements (34–22–36, for instance) require some kind of temporary openings or releases so that one can get a small measurement down over a larger one.

When I tried to pull the green dress down over Estelle, who didn't know any more about dressmaking than I did, all went well until I tried to get the twenty-two-inch waist over her thirty-four-inch bust. She had her arms up over her head and the dress was stuck tight. I told her that she wasn't using any goodwill; just to let the air out of her lungs and there would be nothing to it. She exhaled and I pulled the dress down a little further, and it stuck tight again. This time she became hysterical and began crying and screaming and running around like a chicken with its head cut off because she couldn't see anything either. I had to trip her up and pin her down with a wrestling hold while I cut her carefully out of the dress, down the middle of the back where I could put some hooks in afterwards and not ruin all my work.

The business started going better and better. One day I received a visit from two young men who were with a perfumery distributing company called the Lionel Trading Company and who wanted to be the exclusive distributors of the Desti products. After a long negotiation, I finally signed an exclusive contract with them to be my representatives. In exchange, they agreed to purchase not less than the enormous amount of one thousand dollars' worth of Desti products per month. That was at the end of February 1924. I became dizzy with joy and felt that at last the business I had been in since my boyhood and that my mother had given to me on her departure from America in 1915 was finally going to be successful and bear rich fruit.

Within sixty days, Mother returned from Europe and asked for her business back.

I was aghast, not so much at giving up a profitable business as at giving up the only business I knew, the only business I had ever been in, the only trade or profession with which I was familiar. I pointed this out to my mother, but for the first and only time in her life, she was adamant.

I would gladly have given her, or at least shared with her, the profits, but she was not interested even in discussing such an arrangement.

I had to give the business back to her, of course. I couldn't prove that she had given it to me. Rather than litigating our differences, I gave her the trademark Desti and retained the right to the name Red Red Rouge and the privilege of manufacturing it, Mother binding herself not to use the Red Red Rouge name. The documents were signed in November 1924 and by this time there was no business left. The Lionel Trading Company had withdrawn from the scene and I had closed and dismantled my little factory.

As there was no further reason for living in Brooklyn, Estelle and I found a very lovely studio apartment on Thirty-ninth Street that had once been a stable.

One day Estelle's half-brother asked to buy the James de Wolfe estate in Bristol, Rhode Island, which Estelle had inherited from her mother, now deceased. I handled the matter for her and got her a very fair price. She immediately invested it in a remarkable estate we found between Peekskill and Yorktown Heights in Westchester County.

This extraordinary country place had been put together by a very wealthy gentleman called Edward Harden, who bought many hundreds of acres to assemble it. By the time we bought it, they had sold off all of the acreage except the heart of it, 109 acres with a 19-acre millpond, a marvelous buckwheat mill, and the waterwheel, flume, dam, and waterfall that went with it. It also had a farmhouse and two most attractive, though small, ready-made Bossert houses. These gave us all the rooms we needed. There was a large icehouse on the place, too, where the ice cut from the pond was stored in sawdust and lasted all year. The ice from the pond also supplied all our neighbors' needs for ice.

I have earlier described the insidious and dangerous charm of army life in peacetime. I now became exposed to the dangerous charm of the life of a country gentleman whose wife had a little money.

It is true that I made some inventions: an intaglio photo-etching process that I thought was going to make me rich and for which I received a U.S. patent; a design for a vertical takeoff plane for which I received nothing, but which is just coming into use today; and a design for a very tiny light automobile with a removable and exchangeable power plant in the rear and an air-cooled motor.

All in all, though, I spent most of my time fishing the same fish out of the millpond with barbless hooks and throwing them back in again, or swimming in the pond myself, or teaching people who were persuaded that they couldn't swim how to float. Some of these would float away from the dock occasionally when my attention had been distracted, and become extremely nervous and irritated before I went in and got them. My enemies at this period called me Professor Fish.

Back in New York, my mother had, as usual, found an extraordinary apartment in the very center of things at 603 Fifth Avenue, between Forty-eighth and Forty-ninth Streets. This whole third floor had once been the abode of the ravishing Peggy Hopkins Joyce. Mother had also revived the Desti business to some small extent in a part of that apartment. She was not manufacturing the products, however, nor did she have a chemist, so the business was run in its usual haphazard way. Mother was putting a few strange perfumes into whatever bottles she could find and having a small firm make some powder as much like the Desti powder as possible for her. She did the same thing with the rouges. Of course, the old reliable Secret of the Harem, Desti's Youth Lotion, was still there.

Up at the millpond, life went on its lazy way. We had a bright little neighbor who interested me very much. His name was Andrew J. McCreery. He was a Brooklyn lawyer who had entered politics and, during the time I knew him, became a New York City magistrate who sat in traffic court. It was he who told me about politics and how Tammany got the vote out in bad weather; how repeat voters vote under the names of many people, some of whom are deceased and some only sick in bed. He told me how judges take turns in doing the necessary dirty work, such as dismissing a case against the scion of a powerful family who has unintentionally run over a child and whose case really should be dismissed, except that the Hearst papers are gunning for him. He explained how a judge who deserves a present is given it, not through a traceable amount of cash, but through a completely untraceable tip on the market. Over time I learned from him many other things about politics which would have been of the utmost value to me had I been a writer, for instance, or a motion picture director who wanted to make a film on the subject.

Around January or February it used to get too cold up at the millpond for civilized living. We had central heating of a sort and roaring wood fires, but the water pipes froze if one didn't empty them, and the chemical toilet is an invention of the devil. At that time of year we would go down to our charming apartment on Thirty-ninth Street in New York, and that's where we were at the beginning of 1927.

Since I no longer had a business, I was discussing some plans with Veldheusen, my friend in the perfumery business to whom I had sold all my furniture before moving into Georges Renevant's chicken coop. I suggested going to Paris for him to do some buying and manufacturing to help put his business on a more solid basis than it was at the time, and then to take an active part in it. I told Estelle that we would probably have to pay our own fares, that there was a gambling element to the whole setup which might, quite possibly, not pay off. On the other hand, the chances might turn out to have been pretty good. I then asked her how she felt about going to Paris.

She looked at me strangely and said, "Why don't you go alone?" This does not sound like a particularly startling remark today, but at the time I felt as if she had slashed me across the face.

I had a childlike faith in the institution of marriage then, rather than my present admiration for it based on observation. Two people actually do become one in a true marriage, and that's why it works. While Estelle and I were together, I never looked at another woman, I mean admiringly. I didn't even like to dance with another woman and feel her breasts squashed up against me. That all of this was highly ridiculous and probably some form of arrested development, I am the first to admit. But that's how it was.

I said, "What do you mean? How can you say such a thing?" Then she took a long breath and said, "Because I really don't love you anymore . . ." Then I said that under the circumstances, it would be very immoral of her to continue to frequent my bed, after which I cried like a ninny. It must have been a revolting sight. I left for Chicago the same day, dragging my high principles after me.

Why Chicago? Maybe because it was far away, but probably because I had to see *somebody*. I didn't want to see my mother, who I felt was actually responsible for my predicament, having taken the business away from me, making of me a slightly ridiculous person living on his wife's income.

Father received me charmingly as always, told me how sorry he was, patted me on the back, and opined that I would get over it. My Aunt Mary Sunshine had just returned from Spain and was living with Father, and I was very happy to see her, as she had been a second mother to me when I was a small boy. I thought everything was going to be fine and that after a few days my troubles would be forgotten and that would be that.

In this frame of mind, I went to bed and almost to sleep.

Then it hit me. They say pain carries no memory, that it is impossible to recapture it enough to describe it, but that is not entirely true. I knew that I couldn't stay in bed anymore, but got up and walked up and down the long hallway of our apartment. I went into the dark front room and sat down. I got up and walked up and down the corridor again. Finally I went into Father's room and apologized for waking him, then sat on the floor beside his bed and held his hand. I stayed there all night, probably dropping off occasionally, but not aware of it.

In the morning Father went to his office and I stayed with my aunt for a while, then dressed and went to walk beside the lake. The pain got worse and worse, like an iron bar across my heart, accompanied by the absurd persuasion that it was unendurable. This, of course, was nonsense, because if anything becomes unendurable, one stops enduring it. I went back to our apartment and standing at the window, feeling that I was already dead inside, I decided to go down to the lake that night and get the rest of it over with. At that exact instant, I heard a blood-freezing scream, and a mason who had been working on the sixteenth floor of the Ambassador East fell, passing within six feet of the window where I was standing, and crunched on the sidewalk below me.

All ideas of suicide left me permanently and I left for New York. Before leaving, I sent Estelle a telegram telling her I had misjudged the great depth of my love for her and that I would require a little time living with her to get used to the idea of living without her. It seemed a normal and friendly request, and as the train roared through the night, I rehearsed the impending scene with her over and over again. In my scenario, she invariably acceded to my modest demands. As we had been wonderfully good and tender friends, and her remarks on the morning of my departure the only disagreeable ones that had ever passed between us, I had every reason to believe that she would behave in real life exactly as she was behaving in my mind.

When I got to the apartment on Thirty-ninth Street, however, Estelle had vanished without a trace.

Now began the three most terrible weeks of my life. I don't think I slept or ate, although this is probably an exaggeration because our old Chinese servant used to bring me things on a tray and then cry with me, reassuring me, "Missy come back, Missy come back." I think I went clean off the top. I called every place in America where the girl could possibly have been—relatives, friends, acquaintances, anybody. I got little notes from people I had called, attempting to comfort me, each writer absolutely sure that this was only a lover's spat.

During those three weeks, my entire character changed. Having nothing to be proud about, I had been always unpleasantly prideful. My pride most certainly vanished. I suppose I had some sort of nervous breakdown because ever since, certain chords of music which had not that effect before have made me cry. I subsequently found another thing, too. Whereas other people's troubles had always struck me as being very boring and only symptoms of weakness, I now had sympathy for people and their troubles.

In other words, those three weeks, without teaching me anything about the craft, gave me the heart of a playwright.

Finally one day Father telephoned from Chicago to say that he was coming on to New York and, what was vastly more important and stupefying to me, that he was bringing Estelle with him. So *that* was where she had been, calmly and peacefully, while I had been breaking apart in New York.

I found out subsequently that Estelle had become afraid of what I might do and had boarded the Twentieth Century in New York at about the same time I was boarding it in Chicago. We had crossed paths midway. She had gone to stay with Father who foolishly (but who knows? Maybe not . . .) had given his word not to tell me where she was.

Our meeting at the station was calm and peaceful, too, at least on the outside. I was seething within. We went to the Gotham Hotel, where Father intended to stay. At last I had a chance to state my case and to ask for a short adjustment period which I felt would save my sanity. The lady who had been the apple of my eye, the joy of all my days and the princess of my dreams less than a month before, laughed at my request. I learned for the first time how completely through with a man a woman is, when she is through with a man. None of your masculine namby-pamby, none of that long-drawn-out, sentimental nonsense. She is as businesslike and impersonal as a slaughterhouse employee, scratching the calf's ears at one moment and taking its sweetbreads home for lunch shortly thereafter.

I went back to Thirty-ninth Street, packed my things, and then went over to the Hotel Breslin on Broadway and registered. Don't ask me why. The second night in the Breslin, a bedbug showed up in my virtuous couch. I seemed to have completed some kind of cycle.

I DIDN'T WANT TO SEE MY MOTHER any more now than I had when I left for Chicago. She must have felt a little as I did about her not insignificant role in my present troubles and then have talked it over with Father, who was worried about me, because she telephoned me at the Breslin and asked me to come to see her.

When I got to her wonderful apartment at 603 Fifth Avenue, it was full of female laughter, which I like, and I started feeling a little better right away. Then Mother introduced me to the girls who were laughing with her, and I felt better still. One was a young blonde called Abbie and the other was Jeanne Eagels' kid sister Elaine, also blonde and also young.

Mother remarked that I was looking pretty glum and asked if I would like a drink while she poured a big tumbler full, or nearly full, of bathtub gin for me. Bathtub gin is what we called it during Prohibition because that is where the bootleggers were supposedly concocting it. I looked at the tumbler and said, "I wonder if I really ought to drink that because I haven't eaten anything yet today, and if I take that on an empty stomach, I might feel it." And my mother said, "If you don't want to feel it, why would you drink?"

I drank it and felt better still.

After a while, she told me that she had been talking about me with Father, and they both felt that the sooner I got back to work, the better it would be for me. Father, she told me, had said that if *she* would give the Desti business back to me, *he* would give me an allowance of one thousand dollars a month for a year or so, so that I could rebuild the business and get it into shape. Mother told me she was quite willing to do this. She would go to Europe and stay with Isadora, who was greatly depressed and needed a friend, if I would do my best to send as much of Father's thousand dollars a month to her as I could, retaining only enough of the money to rebuild the business. I said that of course I would and then, to seal the deal, I took her in my arms. We promised each other never to lose our tempers with each other again, and so far as I remember, we never did.

To supplement her quite small revenues, Mother had taken in a bunch of Russian refugees she found somewhere and started them making batiks. The batiks they painted were very pretty and looked like all sorts of things, including stained-glass windows. The batiks were made into shawls, scarves, curtains, cushions, and sometimes special panels for making dresses. Whenever one of the Russians slipped up and made a spot or some imperfection in the design, Mother would say, "That shows it's handwork." After the batiks were painted, they were sent first to a hemstitcher to prevent their unraveling, then to a man who steamed them, removing the wax separations between the colors and the excess dye. If the batiks were to be shawls, they were sent to a man who tied on the long fringes. It was a bright red shawl made here that killed Isadora Duncan.

Of course I wasn't over my broken heart yet, and everybody must have got a little weary of my hangdog expression because I really looked like the last plume on a hearse. One day while Mother and I were walking down Fifth Avenue together, Mother looked at my grim and dismal face.

"You know," she said, "it's a funny thing about smiles . . ."

"Who's talking about smiles?" I growled.

"I am," said Mother, then continued amiably, "When your head is full of happy thoughts, you smile, don't you?"

"I suppose so," I grunted.

"All right," said Mother. "Now listen carefully. It also works the other way! With a smile on your face, your head will fill up with happy thoughts!"

"Where did you hear that nonsense?" I rasped.

"Try it," said my mother. "Go on, see if you can smile."

So I tried to, and the result was I looked like such a gargoyle that my mother burst out laughing in my face, and right after that I was howling along with her, and very shortly thereafter my head was full of happy and cheerful thoughts. There must have been something to her theory.

I had quite a lot to do, of course, which took my mind off my troubles. Also, I was a bachelor again for the first time in three years, or nearly five years, if one looks at it another way. And it's surprising how a young, single male just happens to meet young, unattached

Aboard the Destiny, *1937.*

ABOVE, *going over a scene from* The Great McGinty *with Brian Donlevy, 1940.* RIGHT, *dictating dialogue to my secretary, Jeannie Lavel, 1944.* Facing page, *directing Barbara Stanwyck and Henry Fonda in* The Lady Eve, *1940.*

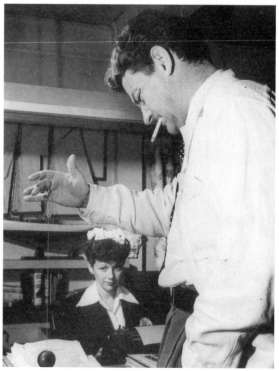

OPPOSITE PAGE, *with Veronica Lake on the set of* Sullivan's Travels, *1941.* RIGHT, *at Paramount with my great friend and ally, Y. Frank Freeman.* BELOW, *on the set of* The Good Fairy *with Margaret Sullavan and Caesar Romero, 1934.*

LEFT, *the rented horse that cost me a movie company, 1946.*
BELOW, *directing Betty Hutton (in bed), Eddie Bracken, and Diana Lynn for* The Miracle of Morgan's Creek, *1942.*

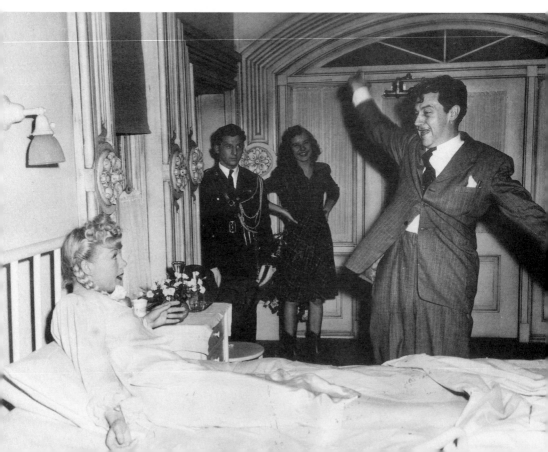

ABOVE, *Los Angeles, 1949.* LEFT,
Anne Margaret Nagle, my Sandy.

Sandy presents Tom-Tom and little Preston to their half-brother, Mon.

females. 603 Fifth Avenue became gayer and gayer and I spent a great deal of time *not* thinking about my lost love.

One of Mother's very charming friends was Jeanne Eagels. According to Jed Harris, she was one of the two *great* actresses he had seen in his lifetime, the other being Laurette Taylor. Jeanne used to come around and take us to a speakeasy called Tomaso's on Forty-fifth Street, west of Eighth Avenue. I mention this because a couple of years later, when I wrote *Strictly Dishonorable,* I laid it in Tomaso's, and the lovely set by Raymond Sovey was an exact duplicate of the little joint. At the time I speak of, Jeanne was in rehearsal for *Her Cardboard Lover.* When the play opened, it was her performance in it that made it appear a lot more important than it was.

Presently Father's first check for a thousand dollars came, and Mother packed her things. Just before locking her trunk, she threw in a beautiful bright red batik shawl for Isadora, who loved everything and anything to do with revolutions, including the symbolic color. Mother sailed on April 23, and joined Isadora in Paris on the thirtieth.

I realize now that my whole life was changing in that spring of 1927. Looking back, every move I made seems to have had a definite place in the scheme of things. I had to be a young man alone on the town to meet a certain young actress. I had to meet this certain young actress for her to irritate me into becoming a playwright. I had to play the piano a little in order to write songs, and I had to write songs a little to invite the young actress up to hear one.

In the back pages of *Popular Mechanics* I saw the advertisement of a gentleman calling himself Piano Bill, who guaranteed to teach positively anyone, down to and including an Albanian busboy, how to play the piano by ear, in any key, in I have forgotten how many days. I sent for more information, but the course at fifty dollars was naturally much too expensive for me, so although tempted, I let the matter drop.

But now a whole selling process began to take shape. Little by little and step by step, as I had not bitten at the first offer, follow-up letters arrived, offering me Piano Bill's course for ever decreasing amounts, always for some splendidly logical reason. There was the reduction before inventory, for instance, which brought the cost down to twenty-five dollars; then the clearance sale of last year's course to make room on the shelves for the new, about-to-be-issued course, which brought the cost down to ten dollars; then the fortunate discovery of a few slightly

fly-specked courses, offered for quick action and for three days only, at
the unheard-of price of five dollars. Finally there came a simple and
straightforward offer to teach me all there was to know about the piano
for one dollar cash. It was obviously not a chance to be missed. If I hadn't
been impulsive and had waited a little longer, I probably would have got
the whole thing for a quarter with an autographed picture of Piano Bill
thrown in. But I was impatient and sent my dollar, and I have never
regretted it.

For some reason, I started out with the master arrow pointing to
the note *G*. After memorizing the twelve passing chords, the rolling bass,
the ragtime bass, the syncopated bass, and the waltz bass, not to mention
the fill-ins, jazz breaks and other musical secrets, all in the key of *G*,
I felt it would be an affectation to study any other key. Instead I bought
a second-hand upright piano for eighteen dollars and founded the
Sturges Music Publishing Company to publish the songs I was now
writing several of a day.

The songs were all in the key of *G*, but I hired a dear little man
called Sammy Grossman, who came to me from the Damrosch School of
Music with the ink still wet on his diploma, to transpose the songs and
to write the orchestrations.

What with songwriting, revitalizing the perfumery business and
catching up on my bachelor days, time melted away until the second
week in September.

37
CHAPTER

SUDDENLY NEWSPAPERS ACROSS THE WORLD headlined the death of Isadora Duncan in an extraordinary automobile accident in Nice in the south of France. I received a telegram from Paris Singer to tell me that Mother was all right; she had not been in the car. I did not know then what had happened or that the bright red shawl Mother had taken to Isadora was the instrument of fate. The papers carried all sorts of explanations of how the thing had happened, but it was not until I got a semicoherent letter from Mother, written while she was still in shock, that I had any picture of the terrible event.

"You will understand why I haven't written," Mother's letter said.

The shock has been too awful. I put Isadora in the car and before she had gone five yards, I called to her that her shawl was dragging. Suddenly the car stopped, I thought because I had called about the shawl. But it was really because the chauffeur saw that her dear head was drawn down beside her knees. She had not been one minute in the car. I ran and thought she had fainted, but I realized her head was caught in the folds of the red shawl she had taken away from me and which she wore always (the painted shawl). The fringes had caught on the side and wound about the wheel, tearing several times about her neck. This, the jerk of the winding, had broken her spinal column instantly, before she could say, "Oh!" It was so instantaneous that the man sitting beside her knew nothing of it, while I called out, "Isadora, your shawl!"

I never lost my head for a second. Fearing she was choking, I ran and got a knife, tried to cut through, then with scissors. All this took only a couple of minutes. Then I helped lift her into a passing car and we rode, she and I alone and the couple who owned the car, I holding her poor head, trying to keep, trying to get her to breathe, never realizing she was already dead, just we two among all the strangers. When we arrived at the hospital, my heart broke when they told me she was dead. I would never have believed that anything so terribly tragic could have arrived so simply. Only that morning

she told me that she could no longer live in a world where there were
little goldenhaired children of three. We had dined with some friends
the night before, and they brought their darling little three-year-old
boy to the table. She ran out screaming. For years she has wanted
to die, but feared suffering. So she got her dearest wish: to die
instantly without being conscious of it. So she ran to the auto
. . . "Mes amis, je vais à la gloire" . . . and she went at 9:10.

At dinner I suddenly saw a cloud come down, turning deadly
white and trembling. Isadora, terribly alarmed, begged me to tell her
what was the matter. I told her I felt some terrible catastrophe has
happened, that perhaps Preston had had an accident. She said,
"Mary, I have never seen such a melancholy face." She asked the
waiter to run quickly and get me a brandy. As we went across the
street to her studio from the restaurant, I begged her not to try out
the little sports auto that night as I feared a tragedy. Taking my
hand, she danced across the street saying, "I would go all the quicker
if I knew it would be my last ride. . . ." We went into the studio,
she turned on the gramophone and began her dance, singing, "I'm
in love again," and declaring it was one of the happiest days of her
life. Suddenly she saw the little auto drive up and ran out, I running
ahead of her, begging her at least to wear my cape as it was cold.
She refused, saying she would only wear her red shawl. I can scarcely
believe yet that she has gone.

We brought her back to the studio at 4:00 A.M., but they refused
to allow anyone in as everything was sealed by the police. They
wouldn't even allow us to wash her darling face. Next day we arranged her on a bed of flowers. She seemed to be sleeping and looked
like a little Tanagra figure, wrapped in her red dress and her voile
shawl. The whole studio studded with candles looked like an ancient
shrine to beauty, no sign of death, just vibrating beauty. Then we
her friends sat beside her. Raymond came. We brought her to Paris
and strewed the box car that held her corpse with a carpet of flowers,
the casket covered with her purple velvet robe that she wore when
she danced *The Resurrection*. Although Paris Singer, who had been
like an angel and who had never left, not for a second day or night
until we left Nice, had got me a sleeper on a fast train, I went with
Raymond on the slow one to accompany her, as they could not take
a casket on the fast one. As the train started to leave the station, the
most unusual hurricane blew everything and every one about, showers. It only lasted a minute but no one will ever forget it.

Isadora's lovely body was burned while they played the air from Bach ("Ni Re"). She had always told me her soul would never leave until it mounted on the strains of that lovely thing, and so we all felt that second it left. There were more than a thousand people in the chamber, women carrying babies, old men, young girls, students, and not a dry eye anywhere. Elizabeth, Raymond, and I looked at her ashes as they drew the asbestos bed out of the furnace and there was just an outline, almost like the breath of one of her dances, all lovely, all beautiful, all sacred. There could never have been decay or decomposition when she was where she was. They say the thousands standing outside never took their eyes from the smoke as it turned from dark to light. . . .

When Mother came back to this country, early in 1928, I got the simple and horrifying story again from her own lips. Actually, said my mother, who by then had recovered from the first shattering shock, it was a good thing. Isadora was drinking heavily, had become as fat as a balloon and was daily destroying the legends of her past loveliness and the dignity of her great position among the artists of the world. As she approached fifty and lost all semblance of a waistline and her last remaining appeal for the opposite sex, a sort of delusion seized her. She believed that she was irresistible to young men.

The night before the tragedy, she and Mother had been in a café bar where a young man had tried to interest Isadora in the purchase of a small French car called the Amilcar. This type of car, which is open and has wire-spoke wheels, was known in Europe as a cycle car. When Isadora kept asking more and more questions on the subject of the car and appeared to be on the verge of purchasing it, Mother drew her aside. The only money they had, Mother reminded her, was what I was able to send over. This would certainly not be sufficient for even so small a car as the Amilcar.

To Mother's considerable embarrassment, Isadora told her that the car was merely a blind, something to talk about, that the young man had not the faintest illusion about selling her a car. It was herself the young man wanted. Mother tried as gently as possible to say that any young man who coveted a woman not only twice his age, but approximately twice his weight, was hardly worth having. This just made Isadora angry. She told Mother that it was her soul the young man saw with eyes of love and that a soul never put on any weight. Isadora moved away from Mother and the ladies spoke no more for the rest of the evening.

The next evening at about six-thirty, Isadora came to Mother's room in the hotel they lived in next to the studio. The two old friends made up, then went across the street to a little café to seal the friendship with a glass of port. Actually it was Mother who had the port. Isadora had something a little stronger. They had a simple dinner, and at nine o'clock they recrossed the street to Isadora's studio, where the young man was to bring the Amilcar for the promised demonstration.

After a while, he arrived. Mother tried one last time to discourage her friend from this nonsense, but Isadora would have none of it. She put the beautiful red batik shawl Mother had given her, two yards long, sixty inches wide, and made of heavy silk, across her shoulders. She climbed into the little two-seater and sat in the bucket seat set about a foot further back than the driver's seat. The young man began a spiel about the mechanical beauties, the riding comfort, and the engine power of the Amilcar. Then he climbed in, started the motor and revved it up thunderously. Mother asked the young man to drive carefully and he told her not to worry, he had never had an accident in his life. Mother stepped back. Isadora called out gaily, "Adieu, mes amis. Je vais à la gloire," and with her right hand tossed the right half of the hanging shawl across her throat and over her left shoulder. The young man let out the clutch, and as the car moved forward, Mother noticed the fringe of the shawl dragging behind in the dirt. She called out, "Your shawl, Isadora, your shawl!" At the same moment, the car stopped. Mother saw Isadora's head bent down and thought that she had fainted. She had not. She was dead.

Silk is terribly strong, and the first full revolution of the wheel caught some of the long fringe in the wire spokes, and instantly tightened the shawl, pulling it like a vise across Isadora's throat, yanking her head down against the side of the car, smashing her face, severing the jugular vein and breaking her neck. It is difficult to imagine a more instantaneous, or less painful, death. It was Mother who went through a rough time trying to get her friend into a hospital or to help her in any way. My mother died three and a half years later of myelogenous leukemia. Nobody knows anything about the condition or what brings it on. It might be shock.

CHAPTER

IN NEW YORK, the excitement about Isadora's death subsided after a while, and I continued to write songs, take care of the Desti business and the various appointments I had with the members of the fair sex.

I got into the office of Mr. Bernstein of the great Shapiro, Bernstein Music Publishing Company on the strength of one of the beautifully engraved calling cards I sent in, its appearance suggesting a man of substance. Sammy Grossman, my arranger, of course had sneaked in behind me. When he came out from behind my overcoat, Mr. Bernstein realized what we were there for and that he was trapped. At the mere prospect of listening to a song, he looked so bitter that I thought it would be useless to push matters further and offered to withdraw. At this, he yelled, "Never mind! Now that you're in, let's have it," and immediately stuck out a weary, hairy paw for the lyric.

In anticipation of this moment and for the purpose of charming the publisher before he had even heard the song, I had had a beautiful cover drawn and artistically colored by one of Mother's Russian batik painters. The sight of this seemed to further infuriate Mr. Bernstein, but not as much as did my title, "Smilin' Your Troubles Away." The song had to do with the fact that if one smiled, his troubles would blow away, or at least be minimized. "Another one of those goddam cheer-up songs," he snarled to his male secretary. Sammy broke into an opening that would have done honor to Rachmaninoff, then vamped till ready. I now gargled the song, after which we took our departure without further comment from Mr. Bernstein.

Another reluctant song publisher endured our renditions of "Ramblin' Along" and "Here's Hoping." "They're amateurish," he pronounced, handing back the lyric sheets, "and you won't know why they're amateurish because you *are* amateurs."

One day Ted Snyder of Waterson-Berlin and Snyder said, "You don't know a goddam thing about lyric writing but you can write short sentences," and then proceeded, every day for about two months, to give me a lesson in the construction of popular songs: how superfluous words, there just for the rhyme, are absolutely forbidden; how the accented syllable of the word must jibe precisely with the accented beat of the music; how a short word phrase must have a short music phrase—and vice versa. And in time I got over most of my amateurishness.

Sammy made a wonderful orchestration of a number of mine called "Sandy Shores," which was played publicly for the first time at the Roosevelt by Ben Bernie's band. The band hadn't had time to rehearse it and had great difficulty playing it. I died a thousand deaths and nine hours later still had a headache. The title was changed to "Asia Minor Blues" and it was broadcast on WRNY a couple of days later. It did not begin a stampede to my door.

Father was getting a little tired of sending a thousand dollars a month and had either stopped doing so or was about to stop doing so, arguing, not without logic, either that the business was a bottomless hole or that he was getting out of the business, he did not know which. In any case, I thought I had better go out and spend Christmas with him and suggested the plan in a letter. He wired back that it seemed like a waste of money, but to come ahead.

Now over the years I worked out a certain technique about going to Chicago, always a faintly delicate visit. Part of this technique consisted of arriving in a horrifying old suit that Father would not care to have me seen in around the University Club. This would startle him into saying, "For God's sake, where did you get that thing?" and then, hardly giving me time to make a hopeless gesture, he would add, "You'd better go down to my tailor first thing in the morning and order yourself a couple of suits. And is that the only shirt you've got, for God's sake?"

I arrived in Chicago about December 18, and was immediately told to go the very next morning to Father's tailor. But the next morning a terrible thing happened. I woke up with a very severe pain in the lower right side of my abdomen and, locating the pain at one-third of the way up from the hipbone to the navel, I realized I had appendicitis.

This presented a severe problem. Appendicitis meant an operation, of course, and operations cost a lot of money. In my mind's eye, I could not see Father, having just paid a whopping hospital and surgeon's bill, sending me down to his tailor to have a couple of expensive suits made. I thought I had better get down to the tailor's and order the suits before I told Father about the impending operation. My theory was that once the tailor had cut into the cloth, there was a pretty good chance that I would get the suits.

I dressed therefore and got into a cab, but I was already much sicker than I had imagined. I started swelling up like a poisoned pup and had to unbutton my pants and half recline on the seat of the taxi. Arriving at Father's tailor's, I made a very poor impression walking in holding my pants together as if they were a little brother's. I made an even poorer impression a few minutes later, when my internal troubles got up a full head of steam and I threw up all over the fitting room, including the mirrors and the ceiling. However, they more or less had my measurements by then, and I had chosen a dark gray, single-breasted sharkskin and a double-breasted blue serge. They helped me out to another cab, probably hoping I would croak on the way home. They nearly got their wish; not on the way home, but about a week later.

As soon as I got home, I telephoned Father and told him that on the way back from the tailor's I had been seized by a terrible pain in my belly, that I had pinpointed the trouble and that it was appendicitis.

"What are you, a doctor or something?" said Father, somewhat irritated by this unpleasant and probably expensive news. "You always exaggerate everything."

I bleated, "I'm not exaggerating anything at all, Father. I tell you I've got appendicitis and unfortunately I need a doctor, and quick!"

"All right, I'll send one," said Father disagreeably.

And he did. The doctor happened to be a cousin of ours and I think he must have been the worst doctor in the world, because he took my temperature, said that I had no fever, that without a fever I couldn't possibly have appendicitis, then departed, telling me to take bicarbonate of soda every half hour until I felt better. The gentleman had apparently never heard of a blood count, nor of people like me who rarely have a fever. I took the bicarbonate of soda every half hour. I don't know why I am alive.

Father came home that night and very cheerfully said, "You see, I told you that you always exaggerate!"

I continued to take bicarbonate of soda. The day before Christmas I was dying. I shook with great chills, then the room blacked out. When I recovered consciousness, I started shaking again. I knew that this was it and made one last effort. I got out of bed, but I couldn't walk anymore, or crawl. I dragged myself down the long corridor to the dining room where the phone was and managed to get Father on the line. I told him very simply that I was dying, that if he wanted to save my life, he'd better send the doctor quickly. He started to tell me that I always exaggerated everything, but I passed out again before he finished. When I came to, he was there with our cousin, the doctor. This gentleman was on the phone in a frenzy of activity. One look had shown him the magnitude of his diagnostic error and he was now trying to get a surgeon and an operating room in a hurry. Father was looking pretty glum and he patted my head and said that he was sorry. I passed out again and when I came to this time, there were some stretcher-bearers putting me onto the kind of stretcher one can get into an apartment and down the stairs. When I saw the waiting ambulance, my heart began to sing and I sang right along with it. I was probably off my rocker a little because now I knew I was going to live.

They didn't waste any time in the hospital either. They took me right in, prepped me and made me swallow a couple of big pills. The next thing I remember was the most beautiful music I had ever heard, the voices of young women singing Christmas carols as they went by my room in the maternity ward the next morning, which was, of course, Christmas. I focused my eyes on them with some difficulty and they were very beautiful, the graduate nurses in white, the two-years girls in blue, and the beginners in tan, all carrying lighted candles, peeking into my room as they went by.

THE FIRST FEW WEEKS of recovery were dangerous and painful; the burst appendix had caused peritonitis to set in, and penicillin was then unknown. One of Father's friends visited one day and brought me Irvin S. Cobb's little book called *Speaking of Operations—*. Nobody who went to the hospital in those days got out without having had several copies of the little work dropped on him by solicitous friends. That wonderful title was inspirational. What a marvelous title it would be for an operetta, for which I would write the book and the songs. I knew I didn't know anything about writing librettos for musical comedies so I asked Father to bring me all the books he could find on playwriting. One of those he produced was Brander Matthews' *A Study of the Drama*, a book of splendidly lucid and sane theatrical advice. Whatever I know about the theatre, whether much or little is a matter of opinion, came out of this book. Among many other things I learned from it and believe fervently, was that when one writes something for the public, aims it at the public, offers it to the public, and the public still doesn't want it, one has missed his aim.

I was sure my aim was true. Toward the end of the six weeks I spent recuperating in the hospital, I wrote a synopsis, a couple of scenes, and the lyrics. It had everything. A semi-invalid millionaire, his young and beautiful daughter, a long-lost wife, and an impecunious young man working as a waiter to pay his way through medical school, as the main characters; and a story with comedy, pathos, and sex. It had places for love songs, a blues number, a sextet from *Lucia,* a chorus of nurses in high-kicking dances, and a boffo finish with the whole cast singing "Speaking of Operations": "They sliced me and they spliced me . . ."

The pretty young nurses and the interns who stopped by to hear the daily installments appeared to be much amused.

Back in New York, I called on Irvin S. Cobb, who was not displeased with the idea of turning the little book into a musical comedy. He said he liked my synopsis. He said he liked my scenes, too, in spots.

He had no wish to collaborate, however, nor to supervise the project, but was willing to let me use the title and his name for a fifty-fifty split of the royalties. Ted Snyder thought the idea was a wow and offered to write the music. I was delighted. Everybody had heard of Irvin S. Cobb, a lot of people had heard of Ted Snyder, but nobody had heard of me but me. I got to work.

It didn't take me very long to conclude that my *Speaking of Operations* must have been conceived and executed in a cloud of anesthesia. What had seemed to me in the hospital the funniest stuff I had ever read seemed to me in New York not only not funny, but heavy with a distinct odor of herring.

I continued to poison the offices of song publishers: DeSylva, Brown, and Henderson; Agar, Yellen, and Bernstein; Leo Feist's; Remick's; Waterson-Berlin and Snyder, presenting them with such little honeys as "Just Like a Thief in the Night (You Stole My Heart Away)", "Just Because You Smiled" and a real lulu called "Even the Skies Are Crying (Now That You've Gone Away)". All I got out of it was the sincere advice to go into some other line of business.

I was not entirely discouraged, however, and the professional reaction to my work had nothing whatsoever to do with the way these numbers were received when warbled by me at 603 Fifth Avenue, accompanied by myself on the piano. All the renditions were in the key of *G,* of course, which was the only one I could play in, although it was a little high for my voice.

Hope Hampton came to hear me and so did Odette Myrtil, and it is doubtful that these thoroughly experienced musicians were much impressed by my naive efforts. But others who came to listen to me bellow "Maybe You'll Be my Baby" in a voice like a goat, at the same time slaughtering the piano, nodded their heads solemnly and approvingly. The news soon went out that holding forth at 603 Fifth Avenue was a young composer whose music the world was waiting to hear.

The residue of this period is a very deep suspicion concerning the opinions of people who tell me about some new and wonderful artist they have discovered.

Tin Pan Alley was the goal, and but for a disagreement with a girl I was taking out, I might never have indulged in another form of self-expression.

The girl was a fairly celebrated young actress when I met her and invited her up to 603 Fifth Avenue to hear some of my songs. The friendship ripened with peculiar rapidity, and the girl, as jealous as she was talented, in no time at all was subjecting me to scenes worthy of more important attachments. The bitterness, the reproaches, the quotes from tragedies in which she had appeared, burst out of her like bandits out of the hills, and with as little warning. Then one day she told me the truth: she had never liked me at all. It appeared she was writing a play and trying out the scenes on me. She could hardly wait until I saw myself portrayed on the stage, saw what an oaf I was, with what boorishness I was accustomed to conducting myself. Oh, she gloated, then I'd see. I meant no more to her than a guinea pig meant to a scientist.

"If *you* can write a play," I told her, "*I* can write a play. And what's more, my play will be produced first and will run longer!"

I went home and wrote the third act of my first play, *The Guinea Pig*, that night. But a third act does not a play make, and it took a month to come up with the first and second acts. I didn't get into trouble until about the third day. Everything had been going smoothly; characters had come on, addressed each other wittily and gone off; page had followed page until I thought there was really nothing to this racket. I was full of confidence and exultation, and then . . . SCRUNCH. Everything came to a grinding halt. The dialogue ceased to flow. My characters stood onstage looking at each other. The clockworks had run down. The marionettes were frozen.

When I was able to turn them into something like real people again, what I called the hook system was born. The hook is a word or an idea spoken by one character which gives the next character something to hook onto when he responds; or, like a trapeze artist, gives him something to swing from on his way to another point of view. From then on, my trouble never lay in inventing dialogue, but in throwing three-quarters of it away.

Of course, that wasn't the only problem I had to solve in becoming a playwright. Avoiding the cardinal sin of having one character tell another character something he already knows, as in, "As you are aware, Mary, the master and mistress have been away for three months . . ." was easy, but I never found a fool-proof method for getting the characters on and off the stage—each entrance and exit was a new challenge to one's inventiveness. I was very, very new to the profession, and there was a lot I didn't know I didn't know.

The young actress who had irritated me into playwriting got over her fit of jealousy, and pretty soon I was taking her out again. One night I brought the script of the just finished *The Guinea Pig* with me and asked her if she'd like to compare the quality of our scripts. She might never have heard of the play she was writing, so uncomprehending was her reaction. It turned out that she wasn't writing a play at all, that she had never intended to write a play, and the fact that I had taken her ravings seriously enough to write one myself was, well, flattering, she guessed. But she didn't want to read it; she never read the works of new playwrights. Besides, she said, if she didn't like it, it might very well spoil our friendship. After a while, I persuaded her to look at just a couple of pages and, with great reluctance, she sank into the couch and held out her hand for the script. She read a couple of pages and a couple more and when she reached the end of the first act, she looked up and said, "But, darling, this dialogue is like champagne!"

Thus began the great adventure.

The Broadway producers I could get to were unanimous in their overpowering desire not to present *The Guinea Pig*. But I talked about it everywhere, looking for backers, looking for somebody who knew somebody who knew a producer. At a dinner one night I met a Mrs. Grace Bicknell from Provincetown, Massachusetts, who had some connection with the Wharf Theatre there. Mrs. Bicknell loved the play, at least as I had told it at dinner, and thought the theatre's reader should have a look at it. When she left for Provincetown the next day, she had a copy of the script with her.

The Desti business kept itself afloat but as usual could never quite make it to a profit position. I wrote some more songs, enjoyed the pleasures of a bachelor's life and looked for backers for my play.

Suddenly out of a clear sky the Wharf Theatre asked for permission to stage *The Guinea Pig;* they had, it appeared, a stinker on their hands and they needed a fast replacement. I borrowed twenty-six dollars to get up there and Mrs. Bicknell, fearful that the presence of the great playwright might unsettle the actors, introduced me to the cast as a friend of hers called Peter Jackson.

On opening night, I learned a little more about the craft of playwriting. The curtain went up on Act I, and the next thing I knew, with the audience hardly settled in its seats, I heard the closing lines of Act II coming across the footlights, and the curtain rang down. When we figured out what had happened, Peter Jackson stepped to the stage and took the audience into his confidence. *The Guinea Pig* was a new play by a new playwright, I explained, and they and the management had just witnessed what happens when a playwright writes exactly the same cue in two different acts. If they would stay in their seats, the play would begin again and the management hoped that they would enjoy it. The audience was charmed with this glimpse of backstage life. They stayed in their seats, and pretty soon I was lost in the great pleasure of hearing people laugh at the lines I had written. The play ran for a week, a triumph by Wharf Theatre standards.

I left my watch as security for the fourteen dollars I owed my Provincetown landlady and drove back to New York, gratis, with a rich friend who owned a car. He dropped me off at Pirolle's Restaurant on Forty-fifth Street to have the sixty-five-cent lunch on the cuff, my credit there being excellent because my French was. Monsieur Pillet, the owner, was persuaded that I had a close connection with Russian nobility, French being the language of choice in those circles, and looked at me knowingly whenever I maintained that I was a simple American born in Chicago, Illinois.

My old friend Georges Renevant, in whose chicken coop I had lived in the fall of 1920, was there polishing off his own sixty-five-cent lunch.

"What are you doing these days?" Georges asked.

"I have just returned," I replied, "from the out-of-town trial of my first play and I am glad to reassure you that it is marvelous."

"What are you going to do now?" Georges wanted to know.

"Have lunch," I said.

"No, I mean to live," he said, and then added, "Why don't you come over and see if Pemberton will give you a job. I'm rehearsing a play for him and I'm a very good friend of Antoinette Perry, who is staging it . . . "

Pemberton was Brock Pemberton, a renowned Broadway producer, and I instantly remembered the first time I had ever seen him, back in 1919. Daisy Andrews had taken me to stand in the back of the theater, where we saw the last act of *Enter Madame* on its opening night. There was a great deal of applauding and hurraying as the curtain fell, and the commotion presently changed into yells for the producer. After some urging, a rather vinegary-looking, bald-headed man sidled out of the wings and riveted his eyes firmly on his shoes. Then, in the warm accents of East Kansas, he froze the audience to its seats by informing it that all this hollering and hand clapping and general hullabaloo was all very well, but that the real story would be told the next night at the box office. Gilda Varesi took one more bow and tried to smile, but the party was over, the lamp was out, and the audience filed out as if it were following a hearse.

"Why should Pemberton give me a job?" I asked Georges.

"Because," said Georges, "you are practically a famous playwright already, embryonically speaking, of course, with one great hit to your credit, nearly, and the one thing they can always use around a theatre is a playwright."

After lunch we walked over to the theatre. I think it was the Biltmore, but it probably wasn't. Georges left me outside on the sidewalk while he went in by the stage door to do things his own way. After a while, he joined me on the sidewalk and we walked completely around the block to the front entrance of the same theatre. We entered the dark auditorium and found Brock Pemberton sitting dismally by himself in the third row watching Miss Perry guide a bi-colored cast through the complexities of a little play called *Goin' Home,* concerned with miscegenation and murder.

"This is Preston Sturges, the playwright," said Georges, presenting me to Mr. Pemberton, "He has just returned from a brilliant success in the provinces and I wondered if there might be something for him here."

"Something like what?" said Mr. Pemberton, looking bitterly at the mop of black hair on the top of my head.

"Oh something like . . . anything," said Georges. "Something like an assistant stage manager maybe, or something like that."

"I am certain we do not need any more assistant stage managers," said Mr. Pemberton, evading my eye, "but I'll ask Tony."

With one slantwise sneer at my wrinkled suit, he wandered down to the footlights and called, "Tony, do we need still one more assistant stage manager who is also a great playwright?"

"My God," said Miss Perry, overdoing it a good deal, "I should say we do! Where in Heaven's name were you able to find one? That's *exactly* what we need. Hire him at once!"

Mr. Pemberton looked longly at his shoes, then balefully at me.

Finally he turned slowly to Georges and contemplated him with the warmth of a cobra gazing at a mongoose.

"I see," he twanged through both nostrils, "that you spoke to Tony first."

He gave me a job as second assistant stage manager, and I learned a lot from him and dear Tony. Jack Gilchrist, who became a great friend, was the stage manager. My first assignment was to keep the author of *Goin' Home* out of the theatre. He was always hanging around making suggestions, and Mr. Pemberton wanted him put in a cage somewhere. Jack advised me to take him to the café around the corner and any time he mentioned getting back to the theatre, to invite him to have another.

Naturally I did not overlook the tremendous advantage working for a great Broadway producer gave me. I revealed to Mr. Pemberton that, right under my arm, I had what would probably be the greatest hit of his career, *The Guinea Pig*. I told him how enthusiastically the play had been received by the Provincetown audiences, that there were lines in it so hilarious that they stopped the show. He looked at me as though he should have known better than to have let me in the door in the first place, and said I could give it to his reader. He, himself, in case I hadn't noticed, was putting on a play.

The reader wasn't bowled over. Tony thought that with some more work, I could make an excellent comedy of it. My boss joined the list of producers anxious not to be connected with the Broadway presentation of *The Guinea Pig*, and I kept on beating the bushes for backers.

Jack Gilchrist couldn't stay on as stage manager when Mr. Pemberton and Miss Perry got ready to produce their next play, and overnight I went from second assistant stage manager to stage manager. The play, written by Paul Osborn, was excellent. The cast was perfect, with the solitary exception of myself, who at age thirty played a boy of fifteen (for fifteen seconds). The sets were artful and pleasing to the eye. The production was first class; the actors, first rank; there was plenty of money for publicity. We opened to a full house with overflow lines at the box office.

And the play flopped.

It was the title that did us in. It was an excellent title, but it corresponded not at all to the content of this excellent play. Mr. Pemberton had chosen the title, *Hotbed*, because it seemed to him a superb title to lure into the theatre not only the audience that the play itself would naturally attract, but also Broadway innocents looking for hot sex.

Actually, the play concerned a university professor who finds himself at the center of a hotbed of intellectual revolution. A piece in which young intellectuals wrestle with philosophical problems addresses itself to the most cultivated strata of the public, a public resolutely hostile to the libidinous vaudeville promised by the title *Hotbed.* That public stayed away in droves. On the other hand, the spectators attracted by the title *Hotbed,* who were licking their lips in anticipation of the titillating scenes they were about to see, left the theatre frustrated and furious before the end of the first act, disgusted and outraged at orgies which were only cerebral. They understood nothing and above all had no wish to understand anything, even supposing that they could have.

In less than three weeks all of us were out on the sidewalk looking for work.

40

CHAPTER

THE BOSS GAVE ME A LETTER of recommendation, remarking as he handed it over that having had a taste of the theatre, I would probably never do another honest day's work in my life.

A bunch of us drifted into a loose federation that got together when the activities of our separate evenings were consummated—or not—drinking coffee at Child's restaurant till nearly daybreak. We were all of the theatre and talked our own language, eventually dubbing ourselves the Broken-Down Stage Managers Club. We argued heatedly, those late nights at Child's, we spun out our dreams and hopes, talked about our ribald love affairs and tried to figure out what was wrong with a theatre that had not found a place for five inspired men like ourselves.

And naturally I talked a lot about raising the fifteen thousand dollars it was estimated that it would cost to mount *The Guinea Pig*. Charley Abramson said he thought it could be put on for a lot less than that. "How much less?" I asked. Charley studied the set designs at the front of my script, counted the number of characters in the cast and said that with a little economizing, it could be done for twenty-five hundred dollars. Jack and Oscar and Jerry said he was crazy. But Charley had been around the business a lot longer than the rest of us and, for me, twenty-five hundred dollars became the talisman figure.

It was the figure I threw out at a dinner party when one of the other guests asked what it would cost to put on the wonderful play I had just told them about. His surprise at the comparatively slight sum was as sharp as mine had been. The hostess, Mrs. Horace Stackpole, excused herself from the table and went down to a desk at the end of the room. When she came back she said, "Here's your play, Preston," and handed me a check for twenty-five hundred dollars.

At Child's that night, Charley lit a cigarette and said I'd better find out first if the check was good. It was, and Charley, who was a lawyer, immediately incorporated the Guinea Pig Company. He also found a three-hundred-seat theatre for three hundred dollars a week. The set designer built the sets in exchange for twenty-five percent of the anticipated royalties. Alexander Carr, the great comedian of *Potash and Perl-mutter*, agreed to play the part of Sam Small for a small salary and ten percent of the gross, provided that we bailed him out of his hotel. The bailout cost us $750. For fifty bucks a week, Oscar Serlin became the stage manager, and I pulled in the same amount as producer. We didn't hire any assistant stage managers.

Trying to walk a tightrope in gale winds is a less precarious venture than trying to get to Broadway on twenty-five hundred dollars, including an out-of-town tryout. We rode out one crisis after another. The leading lady and the leading man quit during rehearsals to take parts in a better-financed production. Their replacements did the same thing. By the time the third leading lady came aboard, we had forty-three dollars left in the till for her costumes; she needed a street dress and an evening gown. I suggested she take the money and outfit herself at Klein's basement. She said she'd cut her throat first.

I stoked the furnace, swept up the stage and did all the odd jobs I had done as Brock Pemberton's second assistant stage manager and some I hadn't, economizing in every way I could.

Rehearsal money ran out. The cast had never performed the play for an audience and, before we opened in New York, we desperately needed an out-of-town tryout, the normal cost of which was about five thousand dollars. We needed a miracle. Instead came inspiration. I remembered having seen a play at the Beechwood Theatre, a beautiful summer playhouse on the old Frank Vanderlip estate in Scarborough, just a few miles out of the city. If I could persuade them of the engaging novelty of a winter production in their summer theatre, they might allow us its use for our tryout. They were captivated. For thirty dollars a night, with the gardeners thrown in as stagehands and furnishings from the mansion lent for the sets, the play opened, greatly charming the residents of Scarborough who came to see it.

The play had been enormously improved since its debut in Provincetown; during rehearsals, Alexander Carr had taught me how to point a joke. In his part as written, the jokes were funny, he said, but they'd be a lot funnier if the point came at the end instead of at the beginning. A joke, like a bee, should carry the sting in its tail. To show me what he meant, he took the speech in which his character assures the leading lady that her job is entirely secure, and winds up his assurances, contradictorily, with: "And if you're still here, maybe even there'll be a

Christmas present." Mr. Carr rearranged it: "And maybe even there'll
be a Christmas present . . . if you're still here." He was right; it was a
great deal funnier that way. I advanced another step toward the mastery
of my craft.

On January 7, 1929, *The Guinea Pig* opened in New York at the
President Theatre. It was an evening of delightful torture. All of us
young, all of us poor; clammy-handed and ashen-faced, hoping for the
best—the chance in a thousand, but fearing the worst: ridicule and
failure. Mine again the memories of my first first night: the little theatre
packed downstairs; Charley Abramson wringing his hands in the empty
balcony; Mother sitting in the third row, laughing with trembling lips;
the great George Kaufman in the worst seat in the house; the asbestos
curtain sticking four feet up from the stage; the man who walked up to
the box office and actually bought a pair of seats; the awful night of
waiting for the morning press to hit the streets.

The reviews were uniformly encouraging and, though not raves,
they were the very balm of Gilead to me. I was a playwright. The little
play ran for sixty-seven performances. I bought a scrapbook and pasted
in it everything I could find that had any connection with *The Guinea
Pig:* reviews, advertising, publicity, tickets, everything. I still have it.

Incidentally, it was in this play that I got the biggest laugh I ever
got in the theatre. It came about this way: The young leading lady, trying
to write a successful seduction scene, asks the youthful leading man just
exactly what a young man would say to a young girl so that she would
give herself to him instantly. I always expected somebody in the audience
to jump the line, but nobody ever did. Everybody's attention riveted on
the young leading man; nobody breathed.

"What would a young man say to a young girl so that she would
give herself to him instantly?" After a moment, the young leading man
looks out over the heads of the audience and sighs, "I wish I knew."

Well, the laughter exploded in the front rows, rolled in a building
crescendo up to the back of the house, poured down to the front, up again
and back, wave followed wave. I can hear it still.

41
CHAPTER

IN APRIL OR MAY, Paris Singer booked passage for me, and I joined him at his wonderful old villa near Beaulieu in the south of France. He was eager to hear all the news and we were very happy to see each other.

One night while I was there, the idea for a play was born. It happened on the road between Monte Carlo and Beaulieu. The night was warm, the air languorous with that suggestion of an African night found only in this one spot in France, and the soft Monegasque moon shone down on me and on the girl beside me in the open car, revealing her cheeks flushed with chaste emotion. We had dined well. We had wined well. Paris Singer's villainous-looking chauffeur was driving. The girl said, "Yes, but if I come to your room, what are your intentions?" I had only one virtue, acquired so young that it was really more of a habit than a virtue: I always told the truth. So I replied, "Strictly dishonorable." Presently she sighed and said, "Well, that sounds rather nice."

Lest I be thought ungallant and the antithesis of the Chevalier Bayard, I will set down what happened next as I set it down for Paris Singer when I wrote to thank him for his great generosity to me: in the form of a playlet, with the names of the principal characters changed to preserve their identity. . . .

The action takes place on the second floor in the wing of a villa. The second floor communicates with the main house by an open-air passageway on the roof over the pantry beneath. It has a private stairway leading to the grounds—a perfect setting for a mystery play, a comedy, a tragedy, or a bedroom farce.

Consider now the actors. They have left the car at the gates. They walk on tiptoe because the world is sleeping and they do not wish to awaken even a titmouse. Two shadows approach the villa, blue-white under the moon, and melt up the little private stair. There is a hasty and fruitless search for a key. Then the taller shadow creeps down the stair and out to the front gate again. He opens the gate. Remaining inside, he slams it shut, then whistling gaily, he crunches his way across the gravel to the main part of the villa. There is no creeping now. He bangs the front door closed behind him, thumps up the stairs, calls a cheery good-night to a slit of light under one of the doors and retires noisily to his own end of the house. As he walks across the open-air passageway, he smiles up at the stars. He is very happy.

Once inside the room, he rushes to the little door, the little door that leads to the staircase from the garden, and to his heart's delight. The key! The key! Thank God, it's here.

The old lock squeaks. He nurses the big bolt out of its resting place, and a trembling wraith steps into the room, slender and fragrant. At last.

They are rather fond of each other. What now? They stand hesitant in the middle of the room. It is nicely but simply furnished. It has a wide bed, a chair, a bureau, and an armoire-à-glace. But the moonlight makes it beautiful. The girl sits. She sits on the edge of the chair. She shows the whites of her eyes, like a frightened animal. The boy sits on the bed. He stretches out a little, lazily. He is in no hurry. Presently it will be over: another memory, another souvenir; a little tender, a little sad. But this, this anticipation, this pause to realize how thirsty one is before one drinks, each nerve tingling, each breath becoming shorter, this is heaven.

"Won't you come over here, my dear? I'm afraid you'll catch cold there, by the window."

His voice sounds strange to him. It belongs to the daylight. Tonight one should sing. Besides, he spoke too loudly. He must watch that.

She rises, fascinated, and lies beside him. Fascinated. Not by him; by something inside her which urges her on and on and on, to do something she knows she mustn't do, something she never has done; something she's thought about since she was ten years old. Fascinated. She lies still. Fear and curiosity mingle with that other thing. Strong, inevitable, like fate itself. What use to struggle? She's struggled so long . . . all these years . . . and for what? It's nice to stop struggling, to float with the current. Restful. She smiles.

How fragrant. How soft these chiffon dresses, so difficult to hook, but so easily opened. How intoxicatingly blends the scent of flowers with the delicate salt odor of life. One more tantalizing bit of chiffon. The last filmy obstacle is crushed aside. The Seventh Gate of Heaven is passed and . . .

"PERONIUS!" and a step on the passageway. "Peronius!"

This time the silver English voice is much nearer. Terror. Horror. Paralysis. No time for the stairs; no time for under the bed; no time for the armoire-à-glace. Perhaps she'll go away. Quiet, she's listening. A step . . . she's going. Then, almost in the room, "Peronius, are you in bed?" The window-door opens slowly.

"DON'T COME IN! I HAVE NOTHING ON!"

Saved. But all atremble.

Very suspiciously, "Are you ALONE, Peronius?"

She must have seen us.

"Am I WHAT?"

"I said, are you ALONE?"

"What a question, my dear Juno, tut-tut, I'm surprised at you."

"Yes, but are you ALONE?"

Singularly persistent, this woman; a one-track mind, apparently.

"Strictly speaking, no. There are three mosquitoes with me, and I think there is a mouse in the corner." That ought to fix her.

With a tinge of vexation, "I wasn't talking about animals. *You* know what I mean."

"I can't imagine what you mean. Surely you didn't think . . . oh, no, it isn't possible . . . you didn't really think I had a GIRL here, did you?" Shivers from the bed.

"Well . . . somehow, I did. That is to say, I don't know *why*, but I was under the impression . . . "

"My dear Juno," quite firmly, "I assure you I am quite alone. And if you will come back later, when I've had time to put something on, I'll prove it to you."

"My dear Peronius, don't think that I *doubted* you. Nothing was further from my thoughts. Well, good-night, my dear."

Slow, and still suspicious, footsteps depart. One cannot tell a lie to take a girl's honor. But to preserve it . . . ?

A groan from the bed. "Christ, get me out of here! I'll never be the same again!"

"But, sweetheart, there's no hurry; it might be dangerous to leave now."

"Danger or no danger, I'm going!"

Two shadows fade down the little stair and out the gate. Presently one shadow comes back. But he is not whistling.

. . .

And that, my dear Uncle Mun, is how a maiden's virtue was saved
for her husband, much may it profit him. Personally, I think Peronius
was guilty of shocking bad taste in taking the girl to his room in the first
place. But you know these mythical characters: they have no manners.

42

CHAPTER

BACK IN NEW YORK, I got a job as assistant stage manager for the road company of a play called *Frankie and Johnnie.* Within a week I was fired because I insisted on getting the eighty-five a week I had been promised, rather than sixty-five a week and a quick shuffle. They didn't know they were fooling with the descendant of a woman born with a caul on her head.

The Chicago police closed the show that night, and everybody had to go back to New York on the Erie, except me. Having been fired, I had to be given my fare back to New York in cash. This meant I had the price and could go back to New York when I liked. It was a bad time to look for a job, and as the beds were soft and the meals regular if uninspired at Father's, I decided to stay with him until I'd written a new play. I thought that task would carry me through the rest of the summer.

Father was kind enough to let me set up shop on his dining-room table, between meals naturally, and there I summoned up that gossamer night on the road between Monte Carlo and Beaulieu. The first lines I wrote down were the two lines of that exchange in the moonlit open car: "What are your intentions?" "Strictly dishonorable."

I had no story in mind, but I knew there were the makings of one in those lines. The creation of dialogue, for me, is an inseparable part of the creation of the story. So many amusing and unexpected things turn up in the dialogue, so many things that one might never have thought of otherwise, that I am convinced the method is good.

I set the play in Tomaso's, the speakeasy on Forty-fifth Street to which Jeanne Eagels had introduced me, and in which the Broken-Down Stage Managers Club had passed not a few convivial evenings. I wrote the male lead with an accent to give the part to my friend Georges Renevant. To the ingenue I gave the maiden name of my Grandmother Biden, Isabelle Parry, and called the play, *Come, Come, Isabelle.*

Once I started to write, I couldn't stop. Considering the bed and board, it was sheer folly to do so, but I finished the play in six working days. I wrote to Brock Pemberton when there were about six pages to go and told him to get excited, the play was practically finished. To Father I confided that I had written probably the best comedy since the memory of man ran not to the contrary; that if the critics thought *The Guinea Pig* showed promise, this play would deliver it in spades. All of this optimism made Father very uneasy. He looked at me as he had when I was a little boy on the back of a pony, prattling about the races I would win when I grew up and became a famous jockey, but without the tender indulgence the look carried in those long-ago days. He thought I was too old for childish crowing; he wondered if I would ever grow up.

Before I sent it on to Pemberton, I changed the play's title to *Strictly Dishonorable.*

When I got back from the mailbox, I calculated for Father how long the manuscript would take to reach Pemberton; how long it would then take him to read it; and predicted that at exactly 11:30 on Saturday morning there would be a telegram from Pemberton telling me that the play was marvelous and that he wanted to produce it. If Father had been given to gestures like grabbing his head, he would have done so, but he just shook it slowly and muttered, "Preston, Preston . . . "

Father went off to his office every morning as usual and I went to the dining-room table as usual and started work on a new play I called *Recapture.*

On Saturday morning, Father and I lingered over breakfast and watched the clock. At eleven he said, "It won't be long now, huh."

"You'll see," I said.

At precisely 11:30, the doorbell rang. I shot out of my chair and yanked the door open. The postman handed me my manuscript stamped Insufficient Postage.

Of course I remailed it, and in just about the amount of time I had calculated, Pemberton wired congratulations, saying the first act was one hundred percent, the second and third acts in need of development, but that the play contained worlds of swell material and he wanted me in New York to try for an August production.

I went back to New York a couple of days before my thirty-first birthday, full of confidence and hope, joyful to be working again with my old employers, Brock Pemberton and Antoinette Perry. This time though, I was the playwright and I wondered fleetingly if a second assistant stage manager might be walking *me* to a café around the corner to keep me out of Pemberton's hair. No such luck. There were three weeks of rehearsal and another week out of town and every day was war. At Pemberton's insistence, scenes were rewritten, dialogue changes went in during rehearsals, and every rewrite and every change was fought over like a fresh kill in a famine. So violent were our disagreements that they resulted in days during which he and I exchanged not a word. As opening night approached, I was absolutely certain that Pemberton had ruined the play; that disaster stood in the wings.

The curtain went up on *Strictly Dishonorable* on September 19, 1929.

I stood grimly at the back of the theatre as Act I unfolded. I heard not even a titter from the audience. Sick with disappointment, I left the theatre and got terribly drunk. I didn't wait up for the reviews; I didn't think I could bear to read the depths of scorn and fury the critics would bring to the attack.

Sometime the next morning a friend called to ask if he could have two tickets to the play. I said of course and telephoned the request to Pemberton. Pemberton called me six kinds of a fool and told me that the play was sold out; that they'd already turned away fifteen hundred people that morning. Didn't I understand, he asked, we had a hit.

And what a hit! The superlatives that the chorus of critics dished out in review after review restored life itself to my battered carcass. I bought another scrapbook and subscribed to a clipping service.

There is nothing like a hit to create between a warring producer and playwright a deep and lasting regard for the talents of the other. And so it was between Pemberton and me.

43

OVERNIGHT MY WORLD had undergone a sea change. I went to bed owing six months rent, having had my last meal on the cuff, and woke up earning fifteen hundred dollars a week. Years of living on the margin, spending whatever I earned and then some, were over . . . for a while anyway. For the first time in my life, I got very cautious. I was afraid that if I bought anything I needed, I would then buy everything I wanted, and that in the momentum thus created there would be no stopping. So I sent my Provincetown landlady the fourteen dollars I owed her, paid up the rent on my apartment at 603 Fifth Avenue, cleared the tab at Pirolle's, and made a vow to buy nothing for a month, or until I got a little more accustomed to having more money than I needed, whichever came first.

The aura of sudden celebrity bestowed on me by *Strictly Dishonorable* attracted photographers, reporters, gossip columnists, professional panhandlers, producers, job offers, and a written demand from my biological father, Mr. Biden, for immediate repayment of the sums he had dispensed on my behalf when I was about a year old.

The market crashed in October, the leading lady got chicken pox in December and was replaced by the understudy, Antoinette Perry's sixteen-year-old daughter, but *Strictly Dishonorable* continued to play to packed houses even during the week before Christmas. The whole business was almost miraculous.

With my play in lights on Broadway, Paramount at Astoria offered me a thousand dollars a week to write a script for a Maurice Chevalier film called *The Big Pond.* I turned it in in two weeks and picked up two thousand dollars. I learned later that the picture company had assumed a ten-week writing period and a tab of ten thousand dollars. When they offered me a thousand dollars a week to write a script for Miriam Hopkins' first picture, *Fast and Loose,* I took their assumptions into consideration and turned in the script in ten weeks and picked up ten thousand dollars.

The other play I had written at Father's dining-room table, *Recapture*, went into rehearsal in the middle of December, did a week out of town in Atlantic City, another in Newark, came into New York on January 29, 1930, and received the most violently destructive notices I had seen in years. It wasn't a bad play, but the liberties I took with its dramatic construction—serving up two acts of comedy and a third act marinated in misfortune—were liberties that the critics might have forgiven O'Neill, but which in me they found brazen. They boiled me in oil and did a swan song on my corpse.

I bought another scrapbook.

Then, on a train south to Palm Beach, I fell in love with a beautiful blonde. She was straight of limb, with a high-bridged nose, a clear forehead, and a sense of humor. As it turned out, a sense of humor was the indispensable attribute required of everyone connected with this little episode, and, as it also turned out, not all of the characters were so endowed.

The beautiful blonde was Eleanor Hutton, the twenty-year-old daughter of Marjorie Merriweather Post and the stepdaughter of her then husband, E. F. Hutton. She was on her way to Mar-a-Lago, a little seventy-bedroom cottage on the sea her mother had built a few years earlier. *Strictly Dishonorable* was the top ticket on Broadway, *Recapture* was teetering, and I was on my way to join Paris Singer at the Everglades Club, which he had built originally as a hospital for shell-shocked British soldiers. He had invited me to visit while I began work on the book of a new operetta called *The Well of Romance*.

Actually, it wasn't a new operetta; it was a face-lift for a used operetta. An immense production with a cast of hundreds called *Silver Swan* had bankrupted its backers, and the composer, Maurice Jacquet, was convinced that a new book and new lyrics for the existing music could make a fortune. The music *was* beautiful, the expensive sets were already built, and back in November I had signed a contract to write the new libretto and the new lyrics. My pals violently counseled against writing a play to accommodate some scenery, but I didn't see it that way.

I didn't get much work done, though. I was in love. She liked me, too, and over the next couple of weeks it was hard to tell which of us was the more besotted. I even went so far as to offer honorable wedlock. I don't remember why we picked that day, but we wanted to get married on June 3. I presented myself to Mr. Hutton to ask formally for Eleanor's hand in marriage. He asked if I were prepared to support the girl in the style to which she was accustomed. I told him that I had proved I could earn my living as a writer, that I had two plays then running on Broadway and that one of them alone brought in fifteen hundred dollars a week. "That's pin money to her," Mr. Hutton said.

Recapture closed on February 13 after twenty-four performances.

The Huttons wanted us to wait for a year or two before there was any serious talk about marriage. When we insisted on June 3, they promptly decided that I was a fortune hunter, a bum, a drunkard, and every other species of lowlife they could think of offhand. They told Eleanor they would cut her off without a cent if she married me without their consent. When I wanted to marry her anyway, it knocked their fortune-hunter theory for a loop, but they weren't finished with me.

At the end of the month, I went back to New York and bought a fifty-two-foot cruiser I called *Recapture*. I had always wanted a boat.

Mr. Hutton put detectives on my trail to try to dig up a bad reputation for me. They didn't find one, of course, but as a result of their snooping, rumors of the romance were all over the papers. I denied anything more than a deep admiration for the young lady, but tales about heiresses, playwrights, and family threats of disinheritance made good copy, and stories continued to appear.

My biological father, Mr. Biden, read the papers too, and a new written demand appeared. He now wanted not only reimbursement for the medical bills I had run up at the age of one, but the thirty years accrued interest thereon, plus reasonable compensation for the setbacks he had suffered when my mother left him. Should I fail to respond promptly, he wrote, he would be forced to reveal to the Huttons that Solomon Sturges of Chicago was not my real father. I had never made a secret of my origins; this letter followed his earlier one into the wastebasket.

Eleanor dodged a hundred objections to my suitability as a husband: I was divorced; I was too old for her—although my eleven years seniority didn't exactly make it a May-December romance; my profession was inherently unstable. I gave her a few things to think about, too, comparing for her the vastly unequal difference between what each of us would have to give up to marry the other. I would have to give up a few women, an amount of money sufficient to feed, lodge and clothe a wife, a few personal liberties like spitting on the floor or going to bed with a hat on. She, on the other hand, would have to give up all the handsome men in Christendom, most of her brilliant friends, an enormously large income, and the name Hutton.

On April 12, 1930, we eloped. Eleanor telegraphed the happy news to her cousin Barbara Hutton at Miss Porter's, and we drove on to Mother's little house in Woodstock. Mother received us with great warmth; champagne and laughter filled the night and we were all very happy.

Around eleven the next morning, there was a knock on the door. We had had a very late night and no one was up. The knocking persisted. I threw on a robe and staggered to the door. A little woman stood on the porch. "Hello, Preston," she said, and asked if Mother were in. It was very early, I said, and Mother had not been well and, as a matter of fact, wasn't up yet. I told the little woman she was quite welcome to come in if she cared to, Mother would undoubtedly be up shortly. She accepted the coffee I offered and after a while she leaned forward in her chair and said, "Preston, don't you know me?" I said that of course I did, it was just that I had such a poor memory for names and that my brain was still swimming in champagne . . .

"I'm Estelle," she said.

There sat the young woman I had loved so much, the girl whose departure a short three years before had nearly destroyed me, looking at me strangely.

It took me a moment to assimilate what had happened and when I had, I realized that it isn't so much that love is blind, it is that love is bewitching. Seen through the eyes of love, Estelle had been to me the fairest of all. Only one thing had changed: I didn't love her anymore. And because I didn't love her anymore, I didn't recognize in this rather ordinary-looking woman the Estelle that the eyes of love had imprinted on my memory. *She* hadn't changed; my perception of her had changed.

This proved an extremely useful insight when I made a little picture called *The Lady Eve,* in which Henry Fonda fails to recognize Barbara Stanwyck, not because she has disguised herself in any way, but because the Lady Eve couldn't hold a candle to the girl in his memory, the girl on the boat.

Presently, Eleanor and Mother got up and joined Estelle and me for coffee. The three ladies found much to laugh about.

. . .

Eleanor came to live with me in my small apartment at 603 Fifth Avenue, and the first thing I had to do was to build some closets for her. Fortunately, she brought with her only a basic wardrobe: morning wear, afternoon wear, evening wear, riding pinks, tennis togs, yachting outfits, bathing costumes, tea gowns, ball gowns, furs, and accessories, just enough to accommodate all climates and all seasons.

We postponed the honeymoon we'd planned, cruising on the *Recapture* for a couple of weeks wherever whim might lead us, so that I could work on *The Well of Romance*. *Strictly Dishonorable,* of course, was still the hit of the season, but we wanted the security that another play on the boards would give us.

One day on her way into the bank, Eleanor met her mother coming out. Hopeful of persuading her that her new husband was a man of substance, Eleanor mentioned our yacht. Her mother asked its length.

"Fifty-two feet," said Eleanor.

"You mean a yole, darling," said her mother, "a yole," relegating the *Recapture* to the class reserved for the sculls I had crewed at La Villa. And so it must have seemed to Mrs. Hutton, builder and owner of the largest ocean-going sailing yacht in the world, the 350-foot, four-masted ship called the *Sea Cloud*.

The Huttons did indeed cut off Eleanor's allowance. There was nothing they could do, however, about the funds that would become available to her under a will on her twenty-first birthday. Although all my pals advised her against it, on the grounds that this operetta starring some leftover scenery was a poor investment, she very sweetly offered to put up the money for the production of *The Well of Romance*. It would be her wedding gift to me, she said. We actually thought that we'd be doing rather handsomely for ourselves, collecting not only the author's royalties, but a share of the producer's as well. Pending Eleanor's receipt of her inheritance, I shoveled in about ninety thousand of my own money for salaries, rehearsals, out-of-town tryouts, and on November 30, 1930, *The Well of Romance* opened at the Craig Theatre in New York. Eight days later it closed.

It was hard for my friends to refrain from saying, "I told you so," but some of them managed it.

44

MOTHER'S HEALTH BEGAN TO FAIL rapidly and in February 1931, I brought her from Woodstock by ambulance to her apartment at 603 Fifth Avenue. She was suffering from myelogenous leukemia, origin unknown. All of her bones ached, and I went in and out of stores all over the city looking for the softest, most comfortable bed and chair made, and brought them to her. When I picked her up to carry her to her new bed, it was like picking up a child; she weighed only about ninety-eight pounds.

Up until this time though, she had enjoyed these years since Isadora's death very much. Suddenly she had started to do all those things she had despised during her entire lifetime. She sewed, she cooked, she cut out clothes, and because she was a talented person, she did these things wonderfully well.

I remembered going to take her to lunch one day about the time that, as an ex-very-pretty woman, she couldn't stand looking at herself in the mirror any more. She put on her lipstick without looking and missed rather badly. I told her I thought she'd better try again. She said, "I just can't bear to look at myself, darling."

She went to the mirror anyway, and she didn't look very good. Her hair had been dyed for so long that it wouldn't take it anymore, and instead of being blue-black, it was purple and orange and green and also a little thin on top. She shook her head ruefully and said, "There's no doubt about it, Preston, I'm breaking up after a hard winter." Then her expression changed and she added with the greatest sincerity and good humor, "But if I'd only known what a heavenly period of a woman's life this is—without husbands, without lovers, without jealousies or stupid angers—believe me, my son, I wouldn't have fought it off for as long as I did."

I always thought that was a remarkable statement for a woman to make. I never heard any other woman say anything that approached it.

I remembered another time, discussing a wife who had left me,

Mother said, "Don't think *she's* having so much fun. Women are absolutely stymied without a man: they can't go *anywhere* or do *anything.*" I don't know how Mother knew this, maybe she read it out of a book, because certainly during the time I knew her, except at the very, very last end of her life, there was always some kind of male around to nail up things or to carry heavy parcels. I cannot remember any time when there wasn't.

Some of the things Mother said a few days before her death echo in my memory, too.

"I know that what I did didn't always make you happy when you were little," she said one day. "I know there were things you didn't understand, but I'm sure they don't bother you anymore. I was only trying to find happiness."

On another day, lying on the bed I bought for her, she said, "Just keep this bed someplace in the house, and if you're ever heartsick or weary, lie down on it and I'll come and put my arms around you, and your troubles will go. . . . "

Mother is still very close to me; her pictures and possessions and ideas and witticisms are everywhere. Not a day passes that she is not mentioned many times. At home in Hollywood, I sleep on her bed.

One afternoon in April, the doctor told me that everything that could be done had been done; it was a matter of a few hours.

Sitting beside Mother's bed as the afternoon waned, I thought about the hungry little girl she had been growing up near the stockyards in Chicago, sent to work in a candy factory for five dollars a week before she was even eight years old. By the time I knew her she had only the nicest things to say about child labor, and she gave me a remarkable scene that I used in *The Great McGinty*. The premises were clean and airy, she said, and the supervisors and overseers all the souls of kindness. Furthermore, the children were allowed to eat absolutely all the candy they wanted on the first day, and were given a free physic on the second, after which they never touched candy again. It was nothing like Dickens' description of child labor.

Then I thought of the remarkable advantages this remarkable mother of mine had managed to wring from a reluctant world and shower upon the head of her unappreciative son. I thought of the oceans I had crossed and recrossed, the countries I had lived in, the operas and concerts I had indignantly attended, the museums and catacombs I had been shoved into, pushed through and dragged out of, the cast of admirable and not so admirable characters who had peopled my early years.

And yet, except that she chose the schools in which I was placed and made a few wise remarks which I remember with pleasure now but thought totally inconsequential at twelve, Mother had absolutely nothing to do with my development or what I grew into. Strangely, Father, who was not my true progenitor, had very much more to do with the shaping of my character than Mother ever had. Mother's admiration meant very little to me and because I had always had it, I took it for granted. But I always had a tremendous desire to be admired by Father. I wanted to be tall because Father was tall, and honorable because Father was honorable, and looked up to and admired because Father was looked up to and admired, and popular with other men because Father was one of the most popular men in Chicago. When Father taught me at the age of four not to tell a lie, I decided never to lie, and I never have. But the things that Mother told me I paid little attention to. I am quite sure that Paris Singer, who replaced Father during my adolescence, had vastly more to do with the shaping of my character than Mother had. Although Mother made innumerable sacrifices for me during thirty-one years of her life and Paris Singer made none, I wanted to be like him. I very much fear that this has something to do with the general esteem in which women are held compared with men. I know it is stupid and unfair, but there it is.

These reflections though were very far from my thoughts that afternoon keeping watch with my mother against the dark. Mother held on to my hand and I leaned over and laid my head down beside hers on the pillow. She had left me behind many times before but both of us knew how terribly final this parting was to be. "There is no tragedy in dying," she whispered to me, "only in never having lived."

At sunset Mother said that she felt that the cord connecting her to antiquity had been cut.

Then in the gathering dusk, Mother slipped away from me. It was April 12, 1931, the first anniversary of my marriage to Eleanor.

ON JUNE 5, 1931, Eleanor slipped away too, sailing for Paris accompanied by my cousin Marian Whitely. She wanted to study for a career as an opera singer, and I promised to do something about the Desti business while she was away. I thought love had ended, but Eleanor told me that I was being foolish.

By August I thought I had figured out why we had both been so unhappy. We had had an awful year. The tiny apartment, the failure of *The Well of Romance,* the weeks of illness and then the death of my mother were, of course, contributing factors, but what became very clear was something else. It was my ready-made conception of marriage, in which the wife plays the role of Chattel and the husband the role of Proprietor, that had nearly done us in. This revelation did not come easily or quickly. I let my romantic life unroll before me from the time I was a half-starved youth to the day Eleanor boarded the ship. With two exceptions, my female companions looked pleased and were apparently enjoying themselves. The two exceptions were my wives. And here a painful fact impressed itself upon my consciousness. It was that although I had always been well-considered and smiled upon as a lover, no one had ever enjoyed me for a single minute as a husband. I finally understood why Eleanor told me, two weeks after we were married, that she'd rather be kept by me than be my wife.

I resolved to change my role to that of Favorite Man, first among my wife's admirers, rather than Owner and Sole Proprietor of this beautiful girl. It was one thing to capture a fort, I realized, and another thing to hold it.

While I sat around ponderously working all that out, I also got to work. Jack Gilchrist's estranged wife, Bianca, who took on the job of my secretary after *Strictly Dishonorable* opened, got behind the typewriter and, though it was hard to get started, we wrote two plays that summer. The first of them, *Cup of Coffee,* took a couple of months to finish. It was probably a little too mild for Broadway, and no producer evinced any interest in staging it. But it was an excellent exercise in writing and served to burn the fat off my brain. I didn't know it then, but a fat-free brain was just what I was going to need.

One evening Charley and I and Arnold Schroeder went down to a dance hall, one of those places, now extinct, where one danced with a hostess for ten cents a dance. We had a lot of fun and we went down again the next night and then for ten nights thereafter. The hostess I drew was a charming little creature who looked like a diminutive Helen Morgan and used such marvelous words as "apperntment" and "berled" eggs and "take yur cherce" and "ersters." Although we spoke supposedly the same language, half the time I didn't know what she was saying and three-quarters of the time she didn't understand me. As a result we found each other very funny.

Then one night I bumped into a reporter friend of mine in a speakeasy on Fifty-second Street. He warned me that one of the tabloids had got wind of how I spent my evenings and had photographers lying in wait at the dance hall to get pictures of me in the arms of a taxi dancer to document the tale of where the playwright played when the heiress was away. I could see the headlines: DANCE HALL DOLLY HEISTS HUSBAND OF HUTTON HEIRESS. I didn't know what to do. I told Charley about the impending story.

"So what?" he said.

"So what?" I said. "It's the worst thing that could happen. The Huttons will seize on a story like this as proof of every unsavory . . . "

"A playwright can go anywhere in search of material," Charley interrupted.

"How was that?" I said.

"A playwright can go anywhere in search of material," Charley repeated.

I got the point. I mentioned my new play and the kinds of places in which I was finding material for it to a columnist, and the story broke without scandal, another item among several others printed that day.

Of course, I then had to write a play. *Cup of Coffee* had limbered me up and got me back into the swing of writing, and I wrote my new play, *Child of Manhattan*, in sixteen days. The basic idea was the attraction between two people opposite in background and education: the leading lady, a beautiful dime-a-dance girl; the leading man, a multimillionaire. Their romance, of course, went a great deal further than the mild adventures of Abramson, Sturges, and Schroeder.

The script was sensational. Everybody who read it wanted to produce it, and even people who had only heard about it made offers. I came to tentative terms with the great producer William Harris and then sailed for Paris on the *Mauretania.*

Eleanor and I had been parted for three months and although neither of us had been very happy in our first year as husband and wife, we were still very much in love. As it turned out, every prince, lord, millionaire, and fortune hunter in Europe was in love with her, too; I couldn't swing a dead cat without hitting a rival. And who could blame them? She was unbelievably beautiful and smart.

I brought my wife back to New York in October, and almost the first thing we did was to buy a five-storey house with an elevator at 125 East Fifty-fourth Street, a house so large that one might not bump into any one of the twelve servants for several weeks. Less than a month later, Eleanor was at Doctors' Hospital on East End Avenue, undergoing an emergency appendectomy. Her recovery was a lot quicker than mine had been for the same operation, because she didn't have my cousin for a doctor and they got to her appendix before it burst. Our plans called for her to spend another year in Paris, where I would join her after the opening of *Child of Manhattan,* probably in March. She sailed in December.

The play went into rehearsal under the aegis of Peggy Fears and A. C. Blumenthal. At the Broadstreet Theatre in Newark, where it did an out-of-town run for a week, the audiences roared with laughter when I wanted them to, cried when I wanted them to, and applauded with many bravos at the end. Nevertheless, the week before a New York opening is not an easy one; the author is assailed with serious doubts.

On the night of March 2, 1932, with such luminaries as Governor Al Smith and Mayor Jimmy Walker in attendance, the curtain rose on *Child of Manhattan.*

The reviews were scalding, the best of them suggesting that I really belonged in some other line of business. "Sheer trash," said one; "As deeply offensive as any ten editions of the low jinks of the Frères Minsky," said another; "Buckety-buckety downhill into bathos and sweetish bosh," wrote a third; "As silly as it is trite," *Time* magazine chimed in. The awful reviews surrounded me like obituaries piled into a funeral pyre. Much of the pain of that dismal morning has subsided as I have advanced through time, but it is still a form of self-torture to page through the scrapbook.

The play ran for eighty-seven performances, but it could not survive the bad press the critics gave it. These doctors of the drama had the final say. Like Molière's physicians, they could not cure but they could kill. I borrowed two thousand dollars from Mr. Blumenthal against my fifty percent share of the movie sale, boarded the *Majestic* and sailed for Paris.

Eleanor and I parted on April 12, 1932, the second anniversary of our marriage. We loved each other sincerely, but we did not like each other. With the dissimilarity of our tastes, our education, and our ideals, there was no hope for us. Accustomed to the way matters of this nature were handled in the rarified circles of the excessively wealthy, she asked, rather vulgarly, I thought, how much I would take to give her a divorce.

I should have replied, "The ninety thousand dollars I spent at your request." But no, a Sturges could never say such a thing, so I didn't either. Instead I said, "It will cost you exactly one courteous request, madame, and a polite thank-you after it is all over."

And that is exactly what I got.

Back in New York, I considered my situation. I was thirty-three years old, I weighed 190 pounds and I was anxious to work. I spoke English reasonably well for a man who had never studied it, having been a melancholy expatriate during my childhood, and I had become accustomed to the lavish style of existence known to the trade as the life of Riley. This because I had written a hit play called *Strictly Dishonorable* and made three hundred thousand dollars out of it. *Strictly Dishonorable* was now gone and so was my three hundred thousand dollars. I had a five-storey house, fifty feet wide. I had a gas bill that I remember as being a thousand dollars a month, although that figure may be a little off one way or the other. I had an intelligent wife divorcing me in Paris, and I had the habit of spending.

I also had before me the unanimous, final, and ironclad decision of the critics, to wit: that whatever else I might be, I was positively not a playwright. Nor was this the first time that they had told me so. With my first play, *The Guinea Pig*, they said my talent was extremely immature, if present at all, which was debatable. With *Strictly Dishonorable,* written six months later, they felt the sure hand of experience and a fertile imagination. With *Recapture,* they said that it was very doubtful that I had written *Strictly Dishonorable.* With *The Well of Romance,* they jumped up and down on my body and tried to squirt the blood out of my jugulars. Now with my fifth play, *Child of Manhattan,* they laid my remains to rest with extreme unction.

All of a sudden I heard laughter, not in my ears but in my memory. The laughter of a large audience, well pleased with what it had paid its money to see, the same *Child of Manhattan.* Then I thought of the people I'd heard laughing at *The Guinea Pig* and *Recapture* and all my other flops, and I began to speculate upon the general health of the theatre when it could be totally controlled by fifteen men, however well intentioned they might be. I knew that Mr. George Jean Nathan referred to himself humorously as The Exterminator, and I knew that he was a sincere man and that he felt that he was doing the theatre a great service by driving the untalented away from it. But I also knew that he couldn't keep a crowd away from a heavyweight fight or a baseball game or even a curling match, no matter what he said or how wittily he said it.

Nor was I persuaded as to my total lack of talent. I was willing to admit that I was not a second Shakespeare, positive that I was not a second Eugene O'Neill, resigned never to scale Parnassus, nor even to get into the Algonquin Grill, but I still thought I ought to be able to earn my living as a playwright.

Then I had a vision.

I saw the theatre as a poor, puny, weak little old man, the last living member of a once rugged dynasty, supported by nurses and peeking out the great gloomy window of a decaying mansion. Surrounding him were fifteen doctors, all well intentioned, who guided, watched over, washed, put to bed, physicked and fumigated the little moribund within an inch of his life. Across his pajamas was printed The Theatre, and what he was peeking out the window at was a big twilly in her working clothes on the sidewalk.

She wore high-button shoes with white tops, a checkered dress, very tight around the *wasistdas,* a wide, patent-leather belt, a feather boa, a big hat with ostrich plumes, and the self-confident smile of a female who knows that what she has, they want. Across her superb frontal elevation was printed The Movies. As I watched, she turned and winked good-

46

IN HOLLYWOOD I STARTED at the bottom: a bum by the name of Sturgeon who had once written a hit called *Strictly Something-or-Other*. Carl Laemmle of Universal offered me a contract, with unilateral options exercisable by the studio, to join his team as a writer. My wife had decamped, my fortune was depleted, and even though I was living on coffee and moonlight, my costs of living continued to cost. I did not have to wrestle with any principles to leap on Laemmle's offer. On September 9, 1932, I arrived in Hollywood with my secretary, Bianca Gilchrist.

I was to write, offer suggestions and make myself generally useful, and for this I was to get a nominal or beginning writer's salary of a thousand dollars a week. Junior writers got less, of course, but I *had* written *Strictly Something-or-Other,* and that made me a kind of senior beginner. I was charmed; it vindicated my contention that writing was my profession, and the money proved it.

There were a great many writers on the lot, and the reason for this was that at the time, writers worked in teams, like piano movers. It was generally believed by the powers down in front that a man who could write comedy could not write tragedy, that a man who could write forceful, virile stuff could not handle the tender passages, and that if the picture was not to taste all of the same cook, a multiplicity of writers was essential. Four writers were considered the rock-bottom minimum required. Six writers, with the sixth member a woman to puff up the lighter parts, was considered ideal. Many, many more writers have been used on a picture, of course; several writers have even been assigned the same story unbeknownst to each other. The Screen Writers Guild of the day had even worked out some rather shameful rules governing the conduct and approach of one writer toward another when he has secretly been given the other's job: he was not in honor bound to volunteer any information, but if asked directly, he must not deny the sad truth.

A man in possession of many bolts of woolen cloth, quantities of lining and interlining, buttons, thread, needles, and padding is not, of necessity, a tailor. A man in possession of many characters, many situations, many startling and dramatic events, and many gags is not, of necessity, a storyteller.

The crafts of the tailor and the storyteller are not dissimilar, however, for out of a mass of unrelated material, each contrives to fashion a complete and well-balanced unit. Many stories are too heavy in the shoulders and too short in the pants, with the design of the material running upside-down.

In constructing a talking-picture play, the basic story to be filmed passes through many hands. Some writer turns out the first manuscript, which, being the first, is condemned even before it is written.

Another writer is called in and the second treatment is made. The second writer is no better than the first writer, but his treatment is vastly different, for the simple reason that every single person in the world will tell the same story differently: see the testimony of various bystanders at the scene of any street accident.

A third writer is now engaged, on the grounds that three are better than one, ignoring the rule that a chain is only as strong as its weakest link. Just as the fourth writer is about to be engaged, with the fifth and sixth creeping over the horizon, word comes from the front office that shooting will begin three days hence.

The script, which is by now voluminous, is carried posthaste to a Funny Man, who believes that only policemen are funny. In two strokes of a pencil, he changes all the male characters to policemen, thus making the script funny.

The script, now funny, requires only a slight tightening up by a Construction Expert in order to be in prime A1 condition. One glance is enough for this expert to detect what is wrong: the end should come first, obviously; the middle should come last; and the beginning should be thrown out. This is accomplished in less time than it takes to tell about it, and the polished script is laid on the desk of the production manager, who takes it home to peruse it. This last, of course, is only a technicality, as the script must surely be right by now.

The production manager, who is not such a sap, returns to the office in the morning, haggard, bulbous-eyed with worry. There seems to be something the matter with the script. It is not that all the material is not there. The proper number of smashed motorcars, the stupendous living rooms, the modernistic bedrooms, the pompous matrons, the sterling workmen, and comic butlers, comic Englishmen, all, all are there. But what in Nick's name are they supposed to be doing?

There is only one thing to be done, and the production manager does it. He calls in another writer. There is no haggling over the fee because time is precious. The story is disentangled and put in proper sequences again. That is to say, it begins at the beginning and ends at the end, passing through the middle. It is now ready for shooting, except for one or two technicalities. First, another Funny Man takes a whack at it and changes the policemen to soldiers. Only one more technicality to clear up and all will be set. Another Construction Expert changes the beginning to the middle; the middle to the beginning; and, now that the play is about soldiers, adds a good rousing battle scene to the end.

Zero hour being at hand, the screenplay is now given to the director, who shoots the script as it stands, excepting only that the locale is changed to the Middle Ages and the lovers meet on bicycles, achieving thus a very comical effect.

The customer walking home in his new suit is razzed by small boys as he passes.

I thought I knew how to put a story together, but it might turn out that I was meant to be a tailor.

Bianca and I were assigned beautiful offices in a little bungalow on the Universal lot affectionately known as the Bull Pen. Its only inconvenience was its location next to the gents' room. All the other distinguished authors who inhabited the Bull Pen had to pass through my office to reach the facilities and on the way out, they always dropped their paper towels on my desk. But at a thousand dollars a week, this was a small matter. I brushed off my desk and counted my money.

I liked the people at the studio and made a lot of new friends. Within a month, I was elected to membership in the Writers' Club. In addition to quarters on Sunset Boulevard housing a bar and a little food where the members could congregate at will, the club had regular Wednesday luncheon meetings of the Corned Beef, Cabbage, and Culture Circle, which I much enjoyed. It was a club for men only, of course, with invitations extended to the ladies on special occasions. Among the active members who became my friends were Rupert Hughes, Doug Fairbanks, Charlie Chaplin, Harold Lloyd, Irving Thalberg, Ernst Lubitsch, John Gilbert, and Will Rogers.

It took me exactly two days on the job as a hired writer, or until I met my first director, to find out that I was in the wrong racket. I had expected my producer to be peculiar, of course, because the facts about Hollywood producers had been well publicized throughout the land. On meeting him, I was not disappointed. About directors, though, I knew very little, and it took me a few minutes to get the point.

It was not so much what the director said, it was the way he said it, especially the way he looked at me (a writer): coolly, confidently, courteously, but with a curious condescension, the way an Englishman looks at an American and an American looks at an Indian. He was a perfectly polite and affable little man and did his best to put me at my ease, but one of my knees kept twitching and I had the uneasy feeling that instead of standing on my feet looking down at him, I should have been on one knee looking up at him. The man was obviously a prince of the blood.

The more directors I met, the more I realized that this was not an isolated case. They were all princes of the blood. Nobody ever had them directing pictures in teams with one of them handling the horseback scenes and another handling the bedroom interludes; nobody ever put them in the Bull Pen or threw paper towels on their desks. The bungalows they lived in on the lot had open fireplaces and private bathrooms and big soft couches. Nobody ever assigned them to pictures they didn't like; they were timidly *offered* pictures. Sometimes they graciously condescended to direct them, but if they said no, a story was a piece of cheese, it was a piece of cheese.

This ennoblement, of course, had been conferred upon directors during the silent days, when the directors truly were the storytellers and the princes of the business. By the time I got to Hollywood, this aristocracy was merely a leftover from an earlier day. The reasons for it were no longer apparent, like the reasons for so many other aristocracies. Years later when I became a writer-director, actually the storyteller again, people said I was doing something new, but I was not; I was doing something old.

As I had never written anything but comedies, my producer assigned me the job of writing the ninth script of a horror picture: an adaptation of H. G. Wells' book, *The Invisible Man.* Hardly any of Wells' story was suited to a motion picture, so it actually meant coming up with an original story. Eight well-known writers had already been paid for adaptations which the studio said could not be used, and I thought that if mine were used, my future at Universal would be assured.

I hurried into the Bull Pen and came out ten weeks later with 180 pages of stuff so chilling that it would cause the hair of a statue to stand on end and cold sweat to stream down its sculptured back. The studio did not pick up its option on my services and I was fired without further ceremony. The director said it was a piece of cheese.

I had just been assigned a rewrite of a continuity for Slim Summerville and ZaSu Pitts when my contract was up, but I stayed on at the studio to finish the job and made them a present of a couple of weeks' work. For this they pronounced themselves grateful, and my hope was that this bread cast upon the waters would return as ham sandwiches.

Although off salary, I was not idle. Thoroughly displeased with the abysmal status of a Hollywood team writer, I considered the benefits of free-lancing, writing scripts on my own time and selling them to a studio later. I could then write anywhere I liked, spend the spring in Paris, for instance, the summer on my boat, the fall in New York and the winter in Palm Beach, coming to California for a couple of days a year to sign contracts for the sale of the scripts.

Free-lancing to me was also a stab at raising the writer's status, if not to the level of prince of the blood, at least to the level of tender of the royal shaving paper or something of equal dignity; anything to get out of the cellar to which custom had assigned the Hollywood team writer.

Bianca got behind the typewriter and I got to work on *The Power and the Glory,* a story inspired by some incidents Eleanor had told me about her mother's father, C. W. Post, founder of the Postum Cereal Company, known today as the General Foods Corporation. The fruits of inspiration bore no resemblance to the actual life and times of Eleanor's grandfather, of course, but I chose the nonchronological structure of the screenplay because I noticed that when Eleanor would recount adventures, the lack of chronology interfered not at all with one's pleasure in the stories and that, in fact, its absence often sharpened the impact of the tale.

The screenplay for *The Power and the Glory* had one thing that distinguished it from other scripts of the time. So far as I know, it was the first story conceived and written directly as a shooting script by its author on his own time and then sold to a moving picture company on a royalty basis, exactly as plays or novels are sold. It established a couple of other "firsts," too. It was the first script shot by a director almost exactly as written. It was also the first story to use what the publicity department dubbed *narratage,* that is, the narrator's, or author's, voice spoke the dialogue while the actors only moved their lips. Strangely enough, this was highly effective and the illusion was complete.

It was neither a silent film nor a talking film, but rather a combination of the two. It embodied the visual action of a silent picture, the sound of the narrator's voice, and the storytelling economy and the richness of characterization of a novel.

The reason for trying this method was to see if some way could be devised to carry American films into foreign countries. It would be extremely easy to put a narrator's voice on the sound track in any language, because the narrator for the most part is heard, but not seen. The further advantage of a narrator is that, like the author of a novel, he may describe not only what people do and say but also what they feel and what they think.

I sold the screenplay to Jesse Lasky at Fox in February 1933 for a large down payment and a percentage of the gross, cast it and directed the dialogue. Shooting started in March.

At that time, very few successful writers had ever watched the whole process of making a picture from beginning to end, including the rushes and the cutting, because they were usually on salary and busy writing something else while their last scripts were being filmed. I, however, was not a successful writer busy writing something else and could do as I liked. I spent six weeks on the set, at my own expense, helping to stage the dialogue and acting as sort of a general handyman, what one might call speculative directing. The director, Mr. William K. Howard, had a nice chair in front of the camera and a property man to take care of his hat and coat. He told everybody what to do and, in general, he had a nice time. Most of my time on the set was spent on top of a green stepladder in the back, watching and learning. Occasionally I would hurry down the stepladder to explain to Mr. Spencer Tracy or to Miss Colleen Moore what I meant by a line and how I thought it should be read, then hurry back up the stepladder and watch it being shot.

And there, on top of the green stepladder, watching Mr. William K. Howard direct *The Power and the Glory,* I got a tremendous yen to direct, coupled with the absolutely positive hunch that I could. I had never felt anything quite like it before. Never while watching a heavy-weight title match had I had the desire to change places with one of the gentlemen in the ring. Nor at the six-day bicycle races, while a fallen rider was picking splinters out of his rear, had I felt impelled to swipe his vehicle and lap the field. Never at the fairgrounds did I envy the man who dove into a barrel of feathers from atop a hundred-foot pole. I am not an envious man. But from the top of the green stepladder, I ached to change places with Mr. William K. Howard, who was doing such an excellent job transferring my screenplay to film.

I did not wish Mr. Howard any hard luck like a bad automobile accident or a seriously broken back or anything like that. I merely wished that some temporary fever would assail him, something not too harmful that would lay him flat for the rest of the shooting schedule, so that the company would implore me, as the only other person thoroughly conversant with the script, to take over the direction in his stead. I have seen that same hopeful look on the faces of my young assistants, and it causes me to watch my step. I watched Mr. Howard with glittering eyes as he nearly tripped over cables, nearly fell off high parallels and sat in countless drafts, which I tested with a wet finger. He unfortunately remained disgustingly healthy, one of the prime requisites of a good director, and I unfortunately remained a writer.

When the picture was released, I naturally received sole credit as the writer, and found my name in the advertisements the same size as the director's.

This, coupled with the deal I made selling the screenplay for large monies up front and a percentage of the gross, made nothing but enemies for me. The directors said, "Who is this bum getting his name the same size as ours?" The producers said, "This sets a very bad precedent; you give these upstarts an inch and they'll want their names up in lights!" The heads of the studios said, "What is this rubbish about giving writers a percentage of the gross which shakes the very foundations of the industry?" The trade press said, "What is this business of shooting a picture by a single writer when we are accustomed to getting ads from six or eight of them per picture?" And the writers, yea, even my breth-ren, viewed with alarm the whittling down of jobs that would ensue if only one writer, God forbid, worked on each script. I was as popular as a polecat and, with all that money in the bank, as independent.

It is true that I was voted that year's equivalent of an Academy

Oscar for the best original screenplay, but it is also true that I didn't get any work for a long, long time. So long that I had to go out and borrow.

Before I got to that stage though, I bought the hull of a seagoing schooner, fifty-two foot overall, which gave me something to live for, filling my mind with repairs and refittings and ropes and chains and teak and mahogany and brass fittings and diesel engines.

It was during this period that I decided to change my profession once more and become a director instead of a team writer. It seemed easier for one man to change his profession than for hundreds of men to so improve theirs that I would be proud to be a screenwriter.

I was sure I could direct because I had just seen it done while I was directing the dialogue on *The Power and the Glory*. I had examined the art at close range and seen no insoluble problems arise. I was sure that I knew more about my own dialogue than anybody else, having heard it in my head before I wrote it down. I was sure I could make myself understood by actors, having done it, and that I could move them around on a stage. I knew I could cast the parts reasonably well, having done it. I knew a little something about photography, having learned a great deal from the photographer I took in at the Maison Desti. I knew a little something about composition, having studied painting for quite a while as a youth. But above and beyond all this was the enormous desire to direct.

Watching the progress of *The Power and the Glory* from the set through the cutting room, I also became aware of the importance of the silent direction that takes place in the cutting room.

Back in 1928, when I was new in the theatre and delighted with my job as assistant stage manager, I used to watch the audience through a peekhole in the tormentor. The thing that astonished me was that all the spectators in the theatre seemed to have their heads attached together so that they all moved in unison. Nine people did not turn to the right while one turned to the left. *Everybody* turned to the right or everybody turned to the left or everybody looked up or everybody looked down. One can see the same thing at a tennis match. I was astonished to see, six nights a week, that one thousand people agreed absolutely exactly on the point of principal interest at any one given moment.

Granted then that there is one point at which an entire audience looks, the next question is, what else do they see while they are looking at this point? And the answer is they don't see anything else.

I experimented by looking at an object in a room and noting what my eyes were doing. I found that I was making for myself an individual shot of the object I was looking at. I use the term *individual shot* rather than *close-up* because, obviously, an object does not come closer by being stared at. What happens is that one's eyes *focus* on that one object and everything else is out of focus and consequently invisible to the mind. Since the mind sees only the object in focus, it becomes larger in *interest*, and in effect a close-up has been achieved.

Incidentally, the phenomenon of the invisibility of everything except the object focused upon is the mainstay of most great tricks of prestidigitation. The magician drops a wand on stage left and while the audience watches him as he leans over to get it, his assistant walks an elephant out of a cabinet on stage right. The audience does not see the elephant, of course, and is deliciously mystified to find the cabinet empty.

Once I became aware of what happens in the cutting room, I began to notice that in some films I was conscious of the cutting and in some films I was not. And then I began to understand that there is a law of natural cutting and that this replicates what an audience in a legitimate theatre does for itself. The more nearly the film cutter approaches this law of natural interest, the more invisible will be his cutting. If the camera moves from one person to another at the exact moment that one in the legitimate theatre would have turned his head, one will not be conscious of a cut. If the camera misses by a quarter of a second, one will get a jolt. There is one other requirement: the two shots must be approximately of the same tone value. If one cuts from black to white, it is jarring.

At any given moment, the camera must point at the exact spot the audience wishes to look at. To find that spot is absurdly easy: one has only to remember where one was looking at the time the scene was made. My friend Rouben Mamoulian told me that he could make the audience interested in whatever *he* showed them. I told him he was mistaken. It is true that he can bend my head down and force me to look at a doorknob when my reflex wants to see the face of the girl saying good-bye, but it is also true that it arrests my comprehension of the scene, destroys my interest and gives me a pain in the neck.

I got to work on my next free-lance project, a screenplay called *The Biography of a Bum* (eventually titled *The Great McGinty*), inspired by the tales told by Judge McCreery back in my millpond days. Jesse Lasky was very much interested in the proposed story, as were the Laemmles, father and son, at Universal. Warner Bros. offered me fifteen thousand to write it and to direct it. It was less than I had received for *The Power and the Glory*, but I was willing to take less in order to direct.

When the screenplay was finished though, all three studios failed to evince any interest in producing it. Everybody said it was beautifully written, but they found the setting too sordid and the story too much concerned with politics. Politics, they were convinced, would not interest women at all, and women made up the majority of the audiences. The day after every studio in town had turned it down, I decided not to sell it unless I was permitted to direct it. It was to be my entering wedge into the profession, my blackjack. After that, it was simple. It only took six years.

At this point, however, I was behind on the rent of my apartment at 603 Fifth Avenue, where Charley and my cat Elmer were keeping things together until my fortunes were repaired and I could get back to a theatre career in New York. I owed thousands on the redesign and refurbishing of my new boat and I had no money left. Nobody had offered me a writing job since Universal fired me, nearly a year earlier. Then my pal Arnold Schroeder, who had followed me to Hollywood in my Lincoln, drove the car off a cliff near the house I was renting up on Bryn Mawr Drive. The hospital bills were heavy, and I realized once again the tremendous expense I had been to Father at various times in my life and wrote to thank him again for his innumerable kindnesses and his great generosity to me.

Foreseeing the worst—no job offers for perhaps months more—I accepted the invitation of William Morris to act as my agent in exchange for his promise to advance the funds necessary for Arnold's hospitalization. He was sure he would have no trouble getting some adaptations for me to do.

William Morris and I were still shaking hands on the deal when Irving Thalberg called to invite me to join his new unit at Metro adapting the book *The Green Hat* as a vehicle for Norma Shearer. Less than a month later I was invited to leave the project. Then came a job adapting the play *Twentieth Century* for Harry Cohn at Columbia. That job lasted four days. Three days later I accepted a two-week job at Universal, which was followed by no work as 1933 came to a close.

In January 1934, I went to Paramount to write an adaptation of a magazine story called *Thirty-Day Princess* for Mr. B. P. Schulberg.

When the details of the deal I had made with Jesse Lasky for *The Power and the Glory* were made public in the pages of the *Hollywood Reporter*, Mr. Schulberg had taken me and the deal on in an editorial in the same publication, excoriating the folly of the single writer arrangement and maintaining, among other things, that any studio supervisor could write as well as any writer anyhow. I disagreed in print with nearly everything he argued. I didn't change his mind, nor he mine. It should not have come as a surprise then that we disagreed on the writing credits for *Thirty-Day Princess*. He, as a producer, was accustomed to accepting praise for pictures as generals accept praise for the valor of their soldiers, and it thus seemed logical to him that the writers should feel the same general sense of shared accomplishment.

I argued that when I cared so little about my work that I became unselfish about sharing credit, that when I was content to hear another man praised for something I had created, and, worse, that when I was willing to accept praise for the work of somebody else, I would have accepted the system and would no longer be worth my salt. Credits to multiple writers, regardless of the quality or quantity of their contribution, robbed one of the pride of achievement. I assured him that when films reached the level of first-class plays and fine books, they would not have been written by pieceworkers. He then hired a fourth writer. When the picture was released, I shared credit with three other writers, although not much of my work was used. Mr. Schulberg was a fine producer, however, and I enjoyed working with him.

An adaptation of *Imitation of Life* at Universal for about a month came next; then I went to work for Sam Goldwyn. Mr. Goldwyn, of course, is always good for a story, although the stories usually center around his supposedly very funny accent. Actually his accent and speaking voice are very charming and have nothing to do with his *Potash-and-Perlmutter*-style of delivery. He is a foreigner and he naturally speaks like one. My good friend Edgar Selwyn previewed what I might expect of the association in a story he told me about him one day.

A rich and powerful New York theatre man was invited by Mr. Goldwyn to come out to Hollywood and join him in his business. Not knowing Mr. Goldwyn intimately, the gentleman, with understandable caution, went to see his friend Mr. Adolph Zukor and asked him his advice about the offer. Mr. Zukor puffed on his one-dollar Corona for a little while, then opined as follows, "From a success point of view, you will reach the absolute top. He is by far the greatest producer in the industry, bar none. From a contractual point of view, he will live up to every comma of every paragraph in every clause on every page. You have nothing to worry about. From an honesty standpoint, you will get absolutely everything that is coming to you down to a fraction of a cent, from every angle of operation, including those that are customarily concealed and impossible to check upon." The old man paused and took a puff of his cigar, then concluded, "But from a happiness standpoint, you will be unhappier than you have ever been in your life. You will never draw a cheerful breath, and each morning you will curse the day that you were born." The theatre man stayed in New York.

I have always enormously admired my friend Willie Wyler's ability to work peacefully and contentedly with Sam Goldwyn for years when his personal loathing for Mr. Goldwyn is surpassed only by Mr. Goldwyn's loathing for him. They loathe and admire each other. It is possible that this total indifference to animosity is a sign of successful men, remote from petty weaknesses. It is an attribute I lack. Animosity directed at me fills my system with adrenaline and I am no longer efficient.

Mr. Goldwyn also loathed *me* and while I was working for him writing the adaptation of Tolstoy's *Resurrection,* released as *We Live Again,* he used to go every morning to the director, my friend Rouben Mamoulian, who had asked for me as a writer, and say eagerly, "When can we get rid of this fellow Sturgeon?" This wouldn't have bothered Willie Wyler at all, but it bothered me, and years later, when Mr. Goldwyn offered to take me on in some sort of a percentage or partnership deal and to actually build a special building for me to assuage my vanity, I turned him down and accepted instead an offer from Darryl Zanuck, a silly thing to have done. And yet, I wonder. I am alive, happy, and reasonably healthy.

Back at Universal, I was hired on at my new rate of fifteen hundred dollars a week to do an adaptation of *Fanny,* the central play of Marcel Pagnol's great trilogy, to be directed by Willie Wyler. Henry Henigson was our supervisor. This story of an older man who marries a young pregnant girl and raises her child as his own, willing to surrender his wife, but not the child, to the young man who impregnated her, could not be written to meet Breen Office standards. The script was revised and revised, but no approach was sufficient to overcome Mr. Breen's threshold objection to a tale connected with out-of-wedlock gravidity, no matter how sweetly resolved. The script was shelved, the project cancelled.

Then on May 28, I signed the contract I had coveted for so long: a contract to become a director at Universal.

TWO DAYS LATER, Henry Henigson asked me as a favor to write one more adaptation before I started my duties as a director. In view of his kindness in securing me a chance to direct, and also because he was paying me fifteen hundred dollars a week, I consented. It was funny, though. Now that I was a director, by contract if not in fact, the attitude had changed. Instead of handing me an assignment, knowing that I would be glad to get it, I was asked if I would be kind enough to help them out by doing the adaptation.

Henry Henigson, Willie Wyler, who was to direct, and I focused our attentions on bringing Ferenc Molnár's play, *The Good Fairy*, to the screen as a vehicle for Margaret Sullavan.

And on that we labored through the spring, the summer, and the fall of 1934. Shooting started in October, and Bianca and I were on the set every day. By this time she and I had fallen into the habit of one another—proximity, I suppose—and had become, without benefit of vows or promises, a duo. She was wonderfully witty, fiercely devoted, jealous, and possessed of a temper that made *my* temper, described by a wife divorcing me some years later as "ungovernable," seem like that of a meadow lark. Two weeks before the picture was finished, Willie eloped with Maggie Sullavan. He asked my opinion of the proposed match beforehand, but he must not have heard what I said.

Near the end of November, I was off salary and started getting *Cup of Coffee* ready for the screen. Shooting was tentatively scheduled to begin around the middle of February 1935, and that meant my directorial debut was only weeks away.

Just when I got a good start on it, Universal asked me if I would take a few weeks off to give them a hand fixing up the *Diamond Jim Brady* script. I consented to do this for a substantial raise, and we ended up signing a contract for four weeks at twenty-five hundred dollars a week, and the same rate per week if additional time were required. This was very important to me because most studios were willing to pay a writer the last salary he received without much quibbling, and this new rate would help me in the writing end of the business if I proved to be a disappointment as a director. Only one or two writers in town were making more.

After *Diamond Jim,* I wrote a couple of scripts, each for a job price rather than a weekly wage. *The Good Fairy* had pleased the critics and when *Diamond Jim* opened to even more critical acclaim, everybody was clamoring for my services. Metro offered me a job; so did Jesse Lasky; Selznick International was talking with my agent, and even Sam Goldwyn wanted to know when I would be available. It was a bull market, but I was loath to go backward in a more or less well-planned career. I was trying for something worth trying for: the chance to direct. I picked up where I'd left off, preparing *Cup of Coffee* for the screen.

Of course, I continued to write songs, too. Ted Snyder, the man who taught me the mechanics of popular songwriting and who had been living in Hollywood since 1930, worked on five of them with me. Willie Wyler used one of them in a picture he directed called *The Gay Deception.*

And every year the Collector of Internal Revenue sent an investigator to call on me to interpret my tax returns with me. In those Depression days, people earning the sums of money Hollywood people did were natural objects of suspicion. Taxes were due on March 15 and were paid on or before that date by the taxpayer, which is why the investigator's visit was only an annual one. The government had not yet made tax collectors out of the employers of the country by instituting the practice of having them withhold and remit taxes from each paycheck before the money reached the hands of the guy who had earned it. The tax rates were cause for complaint in those years of Our Lord in the 1930s; had we known what confiscatory levels they were soon to reach, we might have grumbled less.

Toward the end of the year, I started a small factory in Wilmington called the Sturges Engineering Company, for the manufacture of an extremely efficient, quiet, and vibrationless diesel engine, which, if it turned out to be as quiet as promised, I planned to call the Silent Sturges. The first engines were to be for yachts and for work boats, then stationary engines, and my great hope was to some day make airplane engines.

My new boat, now known as the *Destiny,* was coming along beautifully. Except for changes in the steering wheel, the propeller, the rudder, and the afterdeck, a new and faster-shaped bottom, a thirteen-ton lead keel, higher masts, three squaresails on the foremast, a new suit of sails, and some rearrangement of the main saloon, she was practically as she was when I bought her.

Then Uncle Carl Laemmle, tired of the constant wrangling that had gone on around him since he founded the business, sold the studio. The new owners were a gang called the Standard Capital Company, whose stock I advised Father to steer clear of were he offered any. With their installation in early 1936, *Cup of Coffee* was deleted as a future project and all my preparations and plans to direct were knocked galley west. The new owners did not believe in experiments or youth movements. It was a terrible blow. The hardest thing about directing a picture was finding somebody who would give one a picture to direct, and I didn't know when my chance would come again.

Suddenly a studio said it would let me direct the picture I had written during my long sojourn off salary, *The Biography of a Bum,* if I would sell it very cheap and direct it for nothing. I accepted instantly. The next day the studio narrowly averted bankruptcy and the following week it was sold to a group that did not believe in making pictures with directors who had never made pictures, even if it did cost them nothing.

Henry Henigson, who at Universal had given me my now aborted chance to direct, was over at Paramount and was instrumental in getting me a job to do a story for Charlie Ruggles, Mary Boland, and the radio team of Burns and Allen. My price: $17,500. For their money, the studio got *Hotel Haywire.* By the time it was scheduled for production though, Burns and Allen were no longer with the studio and somebody else was hired to do rewrites for a different cast.

Then another studio said I could direct *The Biography of a Bum* if I sold it for very short money and if, no matter how soon I might be taken off the picture, the story would belong to the studio in toto and forever. They laid a little too much stress on this hypothetical circumstance. There were too many clauses about it in the contract. I envisioned a very short career as a director: I would say, "Roll 'em!" and they would say, "That's all, brother," and give my picture to a director with a track record. I turned the deal down.

The *Destiny* was finally shipshape, and in the summer of 1936, with a miserable captain and a worse cook, I skippered her, engine sealed, to thirty-sixth place in the Honolulu yacht race. She handled magnificently until we ran into the doldrums and spent days looking for the wind. With all that gentle rocking though, I was never again so regular in my life.

Metro signed me on to do a story for William Powell and Myrna Loy, but I found myself in and then out the door, just as quickly as I had when Thalberg had invited me to join his unit back in 1933. I bumped into Nick Schenck, who, after a walk through the MGM lot, said he had never seen so many unhappy people earning a hundred thousand dollars a year. I was one of them, only I earned more than that.

I was not a willing writer. I complained about my stuff not getting on the screen. I asked if it were not obvious that I was a born director and that everything I had done hitherto had unerringly shaped me for this job and for no other. Somebody said that all one needed for success in American life was a bass voice and a muscular handshake, so I seized producers with a powerful grip, looked piercingly into their eyes and asked them in my deepest tones if they doubted for a second that I could direct. When they said, "No," and I said, "Then when do I start?" they said, "As soon as you have directed one picture for somebody else."

That left me out in the alley. I offered to direct pictures for nothing and even to throw in a script—and my scripts had become quite valuable—for nothing. The result was the same. A director is as good as his last picture and it is very hard to have a last picture when one has never had a first.

So I wrote and wrote, but I was not very happy.

That September, Frank Orsatti, my new agent, got me a deal at Paramount for twenty-five hundred a week, naturally with options in favor of the studio at several periods during the run of the contract. My first producer was Mr. Maurice Revnes and my first project was to turn a little story by Vera Caspary called *Easy Living* into a screenplay. Miss Caspary's little story of deceit and disillusion was set aside, but the title was a good one. When I presented the screenplay to Mr. Revnes, however, he told me that 1936 was not the time for comedies and wanted to abandon the whole project. I disagreed. Any time was a good time for comedies. I took the script to Mitch Leisen myself, which resulted in the picture *Easy Living* and in my continued employment by Paramount. I didn't realize it then, but going to a director over the head of my producer was not a sagacious move; I would come to realize it much further down the road.

Around November 1936, I opened Snyder's, a watering hole and eating establishment at 8789 Sunset Boulevard, my first venture in the restaurant business. We offered steak, chops, good liquor, fine wines, music, pool, chess, checkers, dominoes, and culbuto, and a place to eat and drink that stayed open well after midnight. The restaurant was for me a way to repay Ted Snyder for the kindnesses he had shown me in my beginning days as a songwriter. His income at the time was limited to ASCAP royalties: enough to live on, but not enough for the rest. I leased the property, remodeled the structure, bought a liquor license, stocked the kitchen, the bar, and the storeroom, and handed over the management of the business and a salary to Ted. We anticipated a grand time.

Now that I had an engineering company and a restaurant to support, it became apparent, even to me, that I would not be returning to New York to live in the immediate future, and on April 2, 1937, I took title to an improved lot high on a straight hill, one house removed from the corner of Franklin and Ivar in Hollywood, and let my New York landlord know that I would not be renewing my lease at 603 Fifth Avenue. Minutes after Bianca and I and a couple of servants moved in, I had construction started on a swimming pool, a barbecue house, and a badminton court for the backyard. The place was in an uproar all the time with the racket of steam shovels, trip-hammers, and concrete mixers, not to mention the carpenters and the dogs racing around between their legs, barking at the lot of them. The neighbors didn't enjoy it and neither did we.

One night at the house toward the end of July, I was running after Bianca to return a friendly slap and she slammed a door to stop me. The door was ripple glass, and my arm went through it, severing three arteries and cutting halfway through the muscle. Fortunately no tendons or motor nerves were cut so that my piano playing, if I could play the piano, was not impaired. I spent two weeks in the hospital and fattened up to 214 pounds. I began to conclude that I am of the large or streetcar-conductor type of Irish, intended by God to wear size forty-six coats and not to sit on antique chairs.

This occurred to me at dinner with Arthur Hornblow and Myrna Loy. Somebody told a joke and as I laughed, the chair I was sitting on pulverized under me. Nothing was left but a little pile that looked like flea powder. This was sent in an envelope to a cabinetmaker for repair.

He mixed it with glue and returned it as an Italian primitive wood carving of Virgin with Child, about six inches high. It looked very pretty in Myrna Loy's green bedroom.

Snyder's was doing microscopic business, but with weekly infusions of capital from my weekly paychecks we kept the place going. During its first six months, it had twice ended the week without losing money and that made it easy to smell success in the wind.

When I hired some tree surgeons to shuffle around the trees in the backyard of my house to make room for the pool, I discovered an even faster way to get rid of money.

48

CHAPTER

AT PARAMOUNT I WENT TO WORK for Arthur Hornblow, and we spent twenty-six weeks putting together a screenplay based on the play *Never Say Die* as a vehicle for Jack Benny and Franceska Gaal. One week Franceska would spend till five in the morning telling me how bad *her* part was and how good Benny's part was. The next week Benny would spend the evening telling me how bad *his* part was and how good hers was. Arthur Hornblow spent his free time telling me how bad *all* the parts were.

He then postponed shooting the picture so that Jack Benny could appear in a musical comedy first. I argued strenuously to get him to reconsider, warning him that the studio would lose Benny and a valuable star, which, I sincerely believe, Benny would have been after *Never Say Die* as then written. But I did not prevail, and again I had unknowingly bruised the sensibilities of people with long memories.

I did some work on *The Buccaneer* for Mr. Cecil B. De Mille, who got rid of me the minute he read a scene I had written depicting Napoleon in his bath outlining battle plans for his generals on a wall map that snapped up like a window shade every time he touched it. I was turning Napoleon into a comedian, De Mille complained. An assignment to write a script from the old play *If I Were King* for Ronald Colman and Frances Dee came next; then *Broadway Melody of 1939* for practically everybody under contract.

So I wrote and wrote, and my salary went up, and I was increasingly unhappy with my lot as a writer. I wanted to direct. Al Lewin put me to work on a screenplay from the Monckton Hoffe story *Two Bad Hats* for Claudette Colbert. I spent the day at the studio, but most of my writing was done at home, usually after midnight. By this time I had taken on an additional secretary, a young Stanford engineer called Edwin Gillette, known as Gilletti.

In August I bought a wonderful piece of property at 8225 Sunset Boulevard, embellished with a structure that had been the home in which Chester Conklin grew up, and then converted by a later owner into the

Hollywood Wedding Chapel. I didn't have any immediate plans for the property, but its site was a marvelous location for a theatre, a club . . . for almost anything.

My liaison with Bianca, instead of being occasionally stormy, became occasionally serene. Suddenly one day she said she was tired of the whole thing and was leaving for a vacation in Mexico and would come back when she felt like it. And suddenly while she was away, I fell deeply in love. Her name was Louise Sargent Tevis. She was married, but fortunately for me she had been separated from Mr. Tevis for some time.

Within weeks, Louise and I were married in Reno on the same day her divorce from Mr. Tevis was granted: November 7, 1938. She was extraordinarily amiable, tall, beautiful, well-made, and was born in Fort Dodge, Iowa, of pioneer stock that had moved from Maine to the prairie. She was twenty-nine years old.

By the time we came back to the house, Bianca had been apprised of the changed circumstances and had moved her things out and gone to see her mother in New York. Father, who had spent some time with Bianca on a couple of his trips here and who liked her very much, wrote to say that he sincerely hoped that I had treated her fairly and well because she had, after all, devoted her time and talents to my career for nearly ten years.

Louise and I settled in, and my life was smooth and happy, thanks to this calm and lovely girl who had agreed to be my life's companion.

When the lease on Snyder's expired in December 1938, I closed the restaurant and sent the Snyder family on its way. The furniture, fixtures, and equipment put up for sale brought offers of about seven cents on the dollar. I had lost enough money on the enterprise not to wish to crown the achievement with another skinning, so I cut off the sale and had all the stuff moved down to the new property at 8225 Sunset Boulevard and began construction of another restaurant, to be called The Players.

In January, Father, with his new wife, Marie (whom he had married some years after the death of my mother) entrained for California to buy a home out here so that he could spend his last years near me. On the train his blood pressure passed 220, and he was brought to my house in a pretty alarming condition. After Father was settled in, Marie went back to Chicago to arrange the packing and shipping. The whole house was devoted to Father, and the daily condition and progress of Mr.

Senior, as he was called by Edna and Leo Calibo, the Filipino servants, was the main topic of conversation. He enjoyed the bustle and gaiety of this house where he was loved and babied, and I was proud and grateful that I was in a position to do something for this wonderful man, who had done so much for me for so long.

As usual, I was terribly pressed for funds. Not that I was out of work or anything like that, but merely that building five new engines at the Sturges Engineering Company and at the same time building The Players, while also putting aside income-tax money, further complicated by additional tax assessments for 1936 and 1937, had me on the run.

At the studio, writing *Remember the Night* for my new producer, Al Lewin, almost caused me to commit hara-kiri several times, but I postponed it for some later assignment. The trouble was in finding a way to get some pizazz into the story. When I had Fred MacMurray, as the district attorney, take Barbara Stanwyck, the girl on trial for theft, up to the mountains to reform her, the script died of pernicious anemia. When I had him take her up because his conscience bothered him for having had her trial continued until after the Christmas season, it perished from lack of oxygen. When I had him take her up moved by charitable impulse and the Yuletide spirit, it expired from galloping eunuchery. So I thought of a novelty. The district attorney takes her up to the mountains for the purpose of violating the Mann Act. This has always been a good second act. It is an act enjoyed by all, one that we rarely tire of, and one not above the heads of the audience. In *Rain,* for instance, the preacher started to reform her and ended up laying her like a carpet. In *Resurrection,* he got the erection first and hit the trail much later. In *Remember the Night,* love reformed her and corrupted him, which gave us the finely balanced moral that one man's meat is another man's poison, or caveat emptor. As it turned out, the picture had quite a lot of schmaltz, a good dose of schmerz and just enough schmutz to make it box office.

Assessing my career in Hollywood, I felt that I had done wisely in leaving the theatre. Not that I intended to give up playwriting. I thought that I would write plays on the side like a doctor or a barber does. In other words, I would turn amateur.

It took me quite a long time to realize that I had never left the theatre. Literary, or at least literate, friends used to say, "You have lost your honor by coming out here; you have prostituted your art in going to work for this big beazle who appeals only to the lowest and most elemental passions in man; you have despicably abased yourself. In other words, sir, you are nothing but a mackerel. When are you going to pull yourself together, climb out of this slime, and write another play?" As I shared my friends' opinion to some extent, I would turn red and say, "Oh, I'll get around to it one of these days."

Then one day, possibly in self-defense, it occurred to me that I was still writing lines for actors to say in front of audiences gathered in theatres, and the next time somebody said, "When are you going to write another play," I looked him straight in the eye and said, "I've never stopped writing plays."

Starting with this, I worked out a rather deep-dish theory defining the theatre as a form of architecture rather than a form of literature. From this, I deduced that the motion picture was theatre in its modern form, being handy and cheap and necessary and used constantly by hundreds of millions of people worldwide, instead of being something one sees once on a wedding trip, like Niagara Falls or Grant's Tomb.

I compared the theatre to transportation, which evolved from sledges to the helicopter, but remained transportation. And I compared pooh-poohers of the movies to the myopics who used to holler, "Get a horse!" when an early automobile exploded by.

I did not claim that moving out of the legitimate into an illegitimate house was the best thing that could have happened to the theatre. I did not think that a good movie was the equivalent of a good stage play, any more that I thought that an automobile ride was as exhilarating as a drive behind a spirited horse, nor a trip by steam as soul-satisfying as a voyage by sail. I merely claimed that the move had taken place.

I knew all about the enormously successful plays running on Broadway, each with its few road companies straggling up and down the land, and I was delighted to hear of the millions they were making for the authors, backers, actors, and ticket speculators. I wished them well and hoped that they would continue to flourish and multiply and exist forever. And I wished the same to horses and sailboats. But I refused to believe that anything as necessary as the theatre could be available only to the few, at rare intervals, and at prohibitive cost.

I claimed that talking film was one of the great gifts to mankind and the greatest boon the theatre had ever received, making it universal, if two-dimensional, and I wound up by apologizing to the big twilly out on the street whom I had described so vulgarly. She hadn't much of a past, I said, but oh, what a future!

I continued work on *Two Bad Hats* for Al Lewin, then wrote an adaptation of the book *Triumph Over Pain,* the story of the discovery of anesthesia. And at every opportunity, I badgered Mr. William LeBaron, the production chief, to allow me to direct, suggesting those pictures on the roster for future production that no one could direct as well as I, if I could once be allowed to prove it. Always his response echoed the constant advice I received from well-meaning friends: "Shoemaker, stick to your last." It took years before I found the answer to that one: "Show me the man who has stuck to his last, and I'll show you a shoemaker."

Then came the night of nights. Mr. LeBaron, also the executive producer of Paramount studios, was coming to my house for dinner. Here was the great opportunity to convince this shrewd and kindly man that I was destined to direct and that were he to embrace my destiny, it would probably do the studio a little good, too. The seduction of a virgin saint would not have been better planned.

My kitchen was in an uproar for two days before the event. My wife, her angelic disposition a little ruffled for once, almost had hysterics, and Edna the cook nearly had a heart attack, but when Mr. LeBaron arrived, we were ready for him. The hors d'oeuvres gleamed like jewels. The soup was a velvet poem; the fish, a dream; and the roast, a masterpiece. I talked casually about directing and my wife watched Mr. LeBaron anxiously. He seemed undecided.

Then came the salad. Mr. LeBaron weakened visibly. With the dessert, he was almost gone. The Napoleon brandy finished him.

"What was that biography story again that you always wanted to direct," he gasped.

After a dinner like that, I didn't tell the story very well, but it must have been well enough. He said, "I don't see how a man who could produce a dinner like this could possibly fail to make an excellent picture." I helped him into his car, then sank down on the front steps and gulped the night air.

The first round was over.

The next day at the studio Mr. LeBaron sent for me. He said, "I am perfectly willing to stick by my bargain of last night, and what I remember of the story, I remember as being very good, but are you sure you want to become a director? It's a terrible job. You have to get up at six o'clock in the morning and stand on your feet all day listening to a lot of ham actors muffing their lines until rigor mortis sets in. You are already a very successful writer with many credits to your name. If you make yourself ridiculous as a director, you will be less valuable as a writer. You are undertaking a very dangerous thing. You remember the adage, 'Don't change horses in midstream.' To that, let me add, 'Don't change careers in midlife.' "

I told him that I realized all the dangers, but that I had to do it, even if it ruined me. I had wanted to for so long. I was beginning to like the picture business, I told him, but there was only one job in it and that was making them. Everything else was secondary, and I was not by nature a second-fiddle player.

"Be it on your own head," he said. Then as I turned to leave, he added, "By the way, how much do you want for the story? I'll okay any price you say, but let me point out that the less it costs to bring in your first picture, the more it will be admired."

"How about a dollar?" I said.

At the door, I paused and said, "As a matter of fact, I'm going to make a hell of a picture for you."

He looked up from his big desk and smiled. "As a matter of fact, I know it."

49

THE LEGAL DEPARTMENT changed the one-dollar price to ten dollars, which they felt was more legal, and the New York office changed the title *The Biography of a Bum* to *The Great McGinty* because they said "bum" meant something terrible in Australia.

I got to work immediately on the screenplay, on which I had done very little work since I had first written it some six years before. Most of it went easily, but when I got to a new scene in the mayor's mansion, where I was trying to show that McGinty had never taken advantage of his in-name-only role as husband of the young and pretty divorcée with two small children who had married him solely to give him the public image of a family man, I ran into a concrete wall. For four days and nights I wrestled with one idea after another; I wrote and discarded page after page of scene after scene that didn't work. And then, suddenly I had it. And the solution was exquisitely right for film: purely visual. McGinty is shown striding purposefully down the corridor of the living quarters of the mayor's mansion to tell his wife of his displeasure with certain company she keeps. He pounds on her bedroom door. We hear her say "Come in." McGinty yanks the door open and walks into a linen closet, graphically revealing that he doesn't even know where her bedroom is.

I rushed home elated, knowing that Louise would be as happy as I that the wretched problem had been so beautifully solved. She received the news coldly, quietly displeased with me because there were dinner guests waiting and I had forgotten to be home in time to receive them. I realized then that she had no real interest in my work at all.

I went into strict training. This was the big opportunity of my life. I gave up drinking. I gave up smoking. I gave up late hours. After I started shooting, I had a masseur waiting for me every night and when he got through with me, I had dinner in bed. I saved my strength. I treated myself like an egg, and as a result of this totally wholesome and totally unaccustomed manner of living, I was rewarded, on the fourteenth day of shooting, with pneumonia.

My big chance was shot.

I knew that the picture, with Brian Donlevy and Akim Tamiroff and all those people on salary, couldn't be held for me. I knew that pneumonia took six weeks to run its course and that some cheesy old director with a hundred flops to his debit would undoubtedly be called in to take over. And I knew that if the film eventually turned out all right, human nature being what it is, people would say, "Well, you know who is responsible for it. After all, this Sturgeon, or whatever his name is, has never directed before in his life and old Hashface was really due for a hit; somewhat overdue, as a matter of fact." And I knew that when I tried to get another picture to direct, they would say, "Oh, he gets sick all the time."

My fever went higher and higher, about as high as a fever can go. In my delirium, I cursed the luck that had failed me at the crucial moment of my life. Then, fading in and out of focus, I saw a man standing at the foot of my hospital bed. I had difficulty understanding him, but eventually his voice tuned in clearly. He had been sent, he said slowly and distinctly, by Mr. LeBaron of Paramount. He was here to tell me that the studio was enchanted with what it had seen of my picture so far, and for that reason, if I were ill for a week, my picture would be waiting for me. If I were ill for two weeks, my picture would be waiting for me. If I were ill for three weeks, my picture would be waiting for me. After that, if I were still ill, my cutter would have to carry on until my return, but under no circumstances would another director be assigned to the picture.

My fever slid down like a monkey on a flagpole, and I was back on the set in ten days. I had a nurse with me and everybody scolded me all the time about not sitting down enough, but I was pretty much there. I gave up not drinking and not smoking and have not been troubled with pneumonia since. For *The Great McGinty,* I received a statuette of a nude gentleman with a very long sword, known as Oscar, and I am looking at it with considerable satisfaction right this minute.

I reveled in directing.

I thought it would be a good idea to establish myself as a commercial director—that is, a director who makes money for his company—as soon as possible. I knew that if I earned enough money for my company, I would be permitted to do anything I wanted. In rapid succession, I wrote and directed *Christmas in July* (from my play *Cup of Coffee*), *The*

Lady Eve, Sullivan's Travels, The Palm Beach Story, The Great Moment, The Miracle of Morgan's Creek, and *Hail the Conquering Hero.*

I was scared to death about *The Lady Eve.* I happen to love pratfalls, but as almost everything I like, other people dislike, and vice versa, my dearest friends and severest critics constantly urged me to cut the pratfalls down from five to three. But it was actually the enormous risks I took with my pictures, skating right up to the edge of nonacceptance, that paid off so handsomely. There are certain things that will convulse an audience, when it has been softened up by what has occurred previously, that seem very unfunny in cold print. Directing and acting have a lot to do with it, too. I had my fingers crossed when Henry Fonda went over the sofa. I held my left ear when he tore down the curtains and I held everything when the roast beef hit him. But it paid off. Audiences, including the critics, surrendered to the fun, and the picture made a lot of money for the studio.

Barbara Stanwyck had an instinct so sure that she needed almost no direction; she was a devastating Lady Eve.

By the end of 1940, *The Great McGinty* and *Christmas in July* were in release and *The Lady Eve* was in the can. My new restaurant, The Players, with Monsieur Pillet brought out from Pirolle's to run it, had opened without fanfare that summer, and it looked as if the Sturges Engineering Company might sell two diesel engines: one to the City of Los Angeles and one to Pierce Brothers Undertakers, although I couldn't imagine what either party was going to use them for.

But 1940 also brought a change in the warp and woof of my life.

Father, for whose approbation and for whose pleasure I had fought so hard for success, lived to see me attain my ambition of becoming a director, but died before our name was honored with the Oscar. With his death, the absolute security of knowing that in the background of one's life was a man who would *never* let one down, vanished. He was a fine gentleman, this man who had loved me all of my life and whom I loved so dearly. When my first son was born in June of 1941, I named him Solomon Sturges IV in honor of Father.

Directing was easy for me because I was a writer-director and did all my directing when I wrote the screenplay. It was probably harder for a regular director. He probably had to read the script the night before shooting started and do a little homework. The writer-director never has to read anything. Of course, there are some disadvantages, too. There comes the awful day when one has to write a new screenplay and one can't pull any hocus-pocus. One can't page through the script later and say, "Boy, what that fathead writer did to my scene!" And when directing it, one can't say, "Boy, was that cheesy until I took it in hand!" Two of the best alibis in the business are forfeited. But the job has its good points. All the policemen on the lot, the same policemen who wanted to throw one off the lot as a suspicious character when one was only a writer, go out of their way to display their affability and goodwill.

After I saw a couple of pictures put out by some of my fellow comedy-directors which seemed to have abandoned the fun in favor of the message, I wrote *Sullivan's Travels* to satisfy an urge to tell them that they were getting a little too deep-dish; to leave the preaching to the preachers.

    Sullivan's Travels started with a discussion about movie-making, and during its unwinding tried a little of every form that was discussed. It made for some horrible crimes against juxtaposition, as a result of which I took a few on the chin. One local reviewer wanted to know what the hell the tragic passages were doing in this comedy, and another wanted to know what the comic passages were doing in this drama. They were both right, of course. Some of the New York critics felt they had been let down a little by the ending. The ending wasn't right, but I didn't know how to solve the problem, which was not only to show what Sullivan learned, but also to tie up the love story. It would have been very easy to make a big finish either way, but one would have defeated the other. There was probably a way of doing it, but I didn't happen to come across it. It might be profitable for a young director to look at *Sullivan's Travels* and try not to make the same mistakes I did.

    I was shooting the chain-gang scenes for *Sullivan's Travels* in a swamp about fifty miles out of the city when word came over special telephone wires Paramount had strung up for me that the baby Louise had been expecting was about to be born. Leo Calibo, my Filipino man of all work, raced the car into the city at ninety miles an hour to get there in time for the arrival, but when we squealed to a stop at the Good Samaritan Hospital, Master Solomon Sturges IV had already made his appearance. It was June 25, 1941. He only weighed a little more than four pounds and wasn't able to come home with his nurse until about

two months later. By that time *Sullivan's Travels* was in the can and I
was writing *The Palm Beach Story.*

The Palm Beach Story, incidentally, was conceived as an illustration
of my theory of the aristocracy of beauty, or, as Claudette Colbert
expressed it to Joel McCrea, "You have no idea what a long-legged gal
can do without doing anything . . ." The setting was the Palm Beach I
had known during the years when Paris Singer used to invite me to join
him there. The few weeks I spent as Eleanor's house guest at Mar-a-Lago
were not unuseful to the story either. Millionaires are funny.

Writing and then directing *Triumph Over Pain,* rechristened *The
Great Moment* by the studio, and *The Miracle of Morgan's Creek,* not to
mention the construction and opening of a room for live music and
dancing at The Players, juggernauted me through 1942. The Players,
like its predecessor, Snyder's, required a cash infusion every week, but
because it was a lot bigger, it took a lot more of it. Happily, I was making
a lot more of it. Covering the shortfall at the engineering company all
the time seemed negligible by comparison. I had high hopes for The
Players, though. It had attracted on a regular basis not only the celebrated producers, directors, writers, stars, and agents of Hollywood, but
visiting admirals and generals and potentates and old Texas spenders on
double-ended benders and the tourists who wanted to see them all. My
business manager assured me that a solid profit position was just around
the corner.

Louise and I grew apart, but continued to live under the same roof
for a couple of years thereafter, leaving notes for one another on the
newel-post of the staircase. I didn't see much of the little boy; he was
naturally asleep by the time I got in, and his mother didn't think waking
him in the middle of the night for visits was a good idea.

The war was entering its second year, but though I imagined I could still
fly if necessary, I had absolutely no desire to get in. Either this war was
not as well advertised as the last one, or there is a great difference
between the thinking of an eighteen-year-old boy and a man in his early
forties. Or maybe one doesn't fall for the same guff twice or something.
Certainly my life was very much less precious to me at this point than
it had been then, so it couldn't have been that. Maybe if people got to
be old enough, there wouldn't be any wars. Maybe war is just youthful
exuberance, a recurring form of exercise in the spring.

Most of 1943 was spent writing and directing *Hail the Conquering Hero,* and the rest of it in trying to save *Triumph Over Pain* from some savage assaults in the cutting room.

During those exhilarating years, my star shot across the Hollywood firmament like a meteor. I was never interested in time off between pictures. I was always available to help with somebody else's script or picture, always willing to read and recommend stories for the studio to buy. I tried to develop new directors for the studio like Billy Wilder; to bring to the studio some famous ones like René Clair. I was under contract at $2,500 a week, which went up over time to $3,250 a week, with thirty days' notice either way. I was handsomely paid to direct and there were bonuses for bringing the pictures in on time. I loved Paramount.

I didn't know it then, but when Bill LeBaron left Paramount in late 1941 and was replaced by the great songwriter Buddy DeSylva, earlier of the song publishing firm DeSylva, Brown, and Henderson, the beginning of the end of my tenure at the studio was underway.

I have searched my memory and my heart while reflecting on my separation from Paramount, and there is no question that I have given my friends and associates at the studio a few bad moments. That a few fools, crooks, drunkards, and opportunists were injured bothers me not. I was trying to make good pictures, not to win a popularity contest. But that men whom I loved and respected were also hurt, I regret bitterly. The awful day about Ella Raines will be with me always.

Buddy, returning from an absence from the studio, looked at the rushes of *Hail the Conquering Hero* and demanded that Ella Raines, cast opposite Eddie Bracken, be thrown off the picture. She didn't look like a small-town girl to him, and he found her acting wooden. I refused absolutely. I said that had Buddy been there and objected to her casting at its inception, I would of course have agreed. But to have her thrown off the picture after she had been announced for the part and had started shooting, with all the publicity that engendered, would ruin her career, and I refused to do it. It seems very unimportant now whether she was kept in or thrown out. It seemed very important then. I had read Cervantes. I should have known about tilting at windmills.

My bosses could never understand why I kept using practically the same small-salaried players in picture after picture. They said, "Why don't you get some new faces?" I always replied that these little players who had contributed so much to my first hits had a moral right to work in my subsequent pictures. I guess Paramount was very glad to be rid of me eventually, as no one there ever understood a word I said.

Other disagreements with Buddy and his sycophants ensued which culminated in my being forced, very reluctantly, to leave Paramount. The final issue had simply to do with my right to leave the company's service if I were unhappy about the cutting of a picture. I had gone through a long and humiliating series of experiences with Buddy, first with the cutting of *Hail the Conquering Hero*, which I was ultimately successful in having cut the way I wanted it, and then with the cutting of *Triumph Over Pain*. This last was a bitter story about the discovery of anesthesia which I intended to sweeten a little with some funny moments. The studio decided that the picture should be cut for comedy. As a result, the unpleasant part was cut to a minimum, the story was not told, and the balance of the picture was upset. The title, too, was changed to *The Great Moment* over my vociferous objections. I was certain the picture would have a mediocre and shameful career in that form and with that title, a guaranteed gilt-edged disaster that would do neither me nor the studio any good.

I remember very well the final meeting with Buddy and Henry Ginsberg. I told them that I was very anxious to stay at the studio; that I had been very happy even with our initial arrangement of twenty-five hundred a week and thirty days' notice either way. My real contract with the studio was the loyalty and affection I felt for it; the privilege of thirty days' notice was protection for both of us. I said that I realized that I could not demand the decision on the final cut of a picture because that would make the picture my property, which it was not. On the other hand, I said I thought that they should recognize that I worked very hard to make a picture, spent many months with it before it was shot and was certainly closer to it than anyone else. I conceded that their production head was probably a better production head than I, but that I was very probably a better director than he and certainly more familiar with my own immediate problems. My pictures were making money though, and Mr. Ginsberg insisted that for the protection of the studio, I sign a seven-year contract, with options in the studio's favor, like everybody else. I agreed to a seven-year contract, provided that at the conclusion of each picture I shot, I would have the right—for a period of two weeks—to abrogate my contract. This right to leave was not intended to hold a club over their heads, I told them, because I loved Paramount and did not wish to leave, but merely to cause their production head, whoever he might be, to treat me with the courtesy due a grown man of known integrity and not like an irresponsible child. I said no man of value could stand the existing situation very long. If he could stand it, he would no longer be a man of value.

My proposal was deemed unacceptable.

I remember the dreadful hours with Buddy once the break, urged by his sycophants, had occurred; the reasonable and depressing talks we had later, both fond of each other, when it was too late to mend the break. My leaving Paramount, which was my home, the faces on the men, the good-byes in the commissary, all these things come back to me, far from cheerfully. That I broke some records for earning power after my departure means nothing to me. Just plain money never did. I did not care for the places I worked nor the people I worked with after I left. I grew up at Paramount and I was happy there.

Mistakes? I have made plenty of them. By the very nature of his art, though, which depends on invention and innovation, a storyteller must depart from the beaten track and having done so, occasionally startle and disagree with some of his associates. Healthy disagreement we must have. It is its aftermath which is sometimes dangerous, and it is there, beyond question, where I erred.

The only amazing thing about my career in Hollywood is that I ever had one at all.

50

PARAMOUNT RELEASED *The Miracle of Morgan's Creek* in January 1944, about a month after I left the studio. It was extremely well received and was shown throughout the world. As a consequence, I received many letters, including bitterly denunciatory ones from analphabets who believed the sextuplets were the result of the heroine having been promiscuous with six different men. Education, though compulsory, seems to be spreading slowly. An entirely different type of letter was received from servicemen, who said that it was tough enough getting girls to go out with them without pictures like *The Miracle of Morgan's Creek*, which threw parents into a panic and kept girls at home.

Many letters of praise were also received from people who understood what I was trying to do. Some members of the clergy did not fall into this category, and it may be that my intentions were better than my results. I wanted to show what happens to young girls who disregard their parents' advice and who confuse patriotism with promiscuity. As I do not work in a church, I tried to adorn my sermon with laughter so that people would go to see the picture instead of staying away from it.

Scene C-49 from my original script, which was removed at the request of the studio because it was felt that it could be interpreted as showing a clergyman in a humorous light, might be of some interest. The scene was to have depicted Dr. Upperman, the rector of the church, speaking to his congregation from the pulpit, as follows:

DR UPPERMAN

And God blessed them and God said unto them, "Be fruitful and multiply and replenish the earth . . . and subdue it."
(He looks up and removes his spectacles)
Wartime is a dangerous time . . . not only for the brave young men who sally forth to battle . . . but also for their fathers and mothers . . . and for their sisters . . . particularly for their sisters. It is to these I speak today . . . to these and to their parents. God said to be fruitful

and multiply and replenish the earth, and it is a fact that during war, the earth is more fruitfully replenished than during peace. The uniforms, the brass buttons, the bright colors, the helmets with plumes and horses' tails, the music . . . all of these have so captured the imaginations . . . electrified the emotions . . . of all young women from the beginning until now, that more little children, little boys especially, are born in wartime than at any other time . . . which is excellent in itself, but attended, as are so many excellent things, with dangers. Our homes are surrounded by camps. The camps are full of lonely young men . . . let me be the last to speak against them or urge a lack of hospitality . . . but let me be the first to remind you that all is not gold that glitters, that the young are impetuous, that wartime is a thoughtless time, and that in any large group of good men, there are of necessity some fools and scoundrels . . . and against these I warn you. Beware of the spell cast by jingling spurs . . . of the hasty act repented at leisure . . . of confusing patriotism with promiscuity . . . of interpreting loyalty as laxity. Beware, young women.

That was my moral. I am sorry that it was left out. Nevertheless, the picture showed a condition then prevalent in the world. For being shown humorously, it was shown nonetheless, and I like to think it did more good than harm. It is the duty of the theatre to show . . . not to preach.

The picture also brought accusations from parents that I was contributing to the delinquency of minors. To these, my response was, and is, that the picture was playing in a theatre and it was perfectly easy for parents to find out what it was about and to refuse to let their children see it if they thought it might be bad for them. It is this very habit of confusing the theatre with an ice-cream parlor that has caused so much unnecessary misunderstanding between well-meaning people like parents and well-meaning people like me. Efforts to make all motion picture plays suitable to all ages from the cradle to the grave have so emasculated, Comstocked and bowdlerized this wonderful form of theatre that many adults have been driven away from it entirely. It is my intention someday to bring to the screen Ibsen, Shakespeare, Molière, even Sophocles, Aristophanes, and others who do not write for children, in a chain of adult theatres or at least theatres with adult hours. One should hear these voices in Saugerties and Woodstock, where my mother used to live, and in Peekskill and Yorktown, where I used to live, as well as in theatres in New York and London. I hope that I will live long enough to fulfill this ambition.

Although I was no longer associated with Paramount, I still fought to save *Triumph Over Pain.* At a trade showing in New York, the studio cut picked up some confused reviews. The handwriting was on the wall: Paramount, and I, were about to take a bath. I tried to convince my old friend Frank Freeman, the studio chief, that with an expenditure of fifty thousand dollars and some of my time, which I would give them for nothing, it was nearly certain that I could give him a picture of dignity and merit that would reflect credit on all of us and do a lot more business as a result. And again I urged him not to call it *The Great Moment.*

I also had a spoken foreword on the picture which the studio objected to. As it is not heard in the picture, it might amuse a few people to read it here.

On screen, one saw a vast plain, dotted with the wreckage of war—half a cannon, half a triumphal arch, half an equestrian statue (the rear half). There was no sign of life, the only movement coming from swirls of poison gas. Over this one heard a cheerful voice. It said:

> One of the most charming characteristics of Homo sapiens, the wise guy on your right, is the consistency with which he has stoned, crucified, hanged, flayed, boiled in oil and otherwise rid himself of those who consecrated their lives to his further comfort and well-being, so that all his strength and cunning might be preserved for the erection of ever larger monuments, memorial shafts, triumphal arches, pyramids, and obelisks to the eternal glory of generals on horseback, tyrants, usurpers, dictators, politicians, and other heroes who led him, from the rear, to dismemberment and death.
>
> This is the story of the Boston dentist who gave you ether— before whom in all time surgery was agony, since whom science has control of pain. It should be almost unnecessary then to tell you that this man, whose contribution to human mercy is unparalleled in the history of the world, was ridiculed, reviled, burned in effigy and eventually driven to despair and death by the beneficiaries of his revelation.
>
> Paramount Pictures, Incorporated, has the honor of bringing

you, at long last, the true story of an American of supreme achievement—W. T. G. Morton of Boston, Massachusetts, in a motion picture called *Triumph Over Pain.*

The studio felt that wartime was not the moment to say such things and for all I know, they may have been right.

Frank Freeman thanked me for my continued interest in the picture but did not respond to my offer to improve it.

Triumph Over Pain, W. T. G. Morton's story, serious, thrilling, and a little sad, was released in October as *The Great Moment,* cut for comedy by the studio and advertised in some quarters as "Paramount's escapist laugh tonic! Hilarious as a whiff of laughing gas!"

I SPENT THE NEXT THREE YEARS horsing around with independent ventures and stock companies and various other efforts, all to the accompaniment of gentle laughter from the Collector of Internal Revenue. Chief among these was a little partnership I went into with Howard Hughes early in 1944 to form an independent film production company called California Pictures Corporation. Howard wanted someone to manage his motion picture activities while he devoted all of his time to his aviation projects. I wanted to make pictures. The deal on which we shook hands was that I would make movies for the company if I wanted to, reserving the freedom to engage in other ventures under other auspices; and that he would put up the money for the pictures if he wanted to. We also agreed that either of us could sever the partnership instantly by picking up the telephone. And early one morning in October 1946, while one hundred extras gathered on the the set of *Vendetta*, Howard picked up the telephone and the partnership was over.

I never really knew why. Years later, somebody over at Hughes Tool Company, which paid the bills for Cal-Pix, told me it was because of the horses.

We had had some horses brought in to shoot the forest-glade scenes in *Vendetta*, and one day I asked the man who supplied them how much it would cost for me to rent a horse to ride during lunch breaks. "For you, Mr. Sturges, . . ." he said and made a gesture indicating that the question was too foolish to necessitate a response. I rode every day thereafter, sometimes alone and sometimes with a companion or two. I thought supplying me with a horse for an hour or so a day was the gentleman's way of thanking me for the business he was getting from the company. It turned out, though, that day after day this robber had cheerfully billed Cal-Pix fifty dollars an hour for my private use of the horses. According to the fellow from the Hughes Tool Company, when somebody brought the bill to Howard's attention, it dawned on Howard that I probably intended to pauperize him. He picked up the telephone.

Bill Cagney, Jimmy's producer brother, told me another story. Long after California Pictures Corporation had been dissolved, Howard was at Bill's house one night and noticed on the wall one of the solid brass gimbal candelabra I had had manufactured at the Sturges Engineering Company. Howard reached out and tipped it. "Preston give you this?" Cagney said yes. "He gave me one, too," said Howard. "Mine cost me five million."

I suppose five million wasn't too far off the combined costs of *The Sin of Harold Diddlebock* and *Vendetta.*

On behalf of Cal–Pix, I had hired Mr. Max Ophuls, a German who had made his mark as a writer-director in France, to direct *Vendetta,* my screenplay of Prosper Merimée's *Colomba.* I intended to keep myself occupied with cutting *The Sin of Harold Diddlebock.* However, when I introduced Mr. Ophuls to Howard, well after *Vendetta* had commenced principal photography, it was only three seconds after Mr. Ophuls left the room that Howard demanded that I get rid of him. He said he didn't like foreigners and he didn't want any of them working for the company. The talent and the reputation of this fairly celebrated moviemaker cut no ice with Howard. His resolve was unshakeable; the foreigner had to go. Besides, he pointed out, with Max at the helm, *Vendetta* was already thirty days behind schedule.

The whole episode was regrettable from beginning to end.

Vendetta, my version of *Colomba,* which came out better than any adaptation I ever did from another source, never saw the screen. After the dissolution of the company, my ex-partner had the screenplay rewritten and the film reshot.

The story of *The Sin of Harold Diddlebock,* written in part to give the public another romp with the Harold Lloyd it had taken to its heart, was amusing nonsense with a small grain of sense under it all. I must have become fond of the sound of my own words, though, because I shot hundreds of thousands of feet of film and took four months to do it. I had to do some violent pruning in the cutting room afterwards, which could have been done better and done cheaper sooner.

At its trade showing, three or four months after my split with Howard, *The Sin of Harold Diddlebock* got the best reviews I ever received. Mr. Hughes took this as a cue to recut the picture entirely, leaving out all the parts I considered the best in the picture, and adding to its end a talking horse. He changed the title, too, to *Mad Wednesday,* and didn't release it until 1950.

In December 1946, an irritating cough had developed into a racking, violent one, and my friend and doctor Bert Woolfan sent me to see the best chest man in Los Angeles. The specialist took an X-ray, did a bronchoscopy and scheduled me for surgery in exactly one week. He wanted to operate the next day, but gave me a week to arrange for the supervision of my various affairs, although he suggested that the delay was risky. A pulmonary malignancy was present, he told me, and he planned to remove a lobe of my left lung. It was a week of horror.

At The Players the night before the scheduled surgery, I took a deep breath and then tried to imagine what it would feel like the next morning when I regained consciousness in a hospital bedroom, started to take a deep breath and found, halfway through it, that halfway was as far as I could breathe, or would ever breathe again.

At that moment Harold Lloyd came in to have something to eat, and I invited him to join my table. When I told him about the impending surgery, he wanted to know how many doctors had concurred with that opinion. I told him it was the opinion of the best thoracic man in the city.

"If a doctor told me he was going to remove a lobe of *my* lung," Harold said, "I'd go to another doctor. If the second doctor told me the same thing, I'd go to a third doctor. If a third doctor told me the same thing, I'd go to a fourth doctor. If *ten* doctors told me the same thing, I'd begin to consider the possibility that surgery might be indicated. But I wouldn't have even an ingrown toenail surgically treated on the opinion of a single doctor!"

The lofty reputation of my specialist meant nothing to Mr. Lloyd. I took heed, and the next day, with my Los Angeles X-ray and bronchoscopy report in hand, I flew to Chicago to see another highly recommended specialist. This specialist introduced me to the chief of the Billings Medical Clinic, a division of the Department of Medicine at the University of Chicago, and I was admitted to the clinic.

At the clinic, I was thumped and questioned and listened to by teams of earnest doctors. My cough had disappeared, and the doctors theorized that the first bronchoscopy had probably cleared the breathing passages. There were more X-rays, another bronchoscopy, and a battery of other diagnostic tests. Several doctors reviewed the results. Each and every test was negative for any involvement of the lungs in any disease.

I did not have cancer of the lung. I was not a candidate for surgery. I left Chicago enormously relieved and happy.

My Los Angeles specialist, whom I did not see again, was neither relieved nor happy. He wrote a letter to the chief at the Billings Medical Clinic accusing him of trying to steal the California man's patients.

When the break with Hughes hit the headlines, a flattering number of offers for my services came in, and in the spring of 1947 I went to work for Darryl Zanuck, then running Twentieth Century-Fox. I was to write and then direct a picture based on my story *Matrix,* a story originally conceived in 1933. Having paid me fifty thousand dollars for the treatment, Zanuck then asked if I had another story to sell. Neither he nor his advisers liked *Matrix,* and he wanted to trade the rights for the rights to some other story I might have. I guess he had forgotten that he had passed on *Matrix* years before, labeling it even then a trunk item. I offered him a treatment of *The Symphony Story,* an item from an even deeper layer of my trunk. The title was changed to *Unfaithfully Yours,* and we made the trade.

At the risk of sounding pontifical, I believe the success or failure of any writing depends upon the residual. By that I mean what the reader has left in his mind after closing the book; what the spectator takes home with him after leaving the theatre or movie palace. Years ago in Chicago, I went with Father to see a matinee. He laughed so hard that he shook like jelly through the whole comedy, and as we walked up the aisle at the end of the performance, I turned and said to him enthusiastically, "That was some play, wasn't it!" The tears of laughter still wet upon his cheeks, he turned on me and said indignantly, "What are you talking about? I thought it was rotten!"

It was years before I understood what he meant. Then I forgot it and very stupidly made *Unfaithfully Yours.* The audiences laughed from the beginning to the end of the picture. And they went home with *nothing.* Because *nothing* had happened. He hadn't killed *her;* he hadn't killed *himself.* It just looked that way. The audiences ate my seven-course special and went home hungry.

The performances, I thought, were very good, and my favorite parts of the picture are the three prospects of Sir Alfred, which I tried to do as if written and directed by Sir Alfred, who is neither a writer nor a director. Imagining his own roles vividly, the marionettelike behavior of the other characters during the prospects is the natural result of Sir Alfred's ability to have them say and do *exactly* what he wants them to say and do. Only one critic in the world recognized what I was trying to do; I was greatly criticized by a few others for verbosity and for using a static camera in those scenes.

When the picture was released, it was the opinion of almost everybody who knew me that I not only wrote, directed and produced the picture, but that I also played the lead.

Unfaithfully Yours received much critical acclaim and lost a fortune.

The Beautiful Blonde from Bashful Bend got *no* critical acclaim and lost a fortune. The critics didn't care for it any more than I did, and the picture served only to prove that Betty Grable is a splendid actress, capable of any role. I wish the story, an unfortunate hodgepodge, were one-tenth as good as she is.

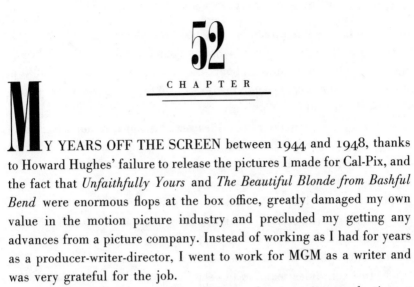

52

CHAPTER

MY YEARS OFF THE SCREEN between 1944 and 1948, thanks to Howard Hughes' failure to release the pictures I made for Cal-Pix, and the fact that *Unfaithfully Yours* and *The Beautiful Blonde from Bashful Bend* were enormous flops at the box office, greatly damaged my own value in the motion picture industry and precluded my getting any advances from a picture company. Instead of working as I had for years as a producer-writer-director, I went to work for MGM as a writer and was very grateful for the job.

I had a meeting with Dore Schary, then running production at MGM, and sold him on the treatment of a story I wrote with Clark Gable in mind. Dore said he'd give me twenty-five thousand for the first draft of the script and another twenty-five thousand when the script was finished, including rewrites, were any needed. The script was written and rewritten and rewritten some more until it suited the tastes of Mr. Larry Weingarten, the producer. At the end, Dore said it was not the story he had paid me to write. And it wasn't. But it was the story Mr. Weingarten insisted on getting.

I got my fifty thousand and they found another vehicle for Mr. Gable.

I have always worked my damnedest to make a good impression at MGM and nothing has ever come of it; first with Thalberg, then with Mankiewicz and Knopf, and this time with Schary and Weingarten.

The picture business was then in a very precarious situation, riddled with fear and with seven-tenths of its personnel out of work. Some years earlier, the United States government had hit all the major studios with a collective antitrust suit and the government had prevailed.

From their beginnings as seat-of-the-pants businesses run in nickelodeons, an industry was brought forth by the early American moviemakers who scratched and struggled and gambled . . . and won. By 1948, motion picture companies were producing pictures in company-owned studios for release by company-owned distribution units to company-owned theatres across the country. In time, there were enough indepen-

dent owners of movie threatres and chains of movie theatres in business
to make the din of their collective hollering audible to congressional ears.
And what they were yelling about was the ability of a major studio to
limit the distribution of its product to its own theatres, generally renting
the films to the independents only after the lucrative first run had played
itself out in the company-owned theatre. This put the independents in
a bad humor, and eventually their screams of unfair competition resulted
in the antitrust suit filed by the government.

The suit concluded with the majors signing a consent decree, the
gist of which was that each studio would divest itself of one of its three
functions: producing films or distributing films or exhibiting films in
their own movie theatres. In the end, the studios chose to divest themselves of their theatres and the nature of the business changed. The huge
production schedules required to keep their own theatres supplied with
new product nearly every week were cut back radically, and, with fewer
films on the rosters, the numbers of employees it took to put them
together shriveled. The studios now tried to make only those pictures
they thought the theatre owners would fight to get. And the theatre
owners, who were trying to predict what the public would pay to see, only
wanted the pictures they thought would make them richer.

As if all of that were not demoralizing enough, the spectre of
television was casting a threatening shadow across the soundstages of
Hollywood.

My agent reported that he was running into some resistance trying
to peddle my services. It appeared that I had developed a reputation for
being too expensive and hard to handle to boot. My last salary at Fox
was $12,500 a week, an amount not only expensive, but bordering on
obscenity when one considered the lifetime earnings of the great writers
of the world. Balzac, for instance, is reputed to have accepted eating
money in exchange for allowing himself to be displayed, writing, in a
store window.

Money? My *God*, I earned so much money, so much that it seemed
unimportant to me and I came to pooh-pooh it . . . the last thing in the
world one should pooh-pooh.

I was perfectly willing to work for less than $12,500 a week, of
course, but the "hard to handle" tag, the residue of several differences
of opinion with the heads of the seven major studios over the period of
my nearly eighteen years in Hollywood, would not be as easily overcome.

Suddenly, for the first time in a very long time, I was earning nothing. Those were the days before residuals, and there was nothing one could look to for income except the next assignment. Others might have looked to the profits from their restaurants or from their engineering companies, but I was not numbered among their happy company.

Without realizing it, I had come to rely on a perpetual income and the ability it gave me to support The Players with its 156 employees; the Sturges Engineering Company with its 10 employees; three boats; a couple of autos; a land yacht; an ex-wife; an eight-year-old son at school in Europe; a household staff; and still to have a little pocket money left over after the several guardians of the public fisc had collected confiscatory taxes on income; taxes on real property; taxes on personal property; taxes on sales; taxes on cigarettes; taxes on gasoline; taxes on telephone calls; alcoholic-beverage taxes; luxury taxes, and excise taxes on nearly everything not already bearing a tax.

I had had so very much luck for so very long that I had managed to forget that it is quite natural for the pendulum to swing the other way.

In an effort to staunch the river of capital flowing out of my pockets to keep the doors open at The Players, I had begun, while I was over at Fox, the design and construction of a theatre on the third storey of the restaurant to attract some paying customers. The theatre seemed to me a plan that could not fail. Instead of having dinner and then driving halfway across the city to see a play, the only option available in those days, my theatregoer would be able to dine in a first-class restaurant and, without leaving the building, see a good play in a first-class theatre. With a population of eight million people in the City of Los Angeles to draw on, I figured a 250-seat theatre with a good play would pack them in for years and, not by accident, turn the restaurant into a geyser of profit.

Since I didn't know where my next job was coming from, it now behooved me to get the theatre built and open as quickly as I could. I invested whatever capital I could lay my hands on, mortgaging the property, among other things, to produce some.

Then a few bills submitted by the purveyors of The Players slipped by the end of the month without being paid. These bills were for some chickens, some pheasants, eggs, steer meat, and several kinds of vegetables, and amounted to sixty-four thousand dollars.

Well, sir, I tried and I tried and I tried and I just *couldn't* gather those measly sixty-four thousand dollars together to pay my bills. It was while I was thus embarrassed that the newspapers of America—and the world, for that matter—came out on their front pages with the interesting list of those men in the United States of America who had, during the preceding year, received the highest salaries. To my horror, I was third, with $407,000, just behind the president of U.S. Steel and Mr. Charlie Skouras of Fox West Coast Theatres. The face on my chicken dealer was really something to see when I continued to tell him I just hadn't the money. He kept waving the newspaper under my nose and saying, "But . . . but . . . but . . ."

My romantic life was in worse shape. In fact, it was over.

I had a girl with the disposition of a viper called Frances Ramsden, and though her temper took a long time revealing itself, things got so bad after a while that when I went over to her house I never knew whether I was going to be greeted with a hug or a nightpot over my head.

In between these spasms, things would be lovely, and it was during one of those lulls that I said that if it would make her happy, I would invite her mother out to see her. This suggestion was accepted with tears of joy, and presently the old crackpot got off the plane. I didn't know she was a crackpot at the time, of course. I saw merely a weatherbeaten version of her daughter.

The ladies had not been under the same roof for more than an hour before they had at each other, and I suddenly realized that the reason they had both been so anxious to be reunited was for the purpose of tearing each other to pieces. This was really something such as I had never seen before: screaming, guttural snarling, almost foaming at the mouth—hatred in its pure state. I invited the mother to leave at once, but it took three weeks more of this kind of stuff before we finally got her back on a plane, yelling that she was going to have everybody arrested.

I don't suppose she was really insane or they would have locked her up, and I was told that she lived very quietly in a small town in the East and had no troubles at all. It was just that her daughter affected her in this way . . . and I was beginning to affect her daughter in the same way.

Finally the divorce mills got through their slow grinding and both the daughter and I were free and unencumbered, as they say in the real-estate world. Almost immediately she started suffering from that old female complaint from which so many of her sex suffer: a ringing in the ears. She began to hear wedding bells. I hadn't heard any myself, so one day she said,

"When is it going to be?"

And I said, "When is *what* going to be?"

"Our marriage, naturally," she said.

And I said, "Where did you get the idea that we were going to be married? I would have to be off my rocker to want to marry a dame I have been getting along with the way I have been getting along with you. Or vice versa."

She said, "It is because we are *not* married that we have not been getting along. I feel the shame of the situation very deeply and this puts me in a bad humor. Every time I see you, I am reminded of the shame of my situation and I am off again. I am naturally a very gentle girl with a sweet disposition."

"I have seen you gentle and sweet," I said, "but I didn't know it came to you naturally. I thought you were making an effort. However, I am willing to believe you, so this is what I propose and what I will do. Since I cannot think of anyone nicer or more attractive than yourself during those periods when you are not upset by the shame of your situation, and since I happen to believe that by making an effort we can control our emotions rather than have them control us, this is my proposal. If you will make this effort I speak of and give me ninety days of absolute courtesy and complete peace and happiness, I will marry you on the ninety-first day. Because if one can control oneself for ninety days, one can do so for the rest of one's life."

"You have no right to ask such a thing," she began indignantly, "and furthermore . . ."

"That is quite possible," I interrupted, "but I am not going to discuss the ethics of the matter with you. Insofar as my own marriage is concerned, I happen to be sitting in the catbird seat, and those are my terms."

Well, sir, she started reluctantly the first day, but one never saw such a difference in a girl! It was as if she had had a lobotomy. Overnight she became utterly charming, kind, and thoughtful for twenty-four hours a day, and life became like unto a stream of perfumed honey. Whereas two weeks before she had tried to kick my brains out from the back of a darkened automobile and had given me the two finest shiners I have ever seen, she was now shoving cushions under me when I sat down and, figuratively at least, strewing my path with rose petals.

At the end of a blissful month, I was congratulating myself upon my wisdom and foresight in choosing this jewel among women. "Just suppose," I said to myself, "I had lost this paragon through a lack of patience and an exaggeration of the importance of the little snits she used to get into a month ago, wouldn't *I* have been an ass?"

We were at a cocktail party one night where I proudly introduced the handsome young lady as the fiancée I was going to marry in sixty days' time. Around the third or fourth introduction, she said,

"Why don't you fly me up to Las Vegas and marry me tonight?"

I said, "Because that isn't the deal, my sweet. I know now after these wonderful thirty days that we can very easily be divinely happy for the rest of our lives, but a deal is a deal and we must stick to it to the letter."

"Oh we must, must we?" said the young lady, and I noticed suddenly, by a demonic glitter in her eye, that she had possibly hoisted one cocktail too many. "I'll tell you where you can stick it, you stupid son of a bitch! I wouldn't marry you if you were the last man on earth! I was just curious to see how far you'd go with your effing psychology and your shortcuts to happiness. I hate your guts and every night when you went home, there was a handsome *young* man waiting in the backyard to do properly what you couldn't even make a stab at! And how do you like that!" with which she slammed out of the party.

I didn't like it at all, of course, especially as all conversation had ceased when she began, and everything she had said was now public property. I was always brought up not to strike women, but I'm not sure this eleventh-century chivalry is always the best thing for their manners. A man standing quietly with a silly grin on his face wiping the insults of a furious woman off his ears is really an abject spectacle. My great friend Gouverneur Morris used to have to do this a couple of times a week for a vixen he had married in his old age, and the spectacle was lamentable. But what can one do? One can't hit them in the face and spoil their prettiness. If one were to hit them on the forehead or on the top of the head, one's knuckles would break. So one stands there and grins . . . and bears it. Like I did.

The next day was a day of desolation. The girl was not only sorry, but inwardly withered. There was not a word of truth in what she had screamed at me, she said, tossing off another Bromo-Seltzer and adding a little ice to the pack on her head. It was all due to the alcohol, man's worst friend. She loved me dearly, she said, and the thought of living without me was just too much to bear.

"That isn't what you said last night," I said.

"I was drunk last night," she said.

"How about *in vino veritas?*" I asked.

"I never met him. I don't know anything about him," she said.

"How about the guy waiting in the backyard?" I said.

"He must still be waiting," she said, "since I haven't got any backyard, and by the time you go home, anybody else would naturally be discouraged."

"How about all those things I make stabs at but am no longer capable of carrying through," I asked.

"Oh, shut up," she said. "I'm a good actress, but I'm not that good."

So since she was very lovely and very charming, unless she was otherwise, we made up, quite tearfully, if I remember correctly.

"Are we back together again now?" she asked through her sniffles.

"Of course," I replied huskily.

"And is everything just exactly the way it was?" she asked tenderly.

"Absolutely and exactly," I replied, "except naturally for one tiny technical difference."

"What is that?" she asked a little apprehensively.

"Well," I said, "it is only that we are naturally now on day *one* of our ninety-day deal!"

"Why, you fat son of a bitch," she began after an instant's shocked silence. Then thinking better of it, she tried another tack. "You have no *right* to ask a girl to go all through that crap again! I *proved* to you how nice I can be for thirty days. You can't ask me to lose all those credits and start the whole goddam thing over again!"

"I'm sorry," I said, "but that's the way I see it. *You* have to learn to get along with *me*, because this is a man's world, and that's how it has to be. I will do everything I can to make you happy for the rest of your life, but first you've got to prove to me that you're on the level. And I insist upon ninety days' trial."

But it was too much for her. In early March of 1950, she went away

to New York, and two days later she was married to the gentleman who
had the hotel suite next to hers, and two days after that she was running
to my friends demanding protection from this bounder she had just
married, who seemed to think the ceremony entitled him to enter her
suite uninvited. Then she had him arrested and as soon as he got out
of the clink, the bounder started calling me up long-distance in the
middle of the night, telling me that the least I could do was to fly to New
York and help put some order in his affairs. I told him he had only to
have looked before he leapt and that insofar as I was concerned, he
could, in Mr. Goldwyn's celebrated remark, "include me out."

However, Miss Ramsden is now very happy, I am glad to report,
but whether because she has turned over a new leaf, or because her even
newer husband has a disposition even viler than hers so that by comparison she is like a ray of sunshine, I do not know.

CHAPTER

A COUPLE OF WEEKS AFTER Miss Ramsden married the bounder in the hotel suite next to hers, a very pretty kid about fourteen years old poked her head into the theatre-a-building at The Players to alert me and the assembled work crew that a fire was about to consume the restaurant. For just an instant, my mother's words after Jack Wright and I had saved the house in Fleurines from burning to the ground came back to tempt me, "We'll never get another chance like this. . . ."

Fortunately, or unfortunately, the danger of fire was small, although I could see why the sparks spitting out of the neon sign would have alarmed a passerby. I thanked the youngster for the warning and invited her to step inside to see the theatre we were building. I invited her to see how it was coming along the next day and the day after that. Pretty soon, showing Sandy the theatre was something I did every afternoon.

She lived at the top of the hill running past that part of The Players where all the construction was taking place and since she had a job with regular hours, she walked up every afternoon at about the same time. Three months earlier she had separated from a college student she had been married to for three months, and I deduced from this information, and with some relief, that she must be older than the fourteen years she appeared to be, indeed that she had reached the age of consent. Still she was very young. One afternoon I told her that I was in two minds: I didn't know whether to adopt her or to marry her. She thought I was joking.

On another afternoon I invited her to have dinner with me some evening at the restaurant on the level below the theatre. When she asked me if I thought they would let me, I realized that she had no idea at all how I earned my living. The next afternoon when she walked by, I was ready with my copy of *Who's Who.* I opened it for her and pointed to my name and told her that I brought the book because I didn't want her to think she was dealing with a total bum. She read the entry, but since she had heard of none of my plays and none of my movies, the information did not electrify her. She wondered why I had switched to a career in construction.

I don't remember exactly when, but one day along the way, something changed. Instead of treating me with that playful flirtatiousness Southern girls bestow on harmless old men, something I said or did, I do not remember what, changed her attitude toward me. I remember only that it had to do with some fierceness in the face of disaster she professed to see in me when my back was against the wall. She couldn't really explain it, but she thought I must have stirred up some blood memory of her Irish ancestors during the Troubles . . . and the women who stood by them.

Things between us were different after that.

My young son, Mon, now about nine, returned with his mother from Europe and went to live in West Los Angeles. He fell in love with Sandy and right under my own roof, the little rat proposed that she wait and marry him instead of marrying me. There was less difference in *their* ages, he told her, than there was between mine and hers. There was a certain logic to his position, but I gave him a good-humored lecture on the proprieties anyway.

When the opera singer Mr. Ezio Pinza arrived in Hollywood to play the part he had created on Broadway in *South Pacific,* I knew that MGM would be looking for a second picture for him, and if ever there was a natural, simple, and foolproof vehicle for an Italian opera singer, it was my old play *Strictly Dishonorable.*

I got in touch with Brock Pemberton, and to help me out, he sold his share of the play to me. Through the good offices of Henry Henigson, I got Universal to agree to sell their rights to MGM for fifty thousand. I brought the package—Brock's share, Universal's share, and my own share—to MGM, naturally suggesting that as the original author, I was probably the best man to turn my little play into a screen musical. They responded to the suggestion that I write the screenplay in exactly the same way Universal had when I offered to write the screenplay for them in 1930 when they acquired the movie rights: they turned me down hastily. But they bought the package for a $110,000: $50,000 to Universal and $60,000 to me.

I immediately ordered the lumber and the motors for the elevating platforms that would constitute the main floor of the theatre.

On the day that the first motor went in and I was demonstrating to everybody and anybody the ingenuity of the invention, the MGM lawyers called to find out what I knew about a little corporation that appeared to have some rights in *Strictly Dishonorable.* I knew nothing about it, of course. It turned out that Brock Pemberton, as an individual, sold me something he had no right to sell because he had formed an obscure corporation twenty years before and this had slipped his mind. While he was trying to straighten out the matter for me, he dropped dead. The MGM money was held up and I was in a terrible financial jam, one of such demoralizing proportions that I did not even answer my mail.

Eventually Charley Abramson got things in hand and the deal went through, but it was August by then. In the meantime, I was hanging on by my teeth, and when I was approached by Hugh Martin, a young composer of considerable talent, to do a Broadway musical based on my old picture *The Good Fairy,* I agreed to write the book. I made it clear to him that getting the theatre up and running was paramount to the play, as the theatre was my only way out of the financial morass that clung to all my days.

Had I been any good at divination, I might have perceived that the state's intention to bury my house under the proposed Hollywood Freeway was the rogue wind heralding the approach of the maelstrom I was headed into. But the omen escaped me.

Around 1949, the state had begun notifying me from time to time that it was considering the use of its power of public domain to acquire my property at Franklin and Ivar. The plans had not yet been approved by all the state and municipal authorities involved, so sometimes the notice was to get ready to lose a corner of the badminton court, at another time to reconcile myself to the loss of ten feet of land adjacent to the house, and at still others, a cheerful notice that the route of the planned freeway had changed; no part of my property was threatened.

But one day in 1950, the state did indeed condemn the property for the public weal and gave me six months to remove from it my house, the barbecue house, the small garage, the three-car garage with apartment, and some trees, and paid me $130,000. Naturally I plowed most of the money into the completion of the theatre, reserving funds sufficient to move and to reconstitute all those structures at a new location.

While the final details of the construction and the furnishing of the theatre went on, I selected, cast, polished, and put into rehearsal five one-act plays. At night, Sandy and I worked on the book of *The Good Fairy* musical. In March we went East for a week or so of rehearsals and an out-of-town premiere and some all-night rewriting sessions. By then the play was called *Make a Wish.* Before its New York opening, I heard that the composer, the set designer, the producer, the director, and, for all I know, a couple of stagehands, had all done a little editing and writing of their own on the book. I never saw the results.

When we got back to Hollywood, the grand event was almost at hand. Mrs. Maxine Merlino had done a magnificent job with the art work. The port-wine velvet curtains drawn back from the gilded peach-toned mirrors, the graceful candelabra suspended along the walls, the deep seats in the orchestra section, the damask-covered tables, the silver and crystal were lovely. The place looked like a Viennese jewel box. The Players Theatre opened with the five one-act plays and Red Nichols and his Five Pennies in the orchestra pit. It was April 4, 1951.

The opening was billed as an Oxnard out-of-town tryout taking place in Hollywood because, when we found out where Oxnard was, it was deemed wiser to hold the out-of-town opening *in*-town. It took a couple of weeks to get the kinks out of the operation, getting the dinners served and cleared before the curtain went up, for instance, but the plays received good reviews and the theatre itself even better ones. After the performances, the theatre seats disappeared, the four sections of the theatre floor, elevated in graduated levels for perfect viewing, were lowered to one level and became a dance floor in a nightclub. The changeover took precisely five minutes.

Of all the innovations the theatre offered, I thought this one would please the customers the most. Having already dined well and enjoyed the plays, they could now have a few drinks, dance a little to the music of a live orchestra and finish off the evening without once having had to check out their wraps and wait for the parking boys to bring up their automobiles.

It took me some time to realize that the reason people weren't staying to drink and dance after the show, my one opportunity to do better than break even at the restaurant, was because they just didn't want to be in the same place for so long and they didn't care if they had to go to the bother of checking out their coats and waiting for their cars.

Enough was enough. But, as I said, it took me a considerable time to recognize the problem.

The five one-act plays were cut to three for the official opening of the theatre on April 24. It quickly became apparent that the bulk of the population of eight million I had counted on to fill the theatre every night for some years either were not theatregoers at all or didn't come to Hollywood to see plays. Most of our audiences were drawn from the threatregoing residents of Hollywood and Beverly Hills and most of these went to the theatre on weekends. We were always sold out on weekends. We got busy finding a new play.

At the end of May 1951, our state-allotted time at Franklin and Ivar was up, and the big move got underway. At midnight one night, the house, cut into three sections, and the barbecue house and the garages, large and small, and some trees and some doghouses inched through the streets of Hollywood on the backs of huge flatbed trucks to the new lot Sandy and I had found at Franklin and Vista. Until the house was reconstructed to the satisfaction of the city, though, we were not allowed to live in it. I didn't know where else we could live. Then my friend Mr. José Iturbi offered me the use of an empty house he owned in Beverly Hills, and we removed to it ourselves and the dogs and all of the furniture, fixtures, and equipment from the several buildings now sitting on temporary log foundations at the new location. On weekends, Mon joined the household too.

By that time, I also had on my hands my half brother (he and I had the same biological father), his wife, his daughter, and their new additions, seven-month-old twins. This was the result of an errant impulse I had to do something for the young man. He was trying to support a wife and daughter managing a soda fountain at a Walgreen's drugstore in New York City and he had written several times asking if I could do anything for him. Maybe it was because I had not responded to the elder Mr. Biden's demands when I had so much and he had so little, or maybe I thought that there was something to the theory that blood is thicker than water. Whatever the case, in late 1947 I invited my half brother to come to California to learn from Monsieur Pillet how to manage a large restaurant. What I failed to take into consideration was the fact that he had been brought up by my biological father, a man who harbored an insane hatred for my mother and who also hated me. Toward the end of 1949, I found it necessary to suggest to my half brother that he find other employment. I also told him that when he did, I expected him to surrender the rent-free occupation of the house I let him use on the lot I owned adjoining the one on which my home stood. I naturally expected that when the state came in to plow that house under, he would find a place for himself and his family. He did not. He moved over to the Iturbi house just as though he had been invited.

When all of the people who wanted to see the one-act plays appeared to have seen them, business at The Players Theatre got a brisk revival with one of the funniest farces ever written, *Room Service,* which opened in July 1951. And this time we had a star. Eddie Bracken played the lead and brought the house down every night. And he did it for nothing, in order to help me bring in enough money to start paying off the creditors and get out of the terrible hole I was in.

Eddie played only a supporting role though on Wednesday, August 15, 1951, giving the bride away when Anne Margaret Nagle, my little Sandy, married me on the stage of the theatre into which we had put so much hope and time and energy. The ring I slipped on her finger was the ring I had removed from my mother's hand just after she died. Sandy had no idea what this love affair meant to me.

The reconstruction of my house and all its satellites was supposed to have taken between four and six months, but nearly two years later, Sandy and I and the five Bidens and the dogs were still living in the Beverly Hills house José Iturbi had been kind enough to lend me until I got a relocation permit to get back into my own house. The costs of reconstruction vastly exceeded the estimates I had relied on, and when I went to the bank to pick up some additional dough it had agreed to lend me in exchange for a first mortgage, I got exactly nothing. Unbeknownst to me, the Collector of Internal Revenue had slapped a lien on all my assets, known and unknown, and even the few thousand dollars I had left in the bank was unavailable to me.

It turned out that Mr. Zanteson, the bookkeeper at The Players for the preceding two years, had failed to file—and naturally failed to pay—one cent of the federal income taxes withheld from the paychecks of the employees. He had also neglected to file or to pay the Social Security taxes withheld from them. The income taxes and unemployment taxes withheld for the State of California had never made it to the state coffers either and, I need hardly add, the employer's required contributions to these various taxes had never been computed, much less paid.

The IRS lien precipitated a rush of creditors' claims and the unpleasant sight of judgments nailed to the front door of my house. I was under siege.

54

C H A P T E R

THERE WERE A COUPLE OF ALMOSTS. In 1952, Frank Freeman invited me back to Paramount to write and direct a picture for Betty Hutton based on the play *Look, Ma, I'm Dancin'*. The script came out marvelously, but Betty, then newly married to a dance director called Charlie Curran, or O'Curran, said that if her husband didn't direct the picture, she wouldn't make it. The studio said that if her husband directed the picture, *they* wouldn't make it. I was asked to stay on at Paramount to do a couple of weeks' work on *Roman Holiday* and a few weeks' work with Billy Wilder on a story he was putting together for Yul Brynner. At the end of that time, Betty Hutton was still insisting that her husband direct *Look, Ma, I'm Dancin'*, and the studio was still adamantly opposed. The script went off the production roster, and that was that.

The relocation permit finally came through, and we moved ourselves and all of our possessions out of José Iturbi's house to our house, which, with its new foundations, didn't look too unsightly from the outside, but was scarred and wounded on the inside. I was positive that when the move from the Beverly Hills house was imminent, my half brother would find himself other accommodations. I was wrong. He moved himself, his wife, and the three children into the dining room, the main kitchen, the laundry rooms, and the maid's quarters of my house. I felt my hands were tied. One can't throw a couple of toddlers and a grade-schooler out on the streets, regardless of the opinion one might have of their parents. Sandy and I moved into the nursery quarters upstairs.

The Players sank under the weight of the four mortgages now burdening its title and its accumulated debts. I tried to persuade the Collector of Internal Revenue to play along with me while I tried to rent the property to another restaurateur, but the first two lessees were unable to meet the nut, and eventually The Players changed hands under an auctioneer's hammer. I didn't lose title to the debts though; there was no corporate veil between The Players and me. The engineering company was sold and the proceeds went to the Collector. Noah Dietrich bought the *Destiny*, which hadn't been out of the harbor since the war had confined it to the dock for the duration, and the Collector got a little more money. It looked as if fate were intent on eradicating every trace of my existence in Hollywood.

But it wasn't all bad news.

On Sunday morning, February 22, 1953, I was just completing my seventh hour of smoking and pacing in the waiting room at the Hollywood Presbyterian Hospital when a voice over the loudspeaker crackled, "Mr. Sturges, come up and meet your son."

At the door of the delivery room, the nurse carrying him out lifted the covering from his face, and Master Preston Sturges looked me dead in the eye. Then he gave me a broad wink. I knew I had hatched a genius.

A couple of hours later I introduced my five-pound son to his mother, who had slept through the whole thing. The hospital nurse trotted him in and laid him, invisible under the light blanket covering him, in his mother's arms. As she reached to turn back the blanket to see what her first-born child looked like, I put my hand over hers and told her, quite seriously, not to get too attached to the little thing, because she couldn't keep him. I did this to try to spare her what I had seen happen to other women I had known, women who were nearly destroyed by the discovery that, purely and simply, children are crops. One raises them and they go away. Little birds fly away and never come back, little rabbits do the same thing, and children are no different. All of this is perfectly normal and according to nature.

The baby was four months old when we celebrated Mon's twelfth birthday that June, and in August I accepted an offer as a play doctor and went to San Francisco to try to save a play called *Carnival in Flanders*. I did the best I could do in a couple of weeks, rewriting the book, restaging the action, but it went to New York without enough rehearsals for the actors to be sure of themselves and it was a total disaster. Charley and I read through the devastating reviews at the Algonquin, and while we were comparing the vitriol of one with another, an offer for my services came in.

George Bernard Shaw's *The Millionairess*, a project proposed by Lester Cowan, was to be written for Katharine Hepburn, who had recently dazzled New York with her performance of the play and who was very anxious to make a film of it. Lester agreed to pay me a thousand dollars a week, plus expenses, for the script, but at the end of the first week, there was no check. Lester said the check was in the mail. Notified the next day that it hadn't arrived, he said his secretary must have forgotten to mail it and that he would see that it was mailed that day. Charley said he had a better idea: he would meet Lester at his office and pick up the check. Thereafter, Charley attached himself to Lester every Friday morning and stuck with him for as much of the day as it took Lester to come up with the money.

When the deal was set, I telegraphed Sandy to bring the baby and to join me at the Algonquin.

The script was written at Katharine's home in Turtle Bay, where I betook myself every day except weekends. One day I looked up from the pages in my hand and caught my breath.

"Katharine," I said, "you look seventeen!"

"Remember the lighting," she said.

Sandy and I stayed at the Algonquin long enough for little Preston to learn to stand up and make speeches on his way down Fifth Avenue to Central Park in his stroller.

His grandmother, a staunch Catholic, was so horrified when she discovered that the baby had yet to be baptized that, to relieve her anxiety, I arranged to have him baptized at Saint Patrick's Cathedral the very next evening. The ceremony brought tears to my eyes, but the baby's shrieks when the water bathed his forehead must have sounded to the few people in the pews that night more as if a circumcision were taking place than a baptism. I presented the baby with a set of calibrated bells for his baptismal gift, just in case. I knew that musical genius manifested itself very early and I didn't want any neglect on my part to postpone its flowering; he was already nearly seven months old. I needn't have worried. He rang the bells without regard to tone or tune or tempo, and I knew that we were not harboring the next Puccini.

The Millionairess got us to London, where it turned out that the English money was ready and that Lester was a little short on the American side of the investment.

A hundred and eighty days later, with the financial shortfall still unresolved and the picture necessarily off the production schedule, we left England. While we were on that side of the Atlantic, I wanted to show Sandy the places I had lived as a boy and the schools I had gone to in

France. We crossed the Channel for Belgium and visited Vely Bey, my old Turkish stepfather, now married to the widow of a chocolate manufacturer, then we drove on to France. When we arrived in Fleurines, I was recognized and warmly·greeted by villagers I hadn't seen in more than thirty years. When they met little Preston, he became le petit Monsieur Preston, and I became, for the first time, Monsieur Preston, le vieux.

In Paris, my arrival generated a lot of publicity and I was received everywhere with great warmth and addressed as "cher maître." The publicity brought an offer from Gaumont to write and direct a picture for them. They had acquired the right to use the title *Les Carnets du Major Thompson* from the author of a series of humorous columns running in *Le Figaro,* and they wanted me to create an original screenplay about an English major called Thompson, any story I wanted to tell.

I accepted the offer, naturally, and Sandy and little Preston and I set out to find living quarters. We quickly discovered that when an apartment to let boasted "tout confort," the comforts, if any, were few. They all had running water, of course, but *hot* running water, as one prospective landlady pointed out when we waved her ad offering "tout confort" under her nose, was not a comfort, *hot* running water was a luxury.

We eventually found a wonderful old hôtel particulier on the boulevard Berthier, built by an English painter in 1903. Since he was a rich English painter, the studio was not in the garret but on the second floor, two stories high with a loggia. The owner, Madame DeMassieux, retained the first floor and its marble bath, and we took possession of the studio and the sous-sol, originally a spacious, white-tiled kitchen, and two tiny rooms at the top of a winding staircase on the third storey.

On the loggia we fashioned a small bedroom for little Preston and installed a bathroom; the tiled kitchen in the sous-sol became my office; and all the other functions of the household were accommodated in the studio and the little kitchen off to its side. We found some extraordinary furniture at the marché aux puces and a toy chest for Preston.

Gaumont provided a bilingual secretary, and we got to work in my white-tiled office.

By the time he was two years old, little Preston was bilingual and had mastered an impressive vocabulary—probably because his mother had been reading bedtime stories to him every night since we first brought him home from the hospital. Every so often it occurred to me that he might be an arithmetical wizard. I don't mean that he had ever done anything that would justify my thinking along these lines, I just happened to note that when genius comes along, it doesn't give much forewarning, it just arrives. So now and then I would interrupt his play to ask him what the square root of sixty-four was. He'd say, "Huh?"

A little time passed, and one morning while he was turning somersaults on my bed, I looked at my little son and very distinctly said, "Baby, what is the square root of sixty-four?"

He said, "Huh?"

I concluded that I didn't have to worry about his getting meningitis or whatever it is children get when they are too intelligent for their age. But the next day, fooling around on the bed with him, I thought I would try once more, on the off-chance that he had grown very intelligent during the night. So again I said, "Baby, what is the square root of sixty-four?"

He said, "Eight."

I grabbed the counterpane as I fell off the bed and was not hurt. Climbing back up, I said, "What did you say?"

He said, "Huh?"

We seemed to be back where we had been the day before, and I thought possibly I had misunderstood him, except that he had said "eight" very clearly. I decided to try just once more.

"What," I asked, "is the square root of sixty-four?"

Again, with the coolness of an Einstein, he said, "Eight," and looked at me as if to say, "What's so hard about that?"

So I yelled for Sandy, and when she came in, I said, "Get a load of this!" and again asked the little boy for the square root of sixty-four.

"Eight," he said and went on playing with whatever he was playing with.

"Isn't that extraordinary?" I said to Sandy.

"Remarkable," she said. "Maybe we could put him in a circus."

"Anyway, on television," I said. "Now I think I'll try him on another one."

"I didn't know you knew any others," said my wife.

"Is that supposed to be funny?" I said. "I think I'll try him on thirty-six."

"Why stretch your luck?" said Sandy.

"What's luck got to do with it?" I said. "Some human beings have no facility whatsoever for arithmetic . . . others have!"

My wife snickered, but I paid no attention to her and turned to little Preston.

"Baby," I said, "what's the square root of—now listen very carefully—thirty-six?"

"Eight," he said without the slightest hesitation.

"You weren't listening to me, darling," I said. "Daddyboy said *thirty-six*. What is the square root of thirty-six?"

"Eight," he said, coldly.

"Why don't you try him on something simpler?" said my wife. "Brilliant as one of your sons would naturally be, he's still a very little boy."

She now appeared to put her hand over her mouth as I turned to the child.

"Very well," I said. "Now listen carefully, darling: as you know, the square root is the number or quantity which, when squared, that is to say, multiplied by itself, will produce a given number or quantity, as eight is the square root of sixty-four."

"Eight," repeated the child.

"Quite right," I said, "but now, let us try another one. Listen carefully to Daddyboy: two squared, that is to say, multiplied by itself, is four. So what is the square root of four?"

"Eight," said the little boy.

This time it was my wife who fell on the floor, after which I got wise to the joke. Possibly it was very funny to teach our son to say "eight" every time he heard the words "square root," but if for the rest of his life he turns out to be a mathematical moron who can't even count his change at a subway booth, he can thank his mother for it, not me.

Gaumont was wildly enthusiastic about the story I created for *Les Carnets du Major Thompson* and they were as sure as I was that we had a hit on our hands. We had hardly begun to count our unhatched chickens when a new book titled *Les Carnets du Major Thompson* by Pierre Daninos, compiled from his columns in *Le Figaro,* became a best-seller.

The studio got very nervous. They imagined the audiences coming to see on film the incidents they had read in *Le Figaro* or in the book.

They imagined the fury of those audiences if they did not get what they expected.

They asked me to write another script.

The new script was to incorporate, as much as possible, the random reflections on the habits of the French made by the Major Thompson of Mr. Daninos' columns. The columns of Mr. Daninos did not tell a story, nor were they intended to; I told Monsieur Poiret of Gaumont that one could as easily make a film based on the telephone directory.

I was in no position to refuse work, however.

My solution was to give the English major, living in France, a French wife and a seven-year-old son. The major and his wife differ violently on whether the child should be raised with a pride in his English forebears or a pride in their hereditary enemies, his French forebears. From this matrix, the major's observations on the French, drawn from the columns, would then be illustrated on the screen.

Summer had come when I finished the second script, in two languages, and little Preston's pediatrician Dr. Auzepy, being a Frenchman, recommended a change of air for Preston. When Sandy and I did not appear to take the recommendation seriously, the good doctor announced that he would not be responsible for the little boy's continued good health were the child deprived of such a change. It was essential to his well-being. So convinced are the French that a change of air is basic to the sustenance of life, that its lack has even been listed as a cause of death. It is not by mistake that Paris empties in August; the citizens are taking a change of air. Sandy and her mother and little Preston took a house in Deauville for the summer, and Bianca, who had become a great friend of Sandy's and who adored little Preston, took a place there too. Every Friday evening I took the wonderful blue train to Deauville to spend the weekend with my little family.

During the week, I shot *Les Carnets du Major Thompson*. In fact, I shot it twice. Each scene was shot first in French and reshot immediately thereafter in English. This was to give the picture the best possible chance in the European and the English-speaking markets.

It wasn't easy.

Martine Carol's speeches in her highly touted perfect English became absolutely unintelligible when the first words out of her mouth were wrongly accented; Jack Buchanan's celebrated perfect French often fell more perfectly on his own ears than it did on those of his listeners.

Making a picture in France is like making a picture on location in America. Gaumont had a studio, of course, but it was equipped and staffed on an as-needed basis. Otherwise it stood empty. It had no permanent departments for props or set construction or lighting or anything else. A call to the wardrobe department, for instance, produced a little woman in black with no wardrobe resources at all except the clothes on her back. The system tests one's mettle, and I found it delightful.

Les Carnets du Major Thompson opened in Paris in December 1955 and pulled in a respectable amount of money for Gaumont in its European release. As 1956 got underway, I turned my attention to preparing the English version for release. In the American market, the book on which the film drew was unknown; neither Jack Buchanan nor Martine Carol had box-office clout in the United States; and I hadn't had a picture on the screen in six years. We proceeded with great care.

Halfway through 1956, at 11:55 P.M. on June 22, Master Thomas Preston Sturges made his first appearance at the American Hospital in Neuilly, weighing in at six pounds. From the father's point of view, the birth was easy, but Sandy didn't sleep through this one, and the baby looked like a casualty. He had no winks for his father on his way to the nursery, as Preston had had; the little thing was so battered, it broke one's heart.

We called him Tom after Sandy's father, and my mother's brother, and the central character in my picture *The Power and the Glory,* and the speakeasy proprietor in whose joint I set my play *Strictly Dishonorable.* We threw in the Preston for good luck. Among ourselves, though, he is known as Tom-Tom. Some months after his birth, José Iturbi, his godfather, held him nervously on a pillow while he was baptized at the cathedral of Notre-Dame. By then he was fat and sassy and had grown considerably less homely than he had been the first time we got a look at him. I am afraid he will never be the male beauty that little Preston is, but he may have just as nice a life.

One may notice that nothing less than a cathedral goes for my little boys, but I hope these Catholic sons of mine don't try to convert me in my old age. They would have a hell of a time of it.

While Tom-Tom was fighting for his rightful place in the family and Preston was making sure that nobody got mixed up about which child it was who had earned priority around the place, I got to work on

J'appartiens à Zozo, a farce I had wanted to write for a long time. I hoped to have it produced in Paris and I wrote it in French.

One of the key scenes, as originally written, had to do with a new bridegroom being caught by hotel detectives on his wedding night in bed with a pretty chambermaid. In New York that romp in the hay would be termed adultery and would constitute grounds for divorce, and I used the scene for that purpose in the script.

The French who read the play, however, were baffled. For them, the play fell apart, depending as it did on the consequences of the adulterous encounter in the hotel room. Zut, alors! A little dalliance in a hotel room wasn't adultery. Perhaps, on one's wedding night, ungallant. But grounds for divorce? Never.

It was my turn to be baffled. I then did a little research into the French marriage laws under the Napoleonic Code, as currently applied. The first thing I discovered was that under the code, the elements of adultery for men differed from the elements of adultery for women.

For a man to be proved guilty of adultery, the accuser must be able to allege and prove three things: first, that the married man *habitually* consorts with a woman other than his wife; second, that he does this under his own roof; and third, that he does it during the daylight hours.

It is interesting to note that the law takes into consideration the natural inclinations of the male of the species and does not try to change by fiat that which springs from the nature of the beast. It is equally interesting to note that, in effect, it puts the male on notice that open contempt of the home or the spouse is not tolerated.

It is a little different for a woman. Only two elements must be alleged and proved here: first, that the married woman consorted with a male other than her husband (and just once is enough; no shilly-shally about the definition of *habitually*); and second, that it happened during the daylight hours (and *where* she does it is irrelevant).

I believe that the definition of adultery when applied to a married woman is stricter because the consequences of her act can change history, not to mention the descent of property.

The mother is always certain that she is the mother; the father can never be quite that cocksure.

Of course, I had to rewrite the script.

In May of 1957, the distributors flew me to New York for the opening of *Les Carnets du Major Thompson,* which we called *The French They Are a Funny Race* in America, to signal to its potential audiences that the film was for adults. The critics found I had "mellowed," and I then deeply regretted having allowed Monsieur Poiret to persuade me not to use the more violent scenes I had shot, particularly the one about the chiropractors.

I sent Sandy a telegram for Mother's Day. I almost didn't. Until Mr. Kassler, the distributor, suggested it, it had never occurred to me that a slender, elegant, and enchanting person like herself could possibly fit into the mother category.

The next evening I got a telephone call from the Coast. It was Mon calling me from his school. He didn't know how to address me: first he called me "Dad," then timidly tried "Father." I didn't know how to speak to him either. I found myself talking to him like one would to a tiny little boy. I kept calling him "Preston" and "Darling" and correcting myself. I was very touched by his call and a little disturbed. One of the reasons I had never worried about my divorce from Louise was because I had no fear whatsoever of being separated from Mon. I could not have known this and been so sure of it except for the fact that I was a child of divorce myself and I remember how close Father was to me all the years that I lived in Paris while he stayed in Chicago. Mon was nearly sixteen now, the age I had been when I was reunited with Father, and though I hadn't seen the boy in four years, he was as much a part of my daily consciousness as were his adorable little brothers. After we hung up, I wondered if Mon felt the unseverable connection to me that I had always felt to Father.

I have always contended that in addition to talent, success depends on a little bit of luck, and my luck seemed to have run out, professionally at least. From a happiness standpoint though, I could not have been more spoiled. I had a beautiful young wife I did not deserve but whom I adored. I had little Preston, a very intelligent, bilingual little boy and a great pal of mine. And I had Tom-Tom, whom I loved very much. It seems absurd for a man of my age to have two little boys as young as they, but the absurdity is made up for by the great joy they bring.

The wracking disappointments I encountered in having got into a position where, to survive, I had to deal with fools, liars, and shaky amateurs instead of against them, were ameliorated by the ecstatic reception I was accorded every time I arrived at my front door: the bear hugs, the shouts, and the tugs to come to see the new cities of pillows and blocks covering the floor. Of course, I didn't have to leave the house to be so welcomed. If I spent some time in the bathroom, my reappearance created the same excitement. It was very heartwarming.

And then one day that was all over, too.

A producer who seemed to have plenty of money to invest in films and a track record in getting pictures made in Europe got very excited about an old story of mine called *Matrix.* He wanted to take a copy of the script back with him that night to show to his group. When I told him the complete treatment and the partial script were in Hollywood, he asked if I could get them to him by the end of the week and left for the airport talking about the fortune we would make together and the money that would change hands when I got the script to him.

Sandy got very excited, too, and talked me into letting her and the boys fly to Los Angeles to find *Matrix* somewhere in one of the hundreds of boxes stacked in our hinged-together house. She promised that *Matrix* would be on its way to me by mail the day after her arrival and begged me to let Preston and Tom-Tom spend a month or so playing in the California sunshine. Both of them must have inherited my lungs because, just as I had been as a boy, they were felled by bronchitis every cold damp Parisian winter. I reluctantly agreed to their soaking up some sun for a couple of weeks, not months. Preston was anxious to meet the big brother in California he had heard about all his life. Tom-Tom, who was only a year old, wouldn't have known his big brother in California from a grand piano.

Sandy looked so lovely that afternoon I put her on the plane, like a young wild thing . . . captured, but not tamed . . . in the woods. I picked Preston up. He held on to me very tight and told me not to be lonesome while he was gone and to take care of his two-wheel bike and his motorcycle, and to dust them every day. I promised. Tom-Tom put his little hand on my cheek and looked at me as if he knew he wouldn't see me again for a long, long time. As I started off the plane, Preston wanted to know if a month was a long time and again admonished me not to be lonesome while he was gone.

As she had promised, Sandy got *Matrix* to me within a week. The great producer professed a continued interest in *Matrix* but said he had a couple of projects to clear up first and that he'd get back to me by the end of the week. He didn't say the end of which week he meant, though, and at this writing about 102 of them have passed.

At the end of six weeks, with no prospects in sight, I dared not spend the money to fly Sandy and the boys back to me. We might need it to eat.

In November, I flew to New York at the expense of a producer who wanted to sign a deal for me to write and direct a screenplay based on the Philip Musica story. He gave me a thousand dollars and a new typewriter with French accents and a ticket back to Paris as earnest money, and put his lawyers to work drawing up the contracts: fifty thousand to write and direct. Charley didn't know anything about the producer but he said the law firm was a reputable one.

The contracts, together with a check for five thousand dollars, didn't show up until mid-January 1958. I crossed my fingers and deposited the check.

It bounced.

NO MATTER HOW ONE LOOKS AT IT, 1958 was a terrible year. Time did not accustom me to the absence of Sandy and my little boys. The quiet house was haunted by the echo of their dear voices and of my own yelling for quiet, for Christ's sake. Their toys and their books and their neatly made beds looked always as though the boys were only out playing at the Parc Monceau as usual. I found a pair of Tom-Tom's little white socks behind the radiator in my reading room and I fastened them to the wall with a thumbtack, so that he would be nearer me.

I do not intend to memorialize here the horrors of that empty time. Suffice it to say that by the end of the year, I faced a black Christmas, without money, without hope. Then suddenly, at the last minute, a cable came telling me that Air France had reservations to New York for me on December 22 and asking me to confirm my arrival with Charley. I didn't know what I was going to do in America but I imagined it had something to do with staging a play. I confirmed my arrival.

I was right. I arrived in New York, checked into the Algonquin and had my first meeting with the two partners putting on a play called *The Golden Fleecing.* I was to stage the play and do any general handiwork on the script I might find necessary. I telephoned Sandy and had a lovely talk with her and another with little Preston and another with Tom-Tom, who could probably not have picked me out of a crowd of two. I hadn't seen any money yet from *The Golden Fleecing* boys, so our reunion was not yet. The distance of only our own country between us obliterated for me the feeling that I was separated from my little family.

Rehearsals began on January 6, 1959. On the same day, one of the partners decided that his mind had become a little too unhinged for his own comfort and he checked himself into a nuthouse. Ten days later he emerged, cured—in his own estimation—and on January 16 told me that he was taking over the direction of the play.

I was out of a job.

More than once over the years I had told Sandy that if worse came to worst, that if we lost *every*thing and found ourselves without a roof over our heads sitting on the curbstone at Franklin and Vista, we would not be without resources. From a car passing to the east, I would borrow a pad of paper; from a car passing west, I would borrow a pencil. By evening I would have written a story and we would be back in business. I always believed this.

1958 did much to destroy the conviction that I could write my way out of trouble. At the beginning of that year I had two of the best plays I have ever written on hand: *I Belong to Zozo* and *The Gentleman from Chicago,* and at the end of the year, despite signed contracts, false starts, and heartbreak, I still had the stories on hand and about $136 total in the bank.

When I found myself out of a job this time, it was not the first-round knockout it might have been. This was because the week before I had accepted an offer from Henry Holt, the publishers, to write my autobiography for them, and on February 11, 1959, the contracts were signed and money changed hands.

I paid off the six-months' back rent on the Paris apartment, paid up my hotel bill and put the change in a safe-deposit box at the hotel. I didn't know if the IRS lien was still lurking out there somewhere and I didn't want to take any chances on finding out the hard way. My first impulse was to fly to California to Sandy and the little boys; my next impulse was to have her bring them to New York. But I had come through a year of such hopelessness that I was just too gun-shy to spend any of what I had left of the advance. I didn't know how long the money would have to last us . . . or how soon I would get any more.

While I got to work on the book, my presence in New York stirred up a lot of activity: there were discussions with Sarnoff's men over at NBC about a couple of ideas for television shows I had put together; meetings with Billy Rose about staging a play for him; Joe Fields was talking about my directing a picture for him in April at the Fox studios in New York. And there were real producers anxious to see *Zozo* and *The Gentleman from Chicago.* It did not seem the right time for me to leave New York and to drop out of sight in California to write the autobiography.

In late May, NBC started negotiations with Charley for me to write, direct, and produce a pilot of one of the television ideas I had presented to them. It's been a couple of months now, but Charley isn't worried.

In April a round of discussions got underway for the production of *I Belong to Zozo* and *The Gentleman from Chicago*. Through May and June, there were long-distance telephone calls from Cincinnati, from Miami, from Canada; meetings in New York, meetings in Miami; and then at the end of June, I signed three separate deal memos: to stage *I Belong to Zozo*, to rewrite *The Gentleman from Chicago* as a musical and to stage it, and then to write and direct a film based on the musical. In July I got some earnest money and paid up the hotel bill. I called Sandy to tell her that she should start thinking about coming to live in New York and about what arrangements would have to be made to preserve the house from burglars and vandals and the effects of some sizeable leaks left over from the move. We decided not to talk about what it would be like to be together again.

The real money will come through when the contracts now being drawn up are signed in triplicate. I made a fortune with *Strictly Dishonorable* in 1929 and lost it. I went to Hollywood and made a larger fortune and lost it, too. I intend to make another one before I kick the bucket and this time, as Al Lewin pointed out the other night, I won't have time to lose it. I might surprise my creditors yet and the good friends who stood by me. I think of Bertie Woolfan and his lovely wife Priscilla Bonner, whose friendship and affection were an integral part of all my years in Hollywood. They were there to cheer me on through the battles I waged and to rejoice in my successes. They took to their hearts the various ladies I took to my own along the way and they are Uncle Bertie and Aunt Priscilla to Mon, and to little Preston and Tom-Tom now. God willing, we will all be together again in the not too distant future.

I know that my life, even in these disagreeably trying times, is *complete*, although I don't know exactly why. Is it because my hopes and disappointments and renewed hopes and ideas and inventions go all the way, the full swing of the pendulum? Is that what energy and vitality really mean: mental energy and vitality? Because a man of sixty very definitely does not jump around as much as a boy of three.

A man of sixty, however healthy, makes me think of an air passenger waiting in the terminal, but one whose transportation has not yet been arranged. He doesn't know just when he's leaving.

While waiting, he thinks back on his life and to him it seems to have been a Mardi Gras, a street parade of masked, drunken, hysterical, laughing, disguised, travestied, carnal, innocent, and perspiring humanity of all sexes, wandering aimlessly, but always in circles, in search of that of which it is a part: life.

Looking back, are there any conclusions to be drawn? Any errors to be avoided the next time around, if there happened to be such a thing? Certainly there are.

There is absolutely no advantage to being poor, for instance. A small income derived in any way that does not make the recipient too ashamed or unhappy is vastly preferable to no income. The Nietzschean theory of living dangerously is splendid, but should possibly be modified to "live dangerously with a small income."

There is no advantage to being without education, either. This pleases no one but your biographer. Education means remembering what you have been told. Remembering what you *haven't* been told, directly out of the human heritage, is called genius.

There can be no question but that it is also an advantage to speak another language besides the mother tongue; two are better, three better still. Theoretically, *ten* should be still better, but for some reason that I have not fathomed, true polyglots seem never to have profited greatly from their ability to converse and read in a multiplicity of languages. Most of the polyglots I have met were sad-eyed guides in caps either too large or too small for them, standing around in drafty customs' sheds.

Money is not star material. One should never have enough of it, or enough lack of it, to allow of its playing a principal role.

I had an idea when I started this that I might pass on, for the edification of my sons at least, the wisdom gained through years of experience. Then a voice within me said, *"What* wisdom? Gained from *what* years of experience? You are as inexperienced and impulsive at sixty as you were at sixteen!"

These ruminations, and the beer and coleslaw that I washed down while dictating them, are giving me a bad case of indigestion. Over the years, though, I have suffered so many attacks of indigestion that I am well versed in the remedy: ingest a little Maalox, lie down, stretch out, and hope to God I don't croak.

fade out

About twenty minutes later, August 6, 1959, Preston Sturges died of a heart attack at the Algonquin Hotel.

THE WORKS OF PRESTON STURGES

STAGE PLAYS

1928 *The Guinea Pig*

1929 *Strictly Dishonorable*

1930 *Recapture*

1930 *The Well of Romance*

1932 *Child of Manhattan*

1951 *Make a Wish*

1953 *Carnival in Flanders*

1988 *Cup of Coffee*

SCREENPLAYS

1930 *The Big Pond*

1930 *Fast and Loose*

1933 *They Just Had to Get Married**

1933 *The Power and the Glory*

1934 *Thirty Day Princess*

1934 *We Live Again*

1934 *Imitation of Life**

1935 *The Good Fairy*

1935 *Diamond Jim*

1936 *The Next Time We Love**

1936 *Love Before Breakfast**

1937 *Hotel Haywire*

1937 *Easy Living*

1938 *College Swing**

1938 *Port of Seven Seas*

1938 *If I Were King*

1939 *Never Say Die*

1940 *Remember the Night*
*Uncredited screenplay contribution

SCREENPLAYS—WRITTEN AND DIRECTED

1940 *The Great McGinty*
(Academy Award winner)

1940 *Christmas in July*

1941 *The Lady Eve*

1942 *Sullivan's Travels*

1942 *The Palm Beach Story*

1942 *Safeguarding Military Information*

1944 *The Miracle of Morgan's Creek*
(Academy Award nominee)

1944 *Hail the Conquering Hero*
(Academy Award nominee)

1946 *The Great Moment*

1957 *The French They Are a Funny Race*
(Les Carnets du Major Thompson)

SCREENPLAYS—PRODUCED, WRITTEN, AND DIRECTED

1947 *The Sin of Harold Diddlebuck*

1948 *Unfaithfully Yours*

1949 *The Beautiful Blonde from Bashful Bend*

1950 *Mad Wednesday*
(Hughes recut of *Diddlebuck*)

PRODUCER

1942 *I Married a Witch*

SONGS

1935 "Paris in the Evening"
(Music by Ted Snyder; Lyrics by PS)
For *The Gay Deception* (Fox) and *Unfaithfully Yours* (1948)

1936 "Secret Rendezvous"
For *One Rainy Afternoon* (Pickford-Lasky)

1944 "The Bell in the Bay"
For *The Miracle of Morgan's Creek*

1944 "Home to the Arms of Mother"
For *Hail the Conquering Hero*

UNPRODUCED STAGE PLAYS

Unfaithfully Yours
I Belong to Zozo

UNPRODUCED SCREENPLAYS

Kiss Me Doctor
Song of Joy
The Invisible Man
(for Universal)

The Mine with the Iron Door
(for Universal)

Broadway Melody of 1939
(for Paramount)

Vendetta
(for Cal Pictures)

Look Ma, I'm Dancin'
(for Paramount)

Nothing Doing
(sold to MGM)

The Philip Musica Story
A Present for Uncle Popo

ADAPTATIONS FROM
THE WORKS OF PRESTON STURGES

1931 *Strictly Dishonorable*
(Universal)
Based on his play.

1933 *Child of Manhattan*
(Columbia)
Based on his play.

1947 *I'll Be Yours*
(Universal)
Based on his screenplay *The Good Fairy.*

1951 *Strictly Dishonorable*
(MGM)
Based on his play.

1956 *The Birds and the Bees*
(Paramount)
Based on his screenplay *The Lady Eve.*

1958 *Rock-a-Bye Baby*
(Paramount)
Based on his screenplay *The Miracle of Morgan's Creek.*

1961 *The Conquering Hero*
(Directed and choreographed by Bob Fosse)
A stage musical based on his screenplay *Hail the Conquering Hero.*

1985 *Unfaithfully Yours*
(Twentieth Century-Fox)

Date shown is year produced (plays) or released (films).

INDEX